VOLUME

5

CREATED BY CHRIS CARTER

THE END AND THE BEGINNING

THE OFFICIAL GUIDE TO

THE X FILES

ANDY MEISLER

HarperEntertainment

An Imprint of HarperCollins*Publishers*

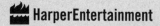 **HarperEntertainment**

An Imprint of HarperCollins*Publishers*
10 East 53rd Street, New York, NY 10022–5299

ISBN 0-06-107595-7

HarperCollins®, ▟®, and HarperEntertainment™ are trademarks of HarperCollins*Publishers* Inc.
First printing: April 2000
Printed in the United States of America
Front cover photograph courtesy of Fox Broadcasting Company
Video grabs provided by Omni Graphic Solutions
Cover Design: Roger Gorman
Interior Design: Roger Gorman
Library of Congress Cataloging-in-Publication Data has been applied for.

Visit HarperEntertainment on the World Wide Web at **www.harpercollins.com**
10 9 8 7 6 5 4 3 2 1

MANY THANKS TO:

David Amann, Daniel Arkin, Dawn Asher, Edward Asner, Laverne Basham, Jeffrey Bell, Anji Bemben, Rob Bowman, Tom Braidwood, Danny Briggs, Harry Bring, Katrina Cabrera, Bruce Carter, Veronica Cartwright, Jodi Clancy, Tom Day, Tom Doherty, Steve Duncan, Michelle Fazekas, Wendy Fishman, Chuck Forsch, Vince Gilligan, Sarah Goldstein, Dena Green, Dean Haglund, Elizabeth Harrison, Bruce Harwood, Ken Hawryliw, Jessica Iverson, Ilt Jones, Corey Kaplan, Kim Manners, Michael McKean, Steven Melnick, France Myung Metz, Bill Millar, Rick Millikan, Cheri Montesanto-Medcalf, Ken Myers, Lori Jo Nemhauser, Chris Owens, Kelly Padovich, Christine Peters, James Pickering, Jr., Paul Rabwin, Holly Rice, Bill Roe, Bob Roe, John Shiban, John Silbersack, Lee Smith, Mark Snow, Frank Spotnitz, Francine and Scott Sprigel, Sarah Stanick, Tim Stepeck, Harriet Sternberg, Duke Tomasick, Sandra Tripicchio, Julia Vera, John Vulich, Michael Watkins, Kevin Westmore, Julie Wilburn, Stacy Wise and Chandra Years.

My admiration for Mary Astadourian and Chris Carter continues to grow—as does my debt of gratitude. Caitlin Blasdell (who launched this book) and Lara Comstock (who steered it to safe harbor) are editors of skill and sensitivity. Maureen and Eric Lasher are great agents; they are even better friends.

ABOUT THE AUTHOR
Andy Meisler writes about television for the *New York Times* and several other publications. He is the author of *I Want To Believe: The Official Guide to The X-Files Volume 3* and *Resist or Serve: The Official Guide to The X-Files Volume 4* as well as the co-author of *The Secret Life of Cyndy Garvey* with Cynthia Garvey and *I Am Roe: My Life, Roe v. Wade, and Freedom of Choice* with Norma McCorvey. He lives with his wife in Los Angeles.

Other *The X-Files* titles published by HarperCollins
    Fiction
The X-Files *Goblins*
The X-Files *Whirlwind*
The X-Files *Ground Zero*
The X-Files *Ruins*
The X-Files *Antibodies*
The X-Files *Skin*

    Nonfiction
I Want to Believe: The Official Guide to The X-Files
Trust No One: The Offical Guide to The X-Files
The Truth Is Out There: The Official Guide to The X-Files
The X-Files *Book of the Unexplained Volume One*
The X-Files *Book of the Unexplained Volume Two*
The X-Files *2000 Desk Diary*
The X-Files *2000 Wall Calendar*
The Official Map of The X-Files
The X-Files *Postcard Book: The Conspiracies*
The X-Files *Postcard Book: Monsters and Mutants*
The X-Files *Postcard Book: Unexplained Phenomena*
The Art of The X-Files
The Making of The X-Files *Film*
The X-Files *Film Novel*

CONTENTS
the sixth season

INTRO

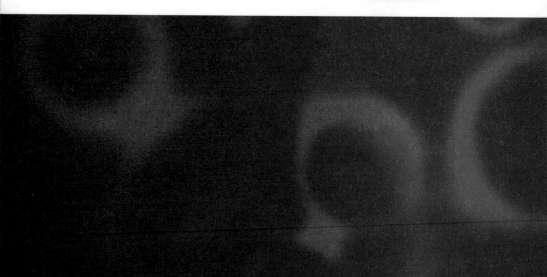

DUCTION

They say art reflects life, but in the case of *The X-Files*, network television's most challenging and provocative series, it is life that has reflected art. Like one of the show's paranormal themes—in this case, reincarnation—*The X-Files* has been reborn in the minds of skeptics, critics, and naysayers many times during the course of its six-year run.

In 1992, when a thirtysomething writer named Chris Carter—who had a few short-lived TV projects to his credit—pitched an idea for an unusual hour-long drama to his bosses at then-fledgling Twentieth Century Fox Television, his idea was not as warmly received as one would think in hindsight. His proposed show would tap into America's fascination with UFOs, paranormal phenomena, and governmental secrecy and lies.

The concept was so edgy and *different* that nervous executives nearly rejected it outright. Opting instead to give Carter a chance, they greenlighted the project, but to keep costs minimal, the production was moved to dark, moody—and, above all, rainy—Vancouver, British Columbia. Chris Carter had no objections to the relocation—Vancouver had a forest which he wanted to use for the pilot episode.

When the pilot episode was finished, it was slotted on the Fox broadcasting schedule after the "hot" new series, *The Adventures of Brisco County Jr.*, for which the network had high hopes. To the programming executives' surprise, *The X-Files* began to attract a small yet significant following.

This success, however, was regarded as an aberration; the naysayers argued that the show would never expand beyond its core audience of sci-fi geeks and conspiracy theorists.

But the unexpected continued. Ratings zoomed. Cover stories about the show began sprouting up in mainstream publications on newsstands across America. The show's two lead actors, David Duchovny and Gillian Anderson, became international superstars. Yet some skeptics still did not want to believe. They theorized that mass public acceptance would be brief, but also powerful enough to alienate the show's original, highly zealous fan base.

Again, the doubters were proven wrong. Not only did the show remain among the most popular with the crucial 18–46 audience, it spawned a lucrative merchandising industry as well. Echoing the success of another entertainment phenomenon, Gene Roddenberry's *Star Trek*, in 1997 Chris Carter announced plans to expand to the big screen in a feature film based on the series. Still refusing to see the truth out there, film industry "experts" predicted that moviegoers would not pay to see a movie version of a currently running television series. When *The X-Files: Fight the Future* became an international blockbuster, pundits seized on yet another reason to forebode the imminent demise of the series—the decision in 1998 by Carter and Twentieth Century Fox Television, at the request of

David Duchovny, to move the show's production from Vancouver to Los Angeles.

According to the critics, relocating to the bright sunshine of Southern California would change the series' dark "look" so drastically that its moody distinctiveness would gradually give way to sitcom sameness, ultimately turning off its loyal viewers. In addition, the Vancouver crew, many of whom had been with the show since the first season, would be replaced. Critics predicted the show and its worn-out producers would rely on standard plotlines guaranteed to become boring and repetitive.

Wrong again.

In case you haven't noticed, most—if not all—of the Vancouver-to-L.A. quibbles died down once the sixth season got underway. Critical reception of the new episodes shot in sunlight, darkness, rain, hail—nearly every weather condition—was almost overwhelmingly positive. The show remained a fixture on most TV critics' "Top Ten" lists and, while U.S. ratings for *The X-Files* did soften somewhat, the slight shift was in accordance with the total decline in television viewership affecting all the networks. *The X-Files* remained the Fox network's top-rated show; won its time period without a struggle; was the second-highest rated network drama among adults (behind the number one show *ER*); and remained solidly in the Top 10 for all desirable demographic groups.

This past year witnessed the finale of several critical and fan favorites—*Melrose Place, Mad About You, Homicide: Life on the Streets*—whose end resulted from viewer desertion or creative exhaustion.

Aware of the pitfalls success brings, Carter dared to keep the show edgy, adding fresh new faces and imaginations to the show's staff, devising new plot twists, and highlighting trademark elements as never before. Balancing hardcore alien/conspiracy episodes with a blend of stand-alone segments, the sixth season showed the further evolution of Mulder and Scully's relationship as partners, friends, and soul mates, emphasized the unique humor of the series, and added even more layers to its mythology.

The sixth season included guest appearances by a wide range of acclaimed actors and comedians, including Lily Tomlin, Ed Asner, Victoria Jackson, Michael McKean, Nora Dunn, Abraham Benrubi, and Darren McGavin. It marked the directorial debut of David Duchovny, as well as his first solo stint as a writer, penning an episode involving two of Mulder's favorite obsessions: aliens and baseball.

From a new twist on the Bermuda Triangle—taking Mulder and Scully back nearly half a century to save the world in an entirely different way—to a "married" Mulder and Scully searching for a monster lurking in suburbia; from a day relived over and over and over to a crime photographer with an uncanny connection to death, *The X-Files* continued to enthrall viewers and critics—and prove the naysayers wrong yet again. Beginning with *The X-Files: Fight the Future* and the seeming end of Mulder's and Scully's careers, the sixth season ended with the birth of a completely new mythology that brings into question the very nature of humanity and its origins.

Where will this new direction take us? While only Chris Carter and the talented staff behind the show can know for sure, it's easy to hazard a guess: further into the unknown, into realms of the imagination to which few works of art—and even fewer television programs—have ever taken viewers before. That is the legacy—and the promise—of *The X-Files*, and the true reason for its continued success . . . and life.

6X01

A vicious creature—possibly of extraterrestrial origin——is cutting a murderous swath through the American Southwest. With Syndicate infiltrators in control of the X-Files, Mulder and Scully must find it—and determine its place in the alien conspiracy.

THE BEGINNING

EPISODE: 6X01
FIRST AIRED: November 8, 1998
EDITOR: Heather MacDougall
WRITTEN BY: Chris Carter
DIRECTED BY: Kim Manners

GUEST STARS:

Mitch Pileggi (AD Walter Skinner)
William B. Davis (The Cigarette-Smoking Man)
Mimi Rogers (Agent Diana Fowley)
Chris Owens (Agent Jeffrey Spender)
Jeff Gulka (Gibson Praise)
Don S. Williams (Elder)
George Murdock (Second Elder)
Wendie Malick (AD Maslin)
James Pickens, Jr. (AD Kersh)
Wayne Alexander (AD Arnold)
Arthur Taxier (AD Bart)
Rick Millikan (Sandy)
Alan Henry Brown (Scientist)
Christopher Neiman (Van Pool Scientist)
Scott Eberlein (Black-Haired Man)
Ralph Meyering, Jr. (Surgeon)
Benito Martinez (Orderly)
Kim Robillard (Homer)
Wayne Thomas Yorke (Power Plant Worker)

PRINCIPAL SETTINGS:

Phoenix, Arizona; Washington, D.C.;
New York City

A relentless sun beats down on the Arizona desert.
On the outskirts of Phoenix, two white-shirted scientists finish an open-air rest stop and run to rejoin their van pool. They climb into the van—it belongs to Roush Technologies, revealed as a Syndicate front in "Redux II" (5X03)— and proceed toward a cluster of generic tract houses.

A scientist named Sandy, visibly ill, gets out, enters his house, and turns his thermostat all the way up. He collapses on his couch, shivering uncontrollably, and watches in horror as his hand morphs into something gruesome and otherworldy.

The van returns early the next morning. A coworker knocks on the door and enters, calling Sandy's name. Silence.

In the sweltering heat he discovers Sandy on the couch—dead, with a gaping hole in his torso where his internal organs used to be. Horrified, he turns away, then freezes. There is a fearsome sound and an explosion of animal violence. The scientist, covered with blood, stumbles toward the front door. He manages to reach the doorknob before he is dragged backward, screaming.

At FBI headquarters in Washington, D.C., Fox Mulder faces a panel of Bureau supervisors, Assistant Director Skinner among them. He explains that a large percentage of the X-Files, burnt in a fire several months ago in "The End" (5X20), are recoverable via a special process.

"And, while this process will be tedious and ongoing," adds Mulder, "what I've already recovered will allow Agent Scully and I to resume work on the X-Files."

Dana Scully enters the room and sits behind him. A middle-aged female AD, whose nameplate reads J. MASLIN, glances up from a file folder and looks at Mulder with disdain.

She says, "Agent Mulder, I'm reading here a very pie-in-the-sky report about global domination plans by vicious, long-clawed spacelings. Is there going to be data to back this vague omnibus account?"

"Yes," says Mulder, matching her tone exactly.

A middle-aged male AD breaks in. "I see your renowned arrogance has been left quite intact," he says. "You're asking us to accept this report of a spaceship buried under polar ice? And your death-defying escape from it?"

Says Mulder, "The ice had become superheated by the ship as it rose beneath us, causing it to collapse."

The second AD reacts scornfully. He declares Mulder's report—which, covering the events of the X-Files movie, concludes that extraterrestrial biological entities are being implanted in humans via genetically altered viruses—unintelligible.

Yet another AD asks Mulder whether the spacelings he saw were from Men in Black.

"I didn't see Men in Black," says Mulder.

"A damn good movie," mutters the bureaucrat.

The confrontation goes downhill from there. Maslin dismisses out of hand Mulder's discoveries. In fact, it appears that the real purpose of the meeting is to discipline Mulder and Scully.

"Let us remind you," says Maslin, "that the FBI is not a school for science. Or for the grinding of personal axes. And hopefully, you will be able to present us with some material evidence to support a continued investigation."

Counters Mulder, "Agent Scully was assigned to the X-Files as a scientist. She was stung by one of those bees and infected by the virus. She is here today with hard and incontrovertible evidence— scientific proof—that the virus she was infected with is in fact extraterrestrial."

At that, Mulder glances at his partner. He and the panelists wait expectantly. But Scully says nothing.

Striding down the hallway a few moments later, Mulder turns to his partner. He is furious.

"Next time I'll wear a clown suit and do balloon tricks," he says. He adds, "The only reason I was in there was because you assured me there was sci-entific basis for what we saw."

Scully shakes her head sadly. "Mulder," she says, "let me remind you once again, what we saw was very little."

"Well, Scully," says Mulder, "that excuse is not going to work this time. You were there, and you were infected with that virus."

Angry herself now, Scully tells Mulder that her tests have not allowed her to identify the virus, but she has determined that its DNA and proteins are found on this world.

Mulder shakes his head. "I saw what that virus did," says Mulder. "I saw it generate a new being—an alien being—inside a human body."

Scully insists that all that modern science—her science—can determine is that the virus attacks and destroys human cells. "That's all it does, Mulder, it creates nothing!"

Mulder glares at her and strides away.

At the Manhattan headquarters of the Syndicate, the Cigarette-Smoking Man—glowing Morley in hand—paces in front of photos of the dead Roush scientists. "There was some sloppiness in Phoenix," he says.

He explains to the assembled Elders that the story has gotten out to the local press—and has been countered by his carefully prepared cover story that a crazed Indian is on a rampage. The real facts are, he says, that Sandy must have accidentally injected himself with the virus—and that the creature, after a twelve-hour gestation, is now on the loose. He adds that he is personally managing the situation.

The First Elder is less than satisfied by this report. "You can manage it all you want," he tells the Cigarette-Smoking Man. "Someone's got to find this thing."

Replies the Cigarette-Smoking Man, coolly, "Someone has to kill it. The response must be equal to the threat."

"Can you dispose of this problem?" asks the First Elder.

"Yes," says the Cigarette-Smoking Man.

In a darkened lab in the FBI Building, Mulder sits at a special optical reader, painstakingly reassembling burnt X-Files. Skinner steps into the room.

"You're wasting your time," says the AD to Mulder.

Mulder disagrees. "We need evidence to justify our reassignment," he says. "I've just got to bring it back from the ashes."

"Nothing you might restore is going to help you, Agent Mulder," says Skinner. "It's over and done. Your reassignment on the X-Files has been denied."

Mulder whirls, furiously. "How can it be denied?" he says. "We're the only reason the X-Files were reopened in the first place! There's no other reason to reopen them!"

"I'm not arguing with you," says Skinner, quietly.

"Then who is!?"

Says Skinner, urgently, "When will you accept that no amount of pressure or reason will bring to heel the members of a conspiracy whose members walk these halls with absolute impunity?"

Still defiant, Mulder asks Skinner how the committee voted on his application.

"Unanimous against," says the AD.

Mulder glares at him, retrieves his papers, and heads to the door.

Says Skinner, "I'm no help to you outside the majority, Agent Mulder," insists Skinner. "Only on the inside." He adds, "You can break their backs. With proof about this virus. Proof that what you say it does is true."

"I don't have that proof yet," says Mulder.

"Maybe I can give it to you," says Skinner, voice

"I SAW IT GENERATE A NEW BEING—AN ALIEN BEING—INSIDE A HUMAN BODY."–Mulder

lowered. "There's a file folder. It's on the desk in your old office."

A few moments later Mulder is at his old desk. He examines a folder. Inside are the same photos of Sandy as in the Cigarette-Smoking Man's display. He notices that he is not alone in the room. Special Agent Jeffrey Spender, last seen in "The End," stands near a wall-mounted light box.

"What are you doing in my office, Agent Spender?" he asks.

A bit nervously, Spender tells him there's been a "miscommunication."

Replies Mulder, scornfully, "If you're about to tell me that they sent you down here to work on the X-Files, I think the failure is simple judgment. I don't care what patronage got you this job. I put my life in here. I'm not going to let some brown nose just slide in here and take it away from me."

Spender replies in kind. "I don't believe in your work, in all the paranormal mumbo jumbo," he tells Mulder. So don't presume I'm going to take your place."

"No? Who is?"

At that moment Diana Fowley—Mulder's old partner and lover, gravely wounded in 5X24—walks into the light.

"Diana. Back on your feet," says Mulder, disgustedly. "I guess that's the only way you could stab me in the back."

He turns and leaves the office. Afterward, the Phoenix file folder is missing from the desktop.

Inside an operating room at an undisclosed location the Cigarette-Smoking Man—smoking cigarette in hand—casually walks among a team of hardworking surgeons. To their shock and frightened dismay, he tells them that their patient's wounds have to be dressed and that he must be made ready to travel immediately.

"But doing that now could kill him!" protests the chief surgeon.

"Let me put it to you simply," replies the Cigarette-Smoking Man. "It's him or it's us."

He turns to leave. The doctors begin their task.

Their patient is Gibson Praise, the empathic chess prodigy from 5X24. Although his brain matter is exposed where his skull has been sawed away, he is awake and calm.

The next afternoon Mulder and Scully, breaking the yellow crime scene tape, enter Sandy's Phoenix apartment. Scully warns her partner that their visit is unauthorized and illegal.

No reaction.

"Why do I bother?" sighs Scully.

Mulder points out bloody gouges in the wall and hardwood floor—deeper, he adds, than any human could make with his bare hands. He pulls a broken

finger- or toenail—it is larger than any human's—out of one gouge. He opens the Medical Examiner's report and notes that the two victims died twelve hours apart.

"So the attacker never left?" says Scully.

"It wasn't an attack," says Mulder. "I think it was celebrating its birthday."

He adds, "The first victim must've gotten infected with the virus somehow. Right here on the sofa is where the creature was born. That would account for the violence done to the man's torso—the virus producing an extraterrestrial entity that ripped away his chest as it birthed itself."

Scully glances, half skeptical and half alarmed, at the crime scene photo. "Forgive the scientific argument for a moment," she says. "You're saying this was done by something newborn?"

At this moment a long gray car glides to a halt in front of the dead scientist's house. At the wheel is a black-haired gunman (from 5X20); in back are the Cigarette-Smoking Man and Gibson, blood oozing through the bandage on his head.

"It was here," says the boy, "but it's gone now."

The Black-Haired Man volunteers to take a look around.

"It's not here!" says Gibson. "Why don't you believe me? Why are you so afraid of me?"

"We're not afraid of you," replies the Cigarette-Smoking Man, unconvincingly,

Gibson ignores him. "You think I can destroy you," he says, with little emotion. "With what I know. Because of what I am. You're thinking you could've destroyed me, too. And if I don't find this creature, you will."

They drive away. A few seconds later the agents emerge from the house, arguing about the validity of Mulder's theory. He angrily cites his experience in Antarctica (in the X-Files movie).

"I saw those creatures, Scully," he says. "I saw them burst to life. You would've seen them, too, if you hadn't been infected, if you hadn't been passed out over my shoulder."

Replies Scully, forcefully, "Mulder, I know what you did. I know what happened to me. But without ignoring the science, I can't—"

She squeezes her partner's hand.

"Listen, Mulder," she says. "You told me that my science kept you honest, that it made you question your assumptions. That by it, I'd made you a whole person. If I changed now, it wouldn't be right. Or honest."

Mulder replies calmly but forcefully. "I'm talking about extraterrestrial life alive on this planet in our lifetime. Forces that dwarf and precede all human history.

"I'm sorry, Scully. But this time your science is wrong."

At the Rolling Hills Nuclear Power Plant, sixty

"THEY WERE USING ME. BECAUSE I CAN COMMUNICATE WITH IT."—Gibson Praise

miles east of Phoenix, the control room operator snoozes at his console. The scene is very familiar. In fact—

"Wake up, 'Homer,'" says a coworker, jostling him awake.

"I was awake," he replies. "I was thinkin'."

"Yeah. That'd be a first," says his colleague.

The coworker grabs a clipboard, checks some gauges, and notices an anomaly in the bleed-cooling system. He tells Homer to check it out. After protesting that it's just a monitoring error, the control room operator reluctantly leaves his post.

Entering the ominous, pipe-filled center of the power plant, Homer hears a faint scratching noise behind him. He turns, worried, and walks cautiously toward the sound. Peering through the thicket of pipes, he catches a quick glimpse of something frightening. Trembling, he pulls a wrench from his pocket and creeps forward. He is lifted off his feet with an unearthly roar. His screams echo, unanswered, through the otherwise unoccupied area.

Later that day, Mulder and Scully arrive at the power plant. They are barred from the teeming crime scene by Spender.

Scully protests. "We received a call that there was a man killed here," she says.

"Received a call from whom?" demands Spender. "Assistant Director Skinner?"

Neither agent answers him. Mulder tries to push past Spender, who blocks his way and accuses him of disobeying orders. Mulder spots Diana Fowley standing nearby and asks her to let them in.

"I can't. This facility has been sealed off by the NRC," she says, grimly.

Says Mulder, "A man's been murdered,"

Fowley answers slowly and carefully, "A workman was killed in an accident," she says. "In a reactor where there was a systems failure."

"Then why are you here?"

"We were called," says Fowley, impassively, "because of a connection to two previous deaths. From a case file stolen from our office."

Mulder nods. "There is a connection. I hope you know what you're doing, Diana. I hope you know whose errand you're running."

"I think I do," says Fowley, coolly.

On the way back to their rental car, Scully criticizes Mulder for his direct approach. Mulder doesn't listen to her.

"It's here. They know it," he says, glancing into the car's rear window.

Lying in the back seat is Gibson, unconscious. Scully rushes to cradle him in her arms, then gently calls his name. He does not respond.

At a nearby motel that night Scully changes Gibson's dressings. He is awake now; there is a bloody, jagged scar on his shaven skull.

"Frankenstein? Really?" says Gibson.

"No, no," protests Scully, soothingly. "You've been worked on by some fine doctors. They've done a fine job on your stitches."

Says Gibson, "You think they were butchers."

"They *were* butchers," says Mulder, bluntly.

Scully grimaces. She tells the boy that he has an infection and a fever. "Why did they do this?" she asks.

"Because I can read people's minds," says Gibson.

He tells Mulder that he ran away from his captors when they weren't looking. "It's easy when you know what they're thinking," he says.

Mulder meets his gaze. "Why are you here?" he asks.

"They were using me," says Gibson. "Because I can communicate with it."

"Communicate with what?" whispers Scully.

"You already know," replies Gibson. "You just don't want to believe it."

Over Scully's objections—that their investigation is completely unauthorized; that Gibson belongs in a hospital; that he is their sole corroborating witness in the case and must be protected—Mulder lifts the boy in his arms and carries him out to their car. Another car drives up to them and stops.

Inside it is Diana Fowley—alone.

"Diana, what are you doing here?" demands Mulder.

Says Fowley, "I couldn't say anything to you earlier. I was given this assignment, Fox. Okay? They offered it to me. I took the chance—to make sure someone served your interests. Someone who believes in the work. Hey, you and I founded the X-Files together. Don't forget that."

Mulder is unmoved. "Who sent you?" he says.

"I'm here on my own."

"To do what? Convince me of your noble intentions?"

"Listen to me!" says Fowley. "That thing is somewhere inside the Number Four Reactor Building. Now, we can let them find it and destroy it, or go find it ourselves.

"You need proof, Fox. You're so close! Why can't you see that?"

Mulder thinks, turns, and walks back to his car. He leans down to talk to Scully.

"You take Gibson," he says.

"Why? Where are you going?" asks Scully.

"To find this thing," says Mulder.

Later that night Mulder and Fowley drive down a deserted rural road. She tells him that she and Spender were on their way to Arizona within an hour of the accident; by the time they got there the body had been removed and the reactor had been sealed off—because, they were told, of a problem with the heat transfer system.

Says Mulder, "That's why it's there. It wants heat. It needs heat. This thing gestated abnormally fast. What if heat activates it?"

"It could spur the virus," says Fowley. "And the rapid development of the entity."

"But it's still seeking heat. Why?"

"What if," asks Fowley, "it's still developing?"

At Phoenix Samaritan Hospital that same evening Scully reassures Gibson as he's wheeled to his room. "We're going to get you well," she says.

Says Gibson, "You want to make me well, but you're just thinking about yourself. And what you can learn from me."

Scully, startled, recoils slightly, then composes herself. "You're a very special boy, Gibson," she says, finally.

"I'm a very special lab rat," says Gibson.

At 11:42 P.M. Mulder and Fowley slip past a security patrol and enter the reactor building. They walk quickly to the area—directly above the reactor core—where Homer was killed. Mulder notes that the temperature is abnormally high; he kneels down and examines a gooey, unidentifiable substance at his feet.

"It's organic," says Fowley, softly.

"Maybe somebody got the flu," whispers Mulder.

Some of this substance is also on the cooling pipes. Mulder reaches into the thicket—just as Homer had—then jumps back, startled.

"There's something in there," he says.

Mulder reaches in again and, with one quick jerk, rips something dark and heavy from the piping. It is a thin slab of organic matter. It lands at their feet with a hideous slap.

From the hospital in Phoenix, Scully phones Mulder. "Mulder, I found something," she says. "Something you won't believe."

"Ditto," says her partner.

Scully says that tests on Gibson's blood have identified a virus—the same virus she had been exposed to.

"What does that mean, Scully?" asks Mulder.

"I don't know," says Scully. "I don't know. But I think we're on to something huge. A link."

Says Mulder, "I'll call that bet and raise."

"What?"

"Never mind. Just take care of the kid."

In Gibson's room the sleeping boy's eyes snap open. A scrub-suited figure pulls open the bedside curtain. It is the Black-Haired Man.

Scully enters the same room several minutes later. To her shock and anger, the little boy is gone.

On the road to the reactor, a paramedic's ambulance—carrying Gibson, driven by his abductor—speeds along.

In the reactor building the agents continue to explore. They hear a door open next to a catwalk above them; it is the Black-Haired Man, with Gibson. Surreptitiously, the agents watch—then follow—them through a maze of corridors and machinery. They lose sight of the pair. A metal door slams shut. The agents run toward the sound.

In the room that holds the coolant-filled reactor core Gibson and the Black-Haired Man stare down into its brilliant blue-white glow.

"Seen it," says Gibson.

"Where?" asks the Black-Haired Man, drawing his gun.

"Somewhere," says the boy.

Shoving Gibson down a stairway in front of him, the Black-Haired Man walks slowly toward the reactor. Mulder—with Fowley behind him—appears behind the thick safety glass window of a door leading to the reactor room. He pounds on it angrily, his cries muffled. Fowley runs away to locate another entrance. Gibson and the Black-Haired Man stare impassively at Mulder through the window.

Gibson turns toward his captor. "I told you it was here," he says.

As Mulder watches helplessly, an alien figure approaches Gibson and his captor. There is an unearthly sound and a scream. The alien and Gibson gaze at each other for a moment. An alarm klaxon sounds; Fowley and a squad of NRC officials run toward the site. Fowley levels her gun at Mulder. Mulder turns back to the safety glass, now smeared with blood.

"Gibson! Gibson!" he yells, screaming helplessly.

Several days later, in a conference room we've seen before, the entire review board—absent Skinner—is present. AD Maslin speaks.

"As I said, and I am forced to reiterate, Agent Mulder, the FBI isn't here for vendettas or for the grinding of personal axes. This holds not just for you, but for everyone at the Bureau. You force us to put a point on this. To make some hard changes."

Behind Mulder sits his partner.

"You and Agent Scully will cease all material association with the X-Files. Refusal to do so will end in immediate dismissal. A probationary period will be set. You will now report to Assistant Director Kersh."

Assistant Director Kersh—a stolid African-American man in his forties—stares impassively at the agents.

Elsewhere in the FBI Building, sitting behind Mulder's old desk, is his brand-new replacement: Jeffrey Spender.

"You're not supposed to come here," says the agent, to a visitor. "It's what was agreed to. It's the deal we made."

Standing in the doorway, cigarette in hand, is the Cigarette-Smoking Man.

"I had to congratulate you," he says smugly. "Commend how you handled it. How you handled Mulder."

Spender rises uneasily and walks toward the Cigarette-Smoking Man. "I did what I was asked," he says.

"You did well, son," says the Cigarette-Smoking Man. "He's on very thin ice now."

Says Spender, "Mulder'll be back. As long as he lives, he won't give up."

The Cigarette-Smoking Man shrugs. "There are solutions, of course. Simple but extreme solutions. I've used these methods. They have their place. But not here."

Spender eyes the Cigarette-Smoking Man, some fear mixed with dismay. "You've killed men?"

The Cigarette-Smoking Man exhales a wisp of smoke. "You can kill a man," he says, "but you can't kill what he stands for."

Then, almost wistfully: "Unless you first break his spirit. That's a beautiful thing to see."

In a lab we've seen earlier, Mulder continues piecing together charred X-Files. Somebody enters the room behind him.

"It'd help if you shut the door, " says Mulder, "and make it harder for them to see that I'm totally disregarding everything I was told."

He turns back to his work. "They can't take away the X-Files, Scully. They've tried."

Scully gazes down at him sadly. "You know," she says, "Agent Fowley's report painted the facts in an

"I DON'T DOUBT WHAT YOU SAW,
MULDER. I DON'T DOUBT YOU.
I'M WILLING TO BELIEVE—
BUT NOT IN A LIE."–Scully

interesting way. I hope you haven't been betrayed."

Says Mulder, "Agent Fowley's report is a means to an end. It's to protect the work. Protect the X-Files."

"Mulder, Agent Fowley's report states that the man you saw attacked was 'bludgeoned by an unknown subject.' She makes no mention of a little boy, who as it happened was nowhere to be found. It would seem the report protects everyone but you."

Mulder shakes his head. "Agent Fowley took me to that plant at great risk to herself. Where I saw something that you refuse to believe in. Saw it again, Scully. And though it may not say it in her report, Diana saw it, too. No matter what you think, she's certainly not going to go around saying that just because science can't prove it, it isn't true."

Scully stares, expressionless, for a second, then speaks with passion.

"I don't doubt what you saw, Mulder. I don't doubt you. I'm willing to believe—but not in a lie. And not in the opposite of what I can prove.

"It comes down to a matter of trust. I guess it always has."

Mulder turns to face her. "You're asking me to make a choice?"

"I'm asking you to trust my judgment. To trust me." Scully extends her hand. In it is a file folder. Her test results.

"I can't accept that," says Mulder. "Not if it refutes what I know is true."

"Mulder, these are the results. DNA from the claw nail we found—matching exactly the DNA in the virus you believe is extraterrestrial—"

Mulder rises, astonished.

"That's the connection," he says softly.

"—which matches exactly," continues Scully, "the DNA I found in Gibson Praise."

Mulder stops short. "Wait a minute. I don't know what you're saying. You're saying that Gibson Praise is infected with the virus?"

"No," says Scully. "It's a part of his DNA. In fact, it's part of all our DNA. It's called a genetic remnant. Inactive junk DNA. Except in Gibson it's turned on."

Says Mulder, "So if that were true it would mean the boy is in some part extraterrestrial."

"It would mean," says Scully, "that all of us are."

Mulder can only stare at her, speechless.

In the nuclear power plant in Arizona, the reactor core still glows blue white. Floating in the nuclear coolant, clinging lightly onto a control rod, is the creature, alive. It is shedding its skin— molting—and turning into a classic extraterrestrial.

BACK STORY/6X01

Are you ready?

"The Beginning" is the 118th episode of The X-Files. It serves as the narrative continuation to both "The End" (5X22)—the final episode of its fifth season—and the X-Files movie. It is a major landmark in the evolution of the series's all-important mythology; the first installment in a grueling twenty-two episode season; and oh, yes: the first forty-six minutes of the X-Files filmed in Southern California with an almost entirely new cast of behind-the-camera artisans.

It was an episode plagued with several serious—perhaps inevitable—production problems

It was also, according to most of the serious fans and TV critics who watched it with special intensity, a particularly artful and effective way to launch the series's new season—and era.

"Obviously," recalls executive producer Frank Spotnitz, "the main problem was to segue from a movie that some people saw and some people did not see, and bring back several characters like Agent Fowley and Agent Spender."

"What we needed to do," says Chris Carter, "was wrap up some important story elements. Gibson Praise needed to return. We needed to see an alien we'd seen in the movie. We wanted to reestablish some of the conspiracy elements, and we wanted to suggest that there was a blurred line between what is terrestrial and extraterrestrial."

According to Carter—who says he began thinking about "The Beginning" even as the X-Files movie was taking shape two years ago—many of the plot points in 6X01 were designed to subtly prefigure the sweeping changes planned for three mythological episodes ("Two Fathers," "One Son," and "Biogenesis"). The very first shot of the season—a long look directly into a bright sun shining on a barren desert—was designed to boldly announce the show's arrival in Southern California.

On the other side of the picture tube, "The Beginning" was a serious search for the newly reconstituted production team. Most of the new hires, recruited and approved by Carter, Spotnitz, and co-executive producer Michael Watkins, adapted quickly to the X-Files work style.

Newly installed costume designer Christine Peters—used to working on comparatively slower-paced TV movies and feature films—recalls realizing immediately "that none of us knew what we were getting into. I'd told everyone who was working with me that this was going to be harder than anything we'd ever done. Now I realized I had no idea just how hard it would really be."

One of her X-Files rookie coworkers, property master Tom Day, spent the better part of his five weeks before filming began merely unpacking and cataloguing more than 400 boxes of props sent down from the former *X-Files* production office in Vancouver. All he remembers of the first episode—in fact, of the first four or five episodes—is a "big blur."

The first nightmare was the facility chosen to play the "nuclear power plant"—a conventional generating facility run by Southern California Edison in Long Beach. Allegedly a backup unit—run only rarely at times of extreme power demand—it would have been perfect, if it hadn't been rented in late July; the entire region hadn't been in the midst of an intense heat wave; and SCE hadn't chosen that particular week to fire up its generator and bring it online. Many of the scenes scheduled for the power plant location had to be filmed in temperatures well above one hundred degrees amidst noise higher than one hundred decibels. Most of the actors' dialogue had to be re-recorded in the studio.

In addition, most of the sequences featuring the power plant's resident alien had to be reshot—sometimes two or three times—because of persistent problems with the nuclear core sets and/or the skin-molting creature. Despite heroic efforts by the *X-Files* second-film unit, plus the art and construction departments, the requisite scenes weren't finished until late October, almost two months after the episode "wrapped" and only days before the season opener's air date.

Canadian actor Chris Owens (Jeffrey Spender), who moved to Los Angeles shortly before the season began, remembers 6X01 mainly for an automotive adventure.

"I'd just bought my new car," he says, "and on my first morning I realized I had to drive myself to Long Beach. I hadn't even been on the freeway yet. And guess what? I didn't have a map and I'd never heard of Long Beach."

At the specific request of Chris Carter and co-executive producer Michael Watkins, the part of Sandy, the Syndicate scientist who unwittingly incubates an alien inside him, was played by longtime *X-Files* casting director Rick Millikan. Millikan is a former actor whose previous onscreen zenith was playing a rapist in *Child Bride of Short Creek*, a 1981 TV movie starring a teenage Helen Hunt. Millikan recalls spending most of his time on the 6X01 location on his cell phone, frantically casting "Drive" (6X02). As for the obvious question: "I paid myself scale," he says resignedly.

The scenes set in the Arizona suburb where Sandy lived were actually filmed in Valencia, a bedroom community north of Los Angeles. "They were looking for something really *Edward Scissorhands*," says location manager Ilt Jones.

The underwater scenes of the alien in the reactor core were filmed in a Marina Del Rey water tank usually employed by the crew of *Baywatch*.

Researcher Lee Smith was assigned the task of finding out whether a child—such as Gibson Praise—could have brain surgery without anesthesia, be sewn up, and be ready to travel in an hour. He called the head of the American Association of Neurosurgeons, who turned out to be an enthusiastic *X-Files* fan. "He told me it was possible," says Smith. "The patient would be a little dizzy—you wouldn't want him to drive or operate heavy machinery—but he would be fine."

A carjacking and subsequent highway chase have an inexplicably deadly ending: an innocent victim's head explodes. **Disobeying FBI orders, Mulder investigates—** and becomes a high-speed hostage himself.

DRIVE

LIVE

SKY 11

6⊗02

EPISODE: 6X02
FIRST AIRED: November 15, 1998
EDITOR: Lynne Willingham
WRITTEN BY: Vince Gilligan
DIRECTED BY: Rob Bowman

GUEST STARS:

Bryan Cranston (Patrick Crump)
Janine Venable (Vicky Crump)
Junior Brown (Virgil Nokes)
Michael O'Neill (Patrol Captain)
James Pickens, Jr. (AD Kersh)
Mindy Seeger (Coroner)
Scott A. Smith (Prison Doctor)

Harry Danner (CDC Doctor)
Linda Porter (Elderly Woman)
Ken Collins (Gas Station Attendant)
Tegan West (Lieutenant Breil)
Art Pickering (Germ Suit Cop)
Mark Craig (Trooper #1)
Tim Agee (EMT)
Wiley Picket (Trooper #2)
Frank Buckley (Nevada News Anchor)
Bob Peters (Idaho News Anchor)

PRINCIPAL SETTINGS:

Elko, Montello, and Wendover, Nevada; Buhl, Idaho; Loleta, California

A local Fox affiliate breaks into regular programming to present an urgent news bulletin. The station's video camera–equipped helicopter swoops over a fast-breaking story:

On a rural road near Elko, Nevada, a stolen Plymouth Barracuda speeds at 100 mph—pursued by police cars behind it. At the wheel is a rough-looking man in his forties; in the back seat, in obvious physical distress, is a woman of his same age and social class.

Further up the road—at Milepost Thirteen—a highway patrolman stretches a spiked chain across the traffic lanes. When the Barracuda runs over it the muscle car's tires are shredded and it swerves to a halt.

The pursuing policemen stop, haul the driver out of the car, wrestle him to the ground, and handcuff him. Still struggling frantically, the man calls out a woman's name. In the back seat the passenger is in more agony than ever.

"Get it out of my head!" she moans, hands pressed to her temples.

The policemen help the woman out of the car and into the back of one of their own vehicles. The handcuffed man's cries grow louder, his struggles more frantic. In the patrol car the woman begins banging her head against a window—once, twice, then many times. A large, bright starburst of blood sprays onto the inside of the window glass. The woman topples over onto the seat, lifeless.

At a weather-beaten farmhouse in Buhl, Idaho, Mulder and Scully knock, identify themselves, and ask a bleary-eyed, bearish character named Virgil Nokes why he recently placed an order for five thousand pounds of ammonium nitrate fertilizer—a prime ingredient for creating a cheap terrorist bomb.

"I grow sugar beets," says the farmer. "Figger I got better things to do with my fertilizer than go around blowin' gummint buildings sky high."

Explains Scully, "This is just routine, sir."

"So routine," mutters Mulder, "that it numbs the mind."

While Virgil searches for his federal fertilizer permit, the agents enter the dusty house. Inside, an account of the high-speed chase is playing on a rabbit-eared television. Mulder watches with fascination, then calls Scully over to watch the replay. She joins him just as the woman's head explodes again.

Says a TV anchorman, "At this time, police officials are refusing to identify the woman or to speculate on how she died, though they do stress it was not the result of a gunshot. A preliminary coroner's report isn't expected for a day or two. Meanwhile, residents of . . ."

A few minutes later Scully leaves the farmhouse—and catches Mulder on his cell phone, volunteering both of them to help the local police solve the mystery. She looks at her partner accusingly.

"Mulder, we're not going to Nevada," she says.

"C'mon, Scully. Just one quick side trip."

"No. Sorry, Mulder. We have a whole new assignment now."

"Running down people that buy fertilizer?" says Mulder, scornfully. "This is scut work, bozo work. This is the FBI equivalent of being made to wear an orange jumpsuit and being made to pick up trash by the side of the highway. They mean to humiliate us."

Scully is unmoved. "Look, Mulder, like it or not, humiliated or not, we're on domestic terrorism."

She adds, "And yes, this is a punishment. But if we want to get back to where we want to be, we have to follow orders. We can't freelance."

Mulder looks Scully in the eye.

"You saw that news report," he says. "What did you make of it?"

"I think that the obvious assumption is that the woman was shot, regardless of what the police say. Maybe it was a sniper."

Now it's Mulder's turn to be unconvinced.

"In the words of their captain," he says, "'She just sorta popped.' And what about this guy who supposedly tried to take her hostage? Her husband. It looked like he was trying to warn the cops before she died."

He adds, "No, the sun will rise in America tomorrow regardless of whether or not we're at yet another farm investigating yet another enormous pile of doo-doo."

Scully says nothing.

"C'mon," cajoles Mulder. "We can be in and out in a day. Nobody has to know."

At a precinct house cell block in Elko, the arrested carjacker lies on his bunk, resting. Blood begins to ooze from one nostril. When he realizes this he sits bolt upright, terrified. He stands and grabs the bars of his cell door.

"Somebody! Please!" he shouts. "It's starting! PLEASE!"

Some time later, in another part of the precinct house, a patrol captain denies Mulder and Scully's request to interview the driver. "He threw quite a fit in his cell, screaming a bunch of nonsense, saying we were going to kill him like we killed his wife," explains the cop.

"You know," he adds, "he's not a particularly stable individual."

He tells the agents that a doctor is examining him,

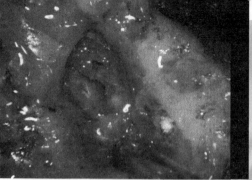

repeats that his wife's death wasn't the police department's fault, and hands Scully a file folder. Inside are the man's mug shots and his name: Patrick Garland Crump, of Montello, Nevada.

Mulder reads over Scully's shoulder. "Forty-year-old roofer. No history of mental illness. No prior record," he says.

"He's got one now," says the captain. "That Barracuda he jacked on the Utah state line? He yanked some teenager out the window, threw his wife in back, and took off."

The policeman walks away. Scully tells Mulder that she'd like to examine Mrs. Crump's body. Mulder nods and walks to a large map of the surrounding area. He and the captain retrace Crump's route: from Montello five miles east to the Utah border, then west through Elko to the point where he was captured.

"Why?" asks Mulder.

The captain shrugs and shakes his head, not overly intrigued. Mulder stares at the map, thinking.

In an examination room at the city coroner's office a female coroner leads Scully to the corpse of Vicky Jenkins Crump.

"I'm hoping you can tell me what I'm looking at," says the coroner. "This is a new one on me."

Scully pulls on a pair of latex gloves and bends down to peer at the shattered side of the corpse's head. "There's no gunpowder residue," she says softly. "No carbon stippling."

She examines the other intact side. "There seems to be no evidence of an entry wound altogether."

"There is none. It's all exit," says the coroner, flatly.

Scully peers through a magnifying glass. "I'm finding what look like fragments of petrous bone embedded in the remaining portion of the auditory canal. In fact, I seem to be looking straight through to the osseous labyrinth—or what's left of it."

The coroner nods. "It's almost like a little bomb went off in her ear," she says.

Using the steel tip of a surgical probe, Scully pushes gently into the affected area. A spurt of blood bubbles up and sprays her. She and the coroner stare at the dead woman, shocked and completely baffled.

At the rear entrance of the precinct house Patrick Crump, strapped to a gurney and wearing an oxygen mask, is loaded into an ambulance. The police doctor shouts orders to a squad of paramedics, while explaining to the patrol captain that the prisoner's condition has suddenly started to deteriorate rapidly.

Mulder runs to the scene, tries to board the ambulance, and is pushed out by a paramedic. He jogs to his rental car, gets in, and follows the police motorcade toward the hospital.

On the highway the ambulance hits 75 mph. Inside, the doctor notes with astonishment that Crump's heart rate is slowing and his condition is miraculously improving. Conscious now, Crump turns his head toward a deputy sheriff at his side, guarding him. He eyes the lawman's revolver in its holster.

At the wheel of his sedan, Mulder sees the ambulance swerve slightly and brake to a halt. He jams on his own brakes, barely avoiding a collision. The back door opens, and Crump gets out—pointing the revolver directly at Mulder.

In the city morgue Scully dials a number on her cell phone. As it starts to ring she spots a lab assistant entering her room.

"Hey, you—out!" she yells. "This lab is quarantined! GO!"

She locks the door behind the fleeing tech. Mulder answers his phone.

"Mulder, it's me," she says, pacing agitatedly. "You know how to pick 'em, I'll tell you that."

She adds, "Look, I have no idea what killed this woman, but I have to assume it's communicable."

"Yeah?" says Mulder.

"Another body's been found, just outside of Montello. Same apparent cause of death—some kind of massive aneurysmal rupture."

"Uh-huh."

"Now, I've called the CDC," adds Scully, breathlessly. "They're on their way. Patrick Crump may be infected. So you need to quarantine his cell, and make sure that anybody who's had any close contact with him whatsoever has been quarantined as well. And that means you, Mulder! You're to have no contact with him whatsoever!"

Silence.

"Mulder?"

"Well, that's gonna be a little tough, Scully," says her partner, at the wheel of his speeding car.

Someone reaches up and over his car's back seat, sticks a gun in Mulder's ear, and pulls away the cell phone. It is Crump. The carjacker glances backward at a phalanx of pursuing police cars, turns back around toward Mulder, and draws another bead on the agent.

"Drive," he says, menacingly.

Behind a plate-glass window in the quarantine lab, Scully scrawls her cell phone number on a piece of paper and holds it up for the police captain to see. He nods, dials, then tells her that Mulder and Crump are heading west; that they're being kept in visual contact; and that the police have pulled some strings to keep the chase off local TV.

"Where are they going?" asks Scully, grimly.

"Crump won't say. Wherever it is, though, he ain't getting there. I'll see to that."

"Roadblock?"

The captain nods. "We'll shut him down east of Tuscarora. Nice, clean, remote space we can own."

Scully sighs and directs that the arrest be made by officers wearing anti-contamination suits, monitored by the CDC and—and that Mulder's car be decontaminated; that Mulder and Crump be decontaminated; and that the men be quarantined separately. The captain agrees, then turns to an officer with a message for him. He puts the phone back to his ear.

"Crump says," he tells Scully, "that if we don't pull back our escort, he's gonna shoot your partner."

In the speeding rental car Crump shouts into the cell phone for the police cars to pull back. They do. He spots Mulder's FBI ID, opens it, and snorts in disgust. The phone rings. To Mulder's shouted dismay, Crump flings it out the window. In obvious pain now, he brandishes the gun. Mulder stops for a red light. Crump screams in agony and rage.

"Keep going! KEEP GOING! GO!"

Losing consciousness, Crump drops the gun. Seeing this in his rearview mirror, Mulder runs the red light and, amidst a cacophony of squealing brakes and tires, speeds down the road.

"Crump?" says Mulder to his passenger. "Is this what happened to your wife? This same thing? If you stop moving, you die?"

Crump stirs slightly, but says nothing.

"I think I saw this movie," says Mulder. "Why didn't you tell anyone? Why didn't you tell the police?"

Again, nothing.

"Hey, look," says the agent. "I don't know how well you recall the last thirty seconds, but your life is in my hands regardless of whether or not you hold that gun. Just tell me everything you know.

That may be the only way I can help you!"

Crump regains the gun. "You people put me here!" he shouts.

"Shut up!" says Mulder, thinking.

He tells Crump that he expects a roadblock in two or three miles. Crump spots a pursuing helicopter, then grimaces in pain.

"If we get stopped—" he groans.

Mulder glances back at him, comprehending. He turns onto a dirt road to avoid the roadblock. This news is relayed from the helicopter to Scully and the captain. Puzzled, the cop asks the agent why Mulder would steer away from the police.

"Maybe he knows something we don't," says Scully.

In another part of the lab a moon-suited CDC doctor, peering through a microscope, tells Scully that he sees no evidence of infection in either victim.

"So then we're in the clear?" asks the coroner.

"No. Not necessarily," says Scully. "*Something killed these people.*"

Scully's phone rings. It is AD Kersh, her new supervisor (from 6X01). He asks her coolly how things are going in southern Idaho.

"Think carefully," he adds.

Nervously, Scully admits that she is not in southern Idaho.

"No. You are not," says Kersh.

Says Scully, "In the course of prosecuting our assignment in Idaho, Agent Mulder and I came across a situation in Nevada which we both strongly felt needed our immediate attention."

"I eagerly await your report," says Kersh, with irony.

He adds that agents from the Las Vegas field office will help her track down Mulder.

"I think at this point," says Kersh, "I want to see him alive even more than you do."

He hangs up abruptly. Chastened, Scully turns back to the second victim. She notes from his chart that he was a meter reader for the local power company.

"Could he have read the meter at Vicky Crump's house?" she asks.

Sheltered from aerial surveillance by a canopy of trees, Mulder guns the car down the dirt road. "Crump?" he says to the agonized man behind him. "What else can you tell about what's happening to you?"

"*Mr.* Crump," snarls the roofer. "You call me by my

"It's west!
WEST. YOU GOTTA HEAD WEST. JUST LIKE YOU DID WITH YOUR WIFE."—Mulder

last name, you say 'Mister' in front of it."

"'Mister.' Gotcha," says Mulder. "I can think of something else to call you. I can put 'Mister' in front of that, too, if you'd like."

Crump sits up with difficulty and glares at Mulder.

"You know, what kind of name is Mulder, anyway?" he says. "What is that, like, Jewish?"

"*Excuse* me?" says Mulder, incredulously.

"Jewish. It is, right?" says Crump.

"It's *Mr.* Mulder to you, you peanut-picking bastard," replies the agent, angrily. "Now, *Mr.* Crump. What can you tell me about what's happeni—"

recounts that when he woke that morning his wife was ill and in pain; when he put her in their truck and drove to the hospital she only seemed to worsen.

Says Crump, "It seemed like the faster we went the better she'd do. But just as soon as I'd try to slow down or stop—"

Mulder looks at the grieving man in the rearview. "I'm sorry about your wife," he says.

Crump looks up, and scowls. "Sure you are," he says. "With the rest of your Jew FBI."

"Crump—"

"Oh, yeah! You think I don't know about it. You think

"I HAVE TO INFORM YOU THAT WE'RE ALMOST OUT OF GAS."–Mulder

At this, Crump screams and doubles over in excruciating pain. "You're goin' the wrong way!" he gasps.

He points to the left. "Go this way! GO THIS WAY!"

Mulder can't turn left. There is no place to turn. Crump starts to pound his head against the car window. Finally, Mulder reaches a turnoff and skids on to the left-hand fork. He looks back at his captor, who is exhausted—but still alive. He makes an important connection.

"It's west!" says Mulder. "West. You gotta head west. Just like you did with your wife. You took her and you headed west. It's not just motion—it has to be in one direction. Is that it, Crump?"

Crump can't speak. But he nods.

Says Mulder, quietly, "What the hell happened to you?"

That night at a trailer park in Montello a moon-suited Scully—accompanied by a phalanx of moon-suited CDC men—examines the Crump residence for evidence of contagion. What they find is a chained attack dog, barking frantically. They approach it to take a blood sample—and its head explodes.

Heading westward on a rural road, Mulder questions Crump, who has partially recovered, and seems to have granted him a grudging measure of trust. Crump

I'm just some ignorant pudknocker, don't ya? But I *get* it, man! I see what this is! I am *not* sick. I do *not* have the flu. Vicky and I were just some kinda government guinea pigs."

"The government did this to you?" says Mulder, with a flicker of interest.

"Well, yeah, man, who else? You see it every day on the TV: They're droppin' Agent Orange, they're putting radiation in little retarded kids' gonads. Yeah, I've watched you sonsabitches, sneakin' around my woods at night. I seen you. You think I don't know?"

Mulder glances down at his dashboard.

"Well, on behalf of the International Jewish Conspiracy," he says, "I have to inform you that we're almost out of gas."

At the Crump trailer neither Scully nor the CDC officials can find evidence of contagious disease. A baffled Scully spots a light shining from a neighboring trailer. The team enters it and loudly announces their presence—to no response. A parakeet lies dead in its cage. Scully enters the trailer's living room and shines her flashlight beam on an elderly lady seated in an easy chair, watching television. Frightened, the woman screams, her cries incoherent. Scully looks at the television screen. A movie is being shown with closed captioning.

The woman is deaf.

In Mulder's rental car the low fuel warning light blinks on. Mulder warns Crump that he will be stopping, then ducks into a gas station for a fill-up. He tries the nearest pump. The hose is too short. He thrusts another nozzle into the filler tube; the attendant shouts at him that he has to pay before he pumps. Frantic now, Mulder hauls the nearly unconscious Crump into an old Chevy station wagon parked at another pump—and takes off, yanking its pump nozzle from its filler tube. The Chevy's owner—a burly ZZ Top type—rushes out from inside the station, yelling for them to stop.

On the front seat of the rental car is a scrawled note addressed to Dana Scully—FBI.

At the Montello house the elderly woman is loaded onto a CDC van. Thinking hard, Scully turns to the CDC doctor. "One deaf woman survives while everything else in the area dies. Why?"

The doctor has no answer. To his horror, though, Scully slowly removes the helmet of her anti-contamination suit. She takes a deep breath.

"The pathology of this thing—it affects the inner ear," Scully says, with conviction. "And this area here is ground zero. What if what we're looking for is some kind of sound?"

Her cell phone rings. Scully unzips her suit and retrieves it. It's the patrol captain, at the gas station. He tells her that Mulder is not only evading his men but has stolen a car. He reads her the note he left behind: "'Crump sick,'" he reads. "'Will die if stopped, same as wife. Must head west to keep alive. No roadblocks,' exclamation point.

"This make any sense to you?" asks the cop.

It doesn't, but Scully tells him to let Mulder keep driving. She looks down. Amidst a pile of dead birds lies a metal access plate, flush with the ground. It reads: U.S. GOVERNMENT PROPERTY: TAMPERING PUNISHABLE BY FINE AND INCARCERATION.

In the back of the battered Chevy, Crump lies in agony. He urges Mulder to go faster—and Mulder pushes the old car past 70. Crump apologizes for his racist remarks, then wonders, anger mixed with sorrow, why the government would strip him of his health and his dignity this way.

Says Mulder, "You've gotta stay alive if you want to stick it to the government. If you die, you let them off the hook. Am I right?"

"Right. Damn straight," croaks the passenger.

Says Mulder, "We'll figure this out."

"Better figure quick," says Crump. "We're runnin' out of west."

Mulder nods. The Chevy rockets past a sign on the side of the road. It reads: WELCOME TO CALIFORNIA: GATEWAY TO THE PACIFIC.

At Horizon View Naval Research Station in Wendover, Nevada, Scully shows up for an appointment with a tight-lipped Navy lieutenant named Breil. On the wall is painted a stylized nuclear sub; part of the insignia for something called "Operation Seafarer."

"My name is Dana Scully," she says. "I called in regard to the electrical equipment that the Navy maintains in the town of Montello."

"Right," says the officer, grimacing.

He recites, "At six-seventeen yesterday morning, in a test of our ground conduction radio system, a situation arose in which our equipment experienced a brief power surge. That's what interrupted television reception in the four-state area. However, steps have already been taken to insure this won't happen again."

Asks Scully, "The ground conduction radio—that would be Project Seafarer?"

Breil replies that the nature of their project is classified.

"Sure, sure," says Scully, reassuringly.

She asks, "Would you happen to know what effect such a surge might have on an organism? Say, a human being? Theoretically speaking."

The Navy man looks at her warily. "Theoretically speaking—that's classified as well."

At dawn, heading westward through California, the Chevy is approached by a pair of CHP officers on motorcycles. Crump curses them under his breath. One of them pulls up to Mulder's window—and hands him a cell phone.

"Mulder, are you okay?" says Scully, on the other end.

"Yeah," says Mulder. "Aside from terminal cell phone withdrawal. That, and I gotta pee. Where are you?"

She tells him she's about to board a Justice Department jet and head to wherever she can intercept her partner.

"I'm guessing wherever the hell Route Thirty-six ends," says Mulder. "But we can't stop, Scully, and I'm kind of at a loss as to what we can do next."

Says Scully, "I think I may have a loose theory as to what caused this."

"Lay it on me," says Mulder.

"Okay. Mulder, do you know what ELF waves are? Extremely low frequency transmissions?"

"Yeah," says Mulder. "It uses an antenna like fifty miles long. The military uses it to communicate with Trident submarines. Project Seafarer, Project HAARP—"

"Mulder, Seafarer has an antenna array stretching beneath the edge of Patrick Crump's property. Now, ELF fields have been shown to produce biological effects on human tissue—inducing electrical currents, altering chemical reactions—"

"Not to mention that it has potential weapons application," says Mulder. "It's been referred to as 'electrical nerve gas.' Or that it may be behind the so-called 'Taos Hum.'"

Says Scully, "What if some overload, some 'hum' from this system, could somehow match the resonant frequency of the human skull? What if it could induce a like 'hum,' that could somehow exert a rising pressure on the inner ear? In a sense, shattering it?"

Says Mulder, "But with constant pressure somehow ameliorating that pressure, making it bearable. But why only westward motion?"

"I don't know, Mulder. Maybe it follows only certain lines of force, electrical or magnetic."

"But the big question is, Scully, what do we do about it?"

Silently, Mulder listens to Scully's explanation.

"We'll be there," he says.

The agent turns around and explains to Crump that his one chance is for Scully to meet them at the end of the highway and quickly, with no time for anesthetic, insert a long, large-bore needle into his inner ear. This process will relieve the pressure, but likely leave him deaf.

"But I'll live, right?" says Crump.

Mulder nods.

"That's what it's all about," says Crump, shakily. "Let's do it."

In Loleta, California, where the highway dead-ends at the Pacific Ocean, Mulder's car, escorted by police, pulls to a halt at the continent's edge—past Scully and a team of waiting paramedics.

Scully jogs to the car. A starburst of blood coats the inside of the window glass. Mulder gets out of the car, takes off his necktie, and stares out at the ocean, his face unreadable.

At FBI headquarters, Mulder and Scully stand in front of Kersh while the AD itemizes the thousands of dollars in unauthorized expenses they've incurred.

"Why don't you bill me," says Mulder, curtly.

Kersh looks up.

"I'm going to bill your partner, instead," he says. "You too obviously relish the role of martyr."

Mulder nods.

"So are we done here? Back to the bozo work? Investigating huge piles of manure?"

"You can always quit," says Kersh, coolly.

Mulder turns on his heel and leaves.

Says Scully, "Sir, Agent Mulder has been through a lot."

"And you apologize for him a lot," says Kersh. "I've noticed that about you."

Replies Scully, "I'm not apologizing for this. Because of his work, the DOD is shutting down their antenna in northeastern Nevada. Our participation in this case will save lives."

Says Kersh, "I can't see you proving that. The Department of Defense admits no culpability whatsoever. Furthermore, they say the closing of that facility is coincidental."

Kersh stares at Scully evenly.

"Don't misunderstand me, Agent. I don't care if you and your partner saved a school bus full of doe-eyed urchins on their way to Sunday Bible camp. You no longer investigate X-Files. You are done. The sooner you and Mulder come to recognize that fact, the better for both of you."

Kersh looks down again, dismissing her. Scully turns and walks away.

"Big piles of manure," she mutters.

Is "Drive" *The X-Files* on *Speed*?

Well, yes and no. Co-executive producer Vince Gilligan, sole writer on the episode, cheerfully admits that 6X02 is partly an "homage" to the 1994 hit action movie. But Gilligan, author of some of *The X-Files's* most popular and idiosyncratic installments, adds that there is an additional—and, typical for the series, comically convoluted—explanation of the existence of "Drive."

"I'd had this idea for a teaser [the short opening scene of an episode] for two seasons," says Gilligan, seated in his office on the Fox lot, his eyes flashing with excitement and mischief.

Gilligan continues, "There's this carnival, see? And it's in full swing and kids are with their parents and everyone's eating cotton candy and having a good time. And through this idyllic scene you see a bunch of SWAT cops, running and carrying submachine guns and giving each other hand signals. And you say to yourself: 'What the hell's going on?'

"Then you cut to this Tilt-a-Whirl that's going full speed. There's a guy on this amusement park ride who's holding a big .44 magnum on a hostage, and he's yelling to the operator: 'If you shut this off I'll kill her!'

"The Tilt-a-Whirl keeps whirling. So the SWAT cops take

action—first yelling at him through a bullhorn; then popping a tear gas canister under the Tilt-a-Whirl—with the centrifugal force the tears come out of his eyes sideways—then watching the bad guy's gun clatter to the pavement; then turning off the ride and taking the guy prisoner.

"What happened next? I had absolutely no idea. So every time I'd mention the Tilt-a-Whirl—and it became a running joke in our story meetings—the other guys would say: 'Where's the rest of the story? Where's the *X-File* here?' So I finally started joking about it. I said: 'His head explodes! That's why he doesn't want to get off the ride!' I didn't mean it seriously, not at all. But at the beginning of the season John Shiban and I were talking about it. We were looking for a story for me to write, and he said: 'Why don't you do something with that crazy Tilt-a-Whirl idea?' And I began to think about it a little more seriously. Why *would* someone's head explode? And the answer, surprisingly, came fairly quickly."

As a long-time connoisseur of dangerous-sounding government experiments, he was well aware of the controversies surrounding the military's use of extremely low frequency radio waves for secret communication. With an upfront thank you to *Speed*—Mulder commenting, in the thick of the action, that "I think I saw this movie"—he neatly reversed its main

drive

"SO ARE WE DONE HERE? BACK TO THE BOZO WORK? INVESTIGATING HUGE PILES OF MANURE?"–Mulder

plot device, making a moving vehicle's inhabitant, not the vehicle itself, a speed-sensitive explosive.

The writing process went smoothly, and by midsummer Gilligan had produced a fast-paced thriller, and, to the admiration of many, a tense psychological drama as well.

"To me," says Rob Bowman, the episode's director, "the high point was the relationship between Mulder and Crump, the man holding him hostage. Their character arcs and attitudes to each other constantly twist and turn; the feelings they evoke in each other going from panic to anger to respect. I think Vince did a great job making the whole thing come full circle."

Gillian Anderson, an unabashed admirer of "Drive," agrees. "It was a great script. A great premise. I thought they carried it off really well, especially the actor who played Crump, the guy in the back seat. He was just phenomenal."

In point of fact, the casting of Bryan Cranston as Patrick Crump nearly didn't occur. "We'd almost decided to go with another guy. I'd called him in for another part entirely," says casting director Rick Millikan.

Millikan adds that he remembered Cranston—a well-regarded young actor best remembered as the one-armed War Department colonel in *Saving Private Ryan*—as a handsome, clean-cut type not suited to play a rough, desperate character like Crump.

"But when he came in, he had a beard and a mustache and really scraggly clothes. Whether through miscommunication or something else, he came to the room prepared to read the part of Crump. I almost decided to stop him, but since he looked so perfect I let him go ahead. And then he sat down, started reading, and hit a major home run. I thought: 'My God! I've got to choose him!' A great story. A great experience."

"Drive" became a series of daunting challenges for a crew working together on only their second episode. The most impressive technical accomplishment of the shoot was the naturalistic lighting and filming of Mulder and Crump as their car sped along the very roads where the action takes place. Amazingly, no external lights were beamed into the car's interiors. The centerpiece of this effort—rarely, if ever, tried before on a weekly television show—was an ingenious assemblage of pipe-mounted sheets of black cardboard (constructed by key grip Tom Doherty's crew), attached to the body of the car and designed to *subtract* excessive sunlight from the shot. It was a brilliant feat of cinematic improvisation—nearly invisible to viewers, as is usually the case in behind-the-scenes miracles—a fact that was duly noted by the American Society of Cinematographers. That organization named "Drive" the best-filmed hour of episodic television of the season. Director of photography Bill Roe received the award.

The episode's difficult air-to-ground scenes—as well as many of the other automotive action sequences—

"Drive" BECAME A SERIES OF DAUNTING CHALLENGES FOR A CREW WORKING TOGETHER ON ONLY THEIR SECOND EPISODE.

were shot in a rural area around Canyon Country, in the Santa Clarita Valley, twenty miles northeast of Los Angeles. (Steven Spielberg fans might recognize it as the site of his 1971 TV movie *Duel.*)

The first attempt at aerial filming was aborted when the rented camera helicopter began spewing oil and had to make an immediate precautionary landing. Virtuosic rescheduling—of a replacement chopper; the *X-Files'* second-unit film crew; and dozens of ground vehicles and other personnel—ensued. The vital footage was obtained without incident several days later.

Automobiles figure prominently in 6X02's plotline. Picture car coordinator Danny Briggs "cast" a couple of vintage Plymouth Barracudas as Crump's getaway car and a pair of *V-8-powered* 1968 Chevrolet Chevelle station wagons—which, during filming, actually went as fast as was indicated in the episode—as the vehicle that Mulder swipes at the gas station during his frantic trip westward. One of the station wagons had its rear seats removed to fit a camera mount. One of the Barracudas had tiny remote-controlled explosive charges attached to its tires to produce on-cue blowouts during filming of the "nail strip" sequence. "It took quite a few takes to get that just right," says mechanic Kelly Padovic. "Luckily, we'd bought about thirty-two identical tires and rims ahead of time."

A scene that was explosive for other reasons—the one in which Scully discovers dozens of dead birds on the grounds of the Crumps' trailer park—was facilitated by props master Tom Day and his helpers renting dozens of stuffed birds from a taxidermist; painting "exploded ear canals" on several for close-up shots; and pasting feathers on toy birds to use as barely seen victims on the perimeter of the shot.

The shot where Crump throws his cell phone out of a moving car was accomplished by . . . throwing a cell phone out of a moving car. (Although, reports second-unit production manager Harry Bring, it might have been nice if they'd remembered to use the rubber dummy cell phone brought for that purpose rather than mistakenly destroy one of their only links to the production office.)

"Drive" marks the first substantial appearance of James Pickens, Jr., as the enigmatically hard-ass AD Kersh. Pickens prepared for his role by observing several of his real-life counterparts at the FBI's Los Angeles office. "The most useful thing I learned was that most of the people at Kersh's level have been with the Bureau for twenty or twenty-five years," notes the actor. "They didn't get where they are by taking their work less than seriously or bucking the system for no good reason."

In most episodes he writes or cowrites, co-executive producer/writer Vince Gilligan salutes his girlfriend Holly Rice.

In "Drive," the gas station where Mulder hijacks the station wagon is named "Holly's."

The scenes in this episode set in the Elko, Nevada, jail were actually filmed in the empty downtown headquarters building of the long-defunct Los Angeles Herald-Examiner. The *X-Files* crew returned much later in the season; parts of the derelict newsroom stood in for a Mississippi prison superintendent's office in "Trevor" (6X17).

To give Patrick Crump the necessary look of desperation and ill health, makeup department head Cheri Monetesanto-Medcalf blew menthol into actor Ryan Cranston's eyes and used liberal amounts of red eyeliner.

The scene where Mulder and Crump's desperate drive comes to an end was filmed at White Point Beach, a seldom-filmed Pacific overlook just south of the Los Angeles harbor community of San Pedro.

Junior Brown, who played the small role of the farmer Virgil Nokes in 6X02, is in real life not an actor but an avante garde country music singer/songwriter/steel guitar player (his best-known song: "My Wife Thinks You're Dead") with a cult following. One of his biggest fans is Vince Gilligan, who thought he would be so right for the part—and so much wanted to meet him—that he put up his own money to fly him in from Oklahoma. "I made sure to visit the set that day to get his autograph," says Gilligan. "He's a great guy!"

"Project Seafarer," the fictional U.S. Navy experimental communications system that explodes the Crumps' brains, has at least two (nonlethal, as far as is known) real life counterparts. Project HAARP—for "High Frequency Active Auroral Research Program"—is a U.S. Army system for bouncing very high intensity beams of electromagnetic radiation off the Earth's ionosphere. Project ELF—for Extremely Low Frequency—is a U.S. Navy project for communicating with submerged Trident submarines by radiating extremely long waves of electromagnetic energy through the Earth.

Researcher Lee Smith contacted the military and several military contractors to get what unclassified facts about these projects that were available. "It's a funny thing," says Smith, "but when I talked to everybody the first time and asked them if the waves put out by the transmitters could harm anyone, they all told me that it was impossible. Then, totally out of the blue, a couple of them called me a few weeks later. They both said something like: 'Look, I couldn't tell you this the first time, but the answer is yes.'"

6 X 03

TRIANGLE

Hauled onto a World War II-era ocean liner trapped in the Bermuda Triangle, Mulder must get his bearings, fight off Nazi raiders—and ensure that democracy survives in the twentieth century.

EPISODE: 6X03
FIRST AIRED: November 22, 1998
EDITOR: Louise A. Innes
WRITTEN BY: Chris Carter
DIRECTED BY: Chris Carter

GUEST STARS:
Mitch Pileggi (AD Walter Skinner/Nazi Officer)
William B. Davis (The Cigarette-Smoking Man/Nazi Officer)
Chris Owens (Agent Jeffrey Spender/Nazi Officer)
Madison Mason (Captain Harburg)
James Pickens, Jr. (AD Kersh)
Tom Braidwood (Frohike)
Dean Haglund (Langly)
Bruce Harwood (Byers)
Robert Thomas Beck (First Mate)
Trevor Goodard (First British Crewman)
G.W. Stevens (Second British Crewman)
Greg Ellis (Third British Crewman)
Nick Meaney (Fourth British Crewman)
Robert Arce (Bald-Headed Man)
Wolfgang Gerhard (First Nazi)
Guido Foehrweisser (Second Nazi)
Kai Wulff (Third Nazi)
Isaac C. Singleton, Jr. (Roughneck)
Arlene Pileggi (Skinner's Assistant)
Laura Leigh Hughes (Kersh's Assistant/Girl Singer)

PRINCIPAL SETTINGS:
Sargasso Sea; Washington, D.C.

In letterbox format: On bright blue tropical waters, the pieces of a wrecked boat—the *Lady Garland*—float placidly. Behind its shattered stern floats a man's body, facedown. It is Fox Mulder.

That night it is raining; the seas stormy. A gang of British sailors hoist Mulder's limp body up and over the rail of a large ship. They deposit him unceremoniously onto the wooden deck; when they see him begin to cough and stir they then regard him suspiciously. Someone kicks Mulder, hard, in the back. He recoils from the blow.

"Sprechen ze deutsch? Ya?" says one of the Englishmen, accusingly.

"I say he's a rat!" says another. "And we throw him overboard like a rat!"

"Right!" says a third. "Let's give him the heave-ho!"

They drag the agent to his feet.

"Oy! What you got to say for yourself, Jerry?" says the first crewman. "Before we throw you back in."

Mulder shakes his head, weak and confused. "My name isn't Jerry," he says.

"What's that, mate?"

"My name's Mulder. Fox Mulder. I got ID in my pocket."

The first crewman removes his waterlogged wallet.

"Fox Mulder," he reads. "Federal Bureau of Investigation."

He pauses, then snarls, "Sorry, mate! Never heard of it!"

The crewmen swarm over Mulder and manhandle him into a passageway.

"Where'd you pick up that accent?" demands the second crewman.

The third crewman answers him. "Probably in the Fuhrer's secret service!"

Threatening him angrily, the crewmen hustle Mulder down a wood-paneled passageway to the captain's cabin. A crewman whispers to the gray-haired skipper that Mulder is probably a German spy. The captain orders Mulder dragged into his room—and slaps Mulder, hard, on the side of his face. Twice.

"Friend or foe?" asks the captain. "To what flag do you pledge allegiance?"

"I think there's been a mistake," says Mulder. "I think the mistake is mine."

Angered, the captain hauls off and slaps Mulder again. "Speak the truth, man!" he says.

Says Mulder, "This is the *Queen Anne,* isn't it? I came looking for this ship."

At this, the crewmen snap open their switchblades and press them against Mulder's neck. This truly gets the agent's attention.

"Hold on a second!" says Mulder, quickly. "I think I can explain what's going on. What's our current position?"

The captain frowns.

"Cut the spy up!" he says, furious.

"No, no! I'll tell you!" shouts Mulder. "We're two degrees above the thirtieth parallel. Sargasso Sea, just above the Tropic of Cancer. Sixty-four degrees west by southwest. Off the Plantagenat Banks, sixty miles south southwest off Bermuda.

"How would I know that if I've been in the water?"

The captain signals his men to let Mulder continue.

"Tell me I'm wrong," says Mulder, carefully. "Tell me that you haven't gotten accurate compass readings, that navigation's been a real bitch. It's because you've been caught in something called the Devil's Triangle. I can show you on the chart here. It goes from Bermuda, down to Puerto Rico, back up to Florida. The *Queen Anne* is stuck here, on the eastern edge of it.

"You've been caught in some kind of time warp—in some kind of limbo dimension. Now you've popped out the other side. Into 1998."

"Nineteen ninety-eight!" snarls the first crewman.

"The man is mad!" says the second.

"Let him tell it to the fishes!" says the third.

DIE WAHRHEIT IST
IRGENDWO DA DRAUßEN

The captain eyes Mulder stonily.

"I'm done fooling about, man," he says. "There's a war on. And in it or no, I don't plan to lose me mind, nor me ship, to a jackal like you."

Mulder laughs, a bit too merrily. "Well, you can relax!" he says. "There's no war going on. The world

is at peace. There's a little trouble at our White House, but that'll blow over. So to speak."

The captain stares at Mulder. "Peace? It's September 3, 1939, man!" he says. "Hitler's entered Poland and we've just been boarded by a bunch of his goose-stepping hooligans! So don't tell me about peace, man! Tell Mother England!"

Mulder tells the captain that it's actually November 16, 1998—but he's interrupted by the ship's first mate, with the news that the Germans have seized the bridge and are steering a course for their homeland.

"Not on the watch of Captain Yip Harburg, they are not," says the skipper. "Lock the prisoner up in here."

The captain and his crew storm out, leaving Mulder alone with an ancient radiotelephone. He grabs its microphone and calls for help. There is no reply. He twirls the dial and hears a nervous-sounding British newsman announce Prime Minister Neville Chamberlain's declaration of war against Nazi Germany. Mulder, shocked, starts to realize what's happened to him. "Oh, sh—" he says.

At that moment he hears someone at the door. A Nazi officer enters the room—and Mulder attacks him from behind, sending him careening into the radio. That changes the station and—to the strains of the Andrews Sisters singing *"Bei Mir Bist Du Schon,"*—Mulder battles the Nazi officer, finally knocking him unconscious. Out of breath, Mulder stares at the German. He has the face of Jeffrey Spender.

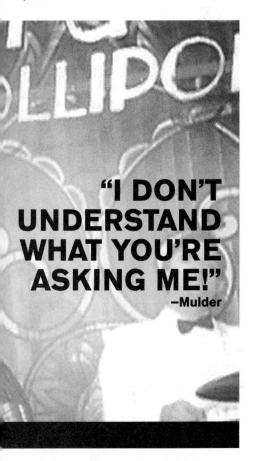

"I DON'T UNDERSTAND WHAT YOU'RE ASKING ME!"
–Mulder

"What the hell is going on?" says Mulder.

He begins to unbutton the officer's uniform. Outside, in the corridor, other German soldiers are methodically checking each stateroom. Mulder emerges from the captain's quarters in full Wermacht uniform. The soldiers call after him in German. When he doesn't reply, they give chase. Mulder sprints through the corridor, gives them the slip, and ducks into the ship's ballroom. A festive formal dance party is underway: Revelers in dinner jackets and evening gowns are dancing to a big band, its girl singer warbling "Jeepers Creepers."

Mulder stares at the singer, who seems somehow familiar. Distracted, he bumps into a fox-trotting dancer: Scully, partnered by a bald-headed gentleman in his fifties.

Mulder grabs her by the shoulders. "Hey, Scully—" he says.

Scully looks at the German officer with contempt. "I suggest you get your Nazi paws off me before you get one in the kisser," she says.

"Huh? It's me, Mulder!"

"Oh, you speak English, do you? Well, how'd you like to see the stars in the American flag?"

Scully holds up a fist. Scully's dance partner, who looks nervous, says nothing. Mulder whispers urgently that he's not really German; that he's stolen the uniform. The commotion catches the attention of the girl singer who, shouting in German, points him out to a squad of soldiers across the dance floor. One of them fires a warning shot at the ceiling. His cronies haul Mulder away.

"See? I told you!" says Mulder to a baffled Scully.

As they drag Mulder outside, he rails against his captors: "Yeah, you're all big men, now—but wait till you get to Russia!" he shouts. "I hope you fellas like the cold!"

A Nazi smacks Mulder on the back of the head with a blackjack. He falls into a clobbered stupor. He's hauled onto the rain-swept deck, where he regains consciousness and struggles free momentarily. The soldiers recapture him, then frog-march him onto the ship's bridge—where Captain Harburg, standing at the ship's wheel, is being berated in staccato German by a Nazi officer. Harburg looks the Nazi—who is obviously in charge—in the eye.

"I'll not give up this ship!" he says.

The Nazi shouts some orders. A soldier draws his luger and aims it at the back of the captain's head.

"Ay, you can put me down, lad," says Harburg, defiantly, "but I'll not let go this wheel. So, till I meet you in hell—"

He spits in the face of the Nazi officer. The German gives the word; the soldier fires a single shot and the captain slumps to the deck, dead. The Nazi commander, unfazed, turns around to face Mulder—who recognizes him as the Cigarette-Smoking Man.

"You!" says Mulder, shocked—but perhaps not surprised.

The Cigarette-Smoking Man barks several rapid-fire questions, in German, at Mulder. Mulder replies that he doesn't understand. The Cigarette-Smoking Man gives an order. A soldier raises his pistol to Mulder's head.

"Wait a minute!" says Mulder, frantically. "Why are you shooting me? What have I done? I DON'T UNDERSTAND WHAT YOU'RE ASKING ME!"

"Halt!" shouts another German voice, from the far entrance of the bridge. It is Walter Skinner, also in

Wehrmacht regalia. He shows the Cigarette-Smoking Man Mulder's FBI ID. The Cigarette-Smoking Man speaks, and the soldier holsters his pistol. Two others grab Mulder and drag him back where he came from.

"Skinner? Where are they taking me?" shouts Mulder, desperately.

AT FBI Headquarters in Washington, Frohike, Byers, and Langley—the Lone Gunmen, last seen in "The End" (5X20)—corner Scully at her small desk in a vast bullpen.

"Mulder's in trouble," says Frohike.

"Big trouble," says Langly.

"What do you mean?" asks Scully.

"Let's take a walk," says Byers, eyes darting in search of eavesdroppers.

At the other end of the room—out of earshot of anyone who might care to listen—they tell Scully that Mulder has disappeared.

"Disappeared from where?" asks Scully.

"From the National Reconnaissance Office's Lacrosse mid-latitude imaging radar satellite," says Langly.

He hands her a satellite photo of the Atlantic Ocean. In tag-team fashion, the Gunmen tell her that earlier that morning they'd seen an image of the British luxury liner *Queen Anne*—a vessel that vanished without a trace over sixty years ago. One theory was that she was torpedoed by a German U-boat. Another was that she vanished into the Bermuda Triangle, off the Plantagenat Banks.

They add that they gave this data to Mulder—who flew to Bermuda, chartered a powerboat, headed for the *Queen Anne's* last position—and disappeared in a storm an hour and a half later.

"But what's happened to him?" asks Scully.

"We can't know that," says Byers. "Not without alternative tracking data.

"What is it you need?"

"Navy AWACS S.L.A.R or S.A.R. 100k swath imaging," says Byers. "You're going to have to find somebody at the Pentagon to get it."

Scully writes down these acronyms, tells the Gunmen to wait for her downstairs, and walks quickly to Walter Skinner's office. She blows past his assistant and interrupts a telephone call.

"I've just received some very disturbing information, sir," she says. "I need your help."

Skinner shakes his head and tells her that since he's no longer her direct superior he cannot help her. Scully refuses to take no for an answer: but not even the news that Mulder may be lost at sea gets Skinner to change his mind.

He walks Scully toward the door.

"I'm not allowed to have contact with you—any contact—with either you or Mulder," he says, loudly.

Skinner's assistant stands in the doorway.

"She walked right past me, sir—" she says.

Scully slams the door in her face.

"You're out of line, Scully," says Skinner, furious.

"No, sir—you're out of line," says Scully, just as angry. "I'm sorry, but I'm coming to you for help and I've got nowhere else to go. I would hope that after everything that we have been through that you would at least have the courtesy and the decency, not to mention the respect, to listen to what I have to say."

Skinner says nothing.

Says Scully, "Now, all I need is information. You don't have to do anything else."

She hands Skinner the piece of paper. "Sir, if you know anybody at the office of Naval Intelligence it would be of great help—"

Skinner looks at the paper, shakes his head, and hands it back to her. "I could lose my job. My pension. Even be subject to legal action."

Disgusted, Scully turns to leave. Skinner stops her.

"Use your head, Scully," he whispers urgently. "It'll save your ass."

"Save your own ass, sir. You'll save your head along with it."

She leaves by another door, stops, thinks, and—in obvious distress—boards an elevator for another floor. She gets out, strides purposefully down another corridor, and enters an office much like Skinner's—belonging to Assistant Director Kersh. She blows past his assistant, who is, incidentally, recognizable as the girl singer with the *Queen Anne's* big band. Inside Kersh's office, she holds the piece of paper in front of her.

"Sir, I need you to get me some information," says Scully, nervously. "I am not at liberty to say why, but I can tell you it is of the utmost importance."

Sensing someone else in the room, Scully glances to her left. The Cigarette-Smoking Man stands silently in a far corner; he returns Scully's gaze. She turns back to Kersh.

"Sorry," she says, subdued. "I shouldn't have come unannounced."

"May I see what you were going to show me, Agent Scully?"

"Uh, it's nothing. Nothing, really," she says.

Kersh steps forward and takes the paper.

"Good," he says, evenly.

Scully turns on her heel and, berating herself, strides out into the hallway at a loss. A lightbulb goes on: She pulls out her cell phone and, on the move, speed-dials a number. She enters the elevator as its doors are closing.

"C'mon, c'mon, Mulder!" The phone rings, and is answered—by a recording saying that "the cellular customer you are trying to reach is not responding."

She rides the elevator to the basement.

In the X-Files office, at Mulder's old desk, sits Spender. In no uncertain terms, Scully tells the startled agent to help her get the intelligence information she needs. He nods, then leaves. Spender's phone rings. She answers it.

"Agent Fowley?" says a male voice—the Cigarette-Smoking Man's.

"Yes," says Scully, carefully.

"I was looking for Agent Spender," says the Cigarette-Smoking Man. "Agent Scully just handed the assistant director a piece of paper with an intelligence system scribbled on it."

"Yes?"

"Who is this?" says the Cigarette-Smoking Man.

Spooked, Scully hangs up. She walks toward the exit—and bumps into Kersh's assistant, who tells Scully she was sent to fetch her. Scully stammers that she was there to meet Spender. The assistant nods curtly and tells her that Spender is with Kersh. Scully bolts for the elevator.

"That rat bastard!" she says.

As the elevator doors close, her cell phone rings. A man's voice, breaking up and unintelligible, comes through faintly from the other end.

"Mulder? Is that you?" she says, frantically.

The elevator comes to a stop. The door opens revealing Kersh, Spender, and the Cigarette-Smoking Man in the hallway. She reaches desperately for the "close" button. The elevator reaches another floor. The doors open again—revealing Skinner, cell phone to ear. He steps into the elevator. The doors close.

"I was trying to reach you," says Skinner. "I got the information you needed."

He hands her a piece of paper. Scully kisses him—directly on the lips—in gratitude. The doors open at the previous floor. Kersh, the Cigarette-Smoking Man, and Spender gaze at the pair quizzically.

Says Skinner, loudly, "If you ever ask me to break policy, I'll have you written up, wrapped up, and tossed out of the FBI for good! Am I understood, Agent Scully?"

"Yes!" says Scully.

She whips back into the elevator, punches up yet another floor, glances at Skinner's message, exits, courses through the corridors, bursts through a door into a parking garage, is intercepted by the Lone Gunmen in their decrepit Volkswagen Van, and sits back, smiling, in their back seat. They speed out, chased in vain by someone in a business suit, on foot, behind them.

On the *Queen Anne*, Mulder and the British crewman are being marched at gunpoint through the bowels of the ship. As they go, Mulder gives the Englishman an advance account of the Second World War. The prisoners are tossed into a machinery-filled belowdeck compartment—and the door is locked behind them.

They join other crewmen, already imprisoned. Mulder's companion, who says he speaks German, tells the agent sarcastically that these are their "new accommodations." He also tells him that the Germans suspect the ship is carrying munitions.

"Are we?" asks Mulder.

The sailor shrugs, and tells Mulder that the ship is too lightly loaded to have much cargo of any kind.

"But the captain knew something," says Mulder. "He wouldn't give up the wheel."

Says the sailor, "The Nazis boarded us after they'd intercepted a radio communication. Some kind of code word they keep asking about: 'Thor's Hammer.'"

Mulder turns to face the sailor, intensely interested.

"You know what that is, mate?" he's asked.

Before Mulder can answer, he is confronted by another bunch of British sailors. Considerably tougher looking, they are led by a large, wrench-wielding Caribbean native—a roughneck. A loud argument ensues, climaxed by a sneering description of what will happen to the black crew members when the ship is taken to Nazi Germany.

Mulder shouts over the confusion. "This ship can't go to Germany!" he says. "It can't happen! I've got news for you—you're not carrying munitions. It's something far more deadly."

"Thor's Hammer?" asks his companion.

"Thor's Hammer isn't a weapon," says Mulder. "It's a man. A man who'll help build a weapon. A bomb that'll win the war for whoever has it."

"And he's on board this ship?"

"I saw him," says Mulder, "in the ballroom."

The sailor smiles, does an abrupt about face, and pushes through the crowd to the door. He pounds on it and shouts in German. As it's opened from the outside, he turns and gives a Hitler salute.

"*Auf widersehn,* mates!" he says smugly.

After the spy leaves—presumably to tell his masters about the vital scientist on board—the crew members argue among themselves as to what to do. They decide to stop the ship—and run to the engine room and confront another Jamaican who seems to be in charge: AD Kersh.

They shout at him to shut down the ship's engines. He replies that he's overridden the ship's steering mechanism and is heading the ship for home: Jamaica. The British crewmen grab him and yell at him to steer a course for England. Mulder shouts above the din.

"Listen to me! Listen to me!" he says. "You can't take this ship to England—you'll never make it! You can't take the ship to Jamaica, either! The Germans will hunt you down no matter what course you steer!"

The crewmen—black and white—shout him down.

"He wants to go back to bloody America!" says a sailor.

"No, I don't! I want you to take the ship and turn it back around the way you came!"

"And what's in that direction?" sneers Kersh.

"The future," says Mulder. "Actually, the past."

The sailors look at him as if he's a lunatic. He tries

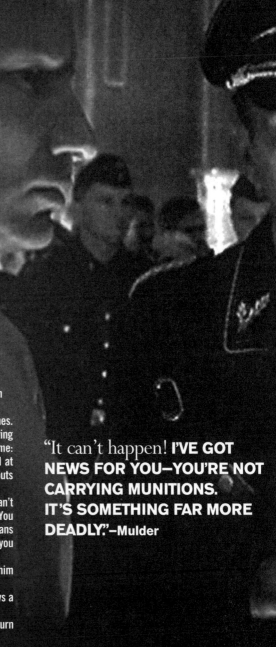

"It can't happen! **I'VE GOT NEWS FOR YOU—YOU'RE NOT CARRYING MUNITIONS. IT'S SOMETHING FAR MORE DEADLY."–Mulder**

in his Nazi uniform. In heavily accented English, he yells at Mulder to get on his feet.

The Cigarette-Smoking Man questions Mulder in German. Spender translates.

"There's a scientist on board who can make a bomb. Who is this man?" he demands.

"I don't know," says Mulder.

The Cigarette-Smoking Man speaks briefly to a soldier, who cocks his pistol. He turns again to Mulder. Again, Spender translates.

"You will answer the question, or we will begin killing passengers," he says. "Which one is the scientist?"

"I don't know," whispers Mulder.

The Cigarette-Smoking Man barks an order. The soldier walks over to the passengers—past Scully and her partner—seizes a white-haired gentleman, and shoots him in the back of the neck. The passengers gasp and scream in terror.

"How many lives," translates Spender, "are you willing to sacrifice?"

"None," says Mulder.

"Then you have the answer?"

Mulder shakes his head.

The Cigarette-Smoking Man speaks. Another passenger is killed. An angry Scully steps forward.

"Stop! This man has no answers!" she says. "You're killing innocent people to learn that he knows nothing!"

Spender shouts at her to shut up and move away. This makes her even angrier. She steps up and into Spender's face.

"Listen to me, you little weasel—"

The Cigarette-Smoking Man calmly assesses the situation, then speaks quickly. Without hesitation, Spender draws his own pistol and points it at Scully's head.

He turns to Mulder. "Answer the question," he says.

A terrifying moment passes. Mulder takes a deep breath.

"I'll answer the question," he says, shoving Spender's gun aside.

He points to one of the dead passengers, lying in a pool of blood on the floor.

"That man is the scientist," he says.

Again Spender raises the gun to Scully's head—then cocks it and tightens his finger on the trigger.

Alongside the *Queen Anne*, a chartered powerboat bobs along unnoticed. On board—and astonished at seeing this ghost ship—are the Lone Gunmen and Dana Scully, 1998 version.

Inside the ballroom, Spender's gun is still pointed at the 1939 Scully's head.

"You're lying!" Spender tells Mulder.

to explain—but is interrupted by a squad of Nazis, who seize him.

"Turn the ship around!" he yells, as he's hauled out of the engine room. "Or Hitler rises, Germany wins, and your children will never know what freedom is!"

Mulder is hauled through the metal labyrinth and back into the ship's ballroom. The dancers have been pushed into a cowed mass; the Cigarette-Smoking Man, accompanied by the traitor crewman, is clearly in charge. Mulder is dumped at the feet of Spender, back

"He's telling the truth!" says Scully.

"Shut up! Who is the scientist?"

Mulder angrily tells him the dead man is the scientist. A soldier pulls a wallet out of the corpse's breast pocket and, at the Cigarette-Smoking Man's order, asks Mulder to give him the man's name.

"John Brown," says Mulder, defiantly. "Ask me again and I'll knock you down."

"What's his name!?"

"Puddintame. Ask me again and I'll tell you the same."

Spender is just about to fire when a male voice breaks in. It is Scully's partner, the bald-headed man. He admits that he is the scientist. Scully tells the Nazis that he is lying.

"Please," the scientist begs Scully, "tell them the truth before someone has to die."

He turns to Spender. "She's traveling with me to protect me. She works for the OSS."

The Cigarette-Smoking Man speaks briefly, and the bald-headed man is led away. He speaks again, and Mulder and Scully are shoved down onto their knees. They bow their heads, waiting for the end. Everything goes silent.

"What's happening?" breathes Scully.

"The engines just shut down," says Mulder.

The Nazis freeze, and look up. Through the door pour the British crewmen—they've escaped from the engine room. A wild melee ensues. The passengers join in, wrestling the Nazis and bopping them over the head with champagne bottles.

Elsewhere on the ship, the Gunmen and the 1998-model Scully, flashlights in hand, creep cautiously through the ship's corridors. Mulder—insisting that she is the only person who can save the ship—gets the 1939-model Scully to follow him. They crawl on their hands and knees out of

They take off running.

The screen splits, with a vertical line running top to bottom.

On the left, 1998 Scully and the Gunmen are searching the corridor Mulder and 1939 Scully have just vacated. On the right, Mulder and 1939 Scully are evading the pursuing Nazis. In the ballroom, the battle still rages.

In full screen, 1998 Scully and the Gunmen enter the ballroom. It is deserted; cobwebbed and faded. On deck, Mulder leads the 1939 Scully by the hand. She struggles against his grip.

"I'm going to tell you how to save this ship," he says.

"Out here?" says Scully.

"I can't stay," says Mulder. "I've got to get back to history—"

"What?"

"—and you've got to rescue it. Listen to me: The ship's been caught in something called the Devil's Triangle. It's some kind of time warp. A rift in space."

"Are you crazy?"

"You know Einstein, right? He predicts the theoretical possibility. He also predicts an atomic weapon that destroys the world."

"Yeah? So what?"

"If you don't go back, and convince the crew of this ship to turn it around and head back into the Devil's Triangle, everything Einstein predicted will come true—except for the outcome of history."

Scully wavers. "So, if I don't turn this ship around—"

"In all likelihood," says Mulder, "I won't exist. And neither will you. So, in case we never meet again—"

He pulls Scully close to him and kisses her on

"LISTEN TO ME: THE SHIP'S BEEN CAUGHT IN SOMETHING CALLED THE DEVIL'S TRIANGLE. IT'S SOME KIND OF TIME WARP. A RIFT IN SPACE."–Mulder

the ballroom, flee down another corridor—and are brought up short by a pistol-wielding Nazi standing behind them.

"Now what, Einstein?" asks Scully.

A shot rings out, and they wince. They look behind them, and see the Nazi lying dead on the floor. Behind the dead man, smoking gun in hand, is Skinner.

"God bless America!" he says, in accented English. "Now get your asses out of here."

the lips. After a few seconds Scully pulls away and gives Mulder a right cross to the kisser.

"I was expecting the left," says Mulder.

To Scully's startled shouts, Mulder climbs over the ship's rail and leaps into the ocean. The 1939 Scully peers over the rail and tosses a life ring over. Mulder sinks into the water, and floats face-down amidst jetsam and wreckage. The 1998 Scully and the Gunmen struggle to bring Mulder aboard their chartered powerboat.

He regains consciousness in a hospital room, circa 1998, with Scully at his bedside.

"What happened to me?" groans Mulder.

"You did something incredibly stupid," says Scully. "You went looking for a ship, Mulder, in the Bermuda Triangle."

"Say that again?" says Mulder, not totally uncomprehending.

Frohike, Langly, and Byers enter. Mulder stares at them for a second, then speaks.

"You were there, Scully!" he says, excitedly.

Says Langly, "He's delirious."

"And he was there, too!" says Mulder.

Walter Skinner enters and joins the group.

"Right. Me and my dog Toto," scoffs the AD.

Mulder stares at him, too. "No, you were there with the Nazis—"

Says Scully, "Mulder, will you settle down? It's an order."

"Not that he takes orders," says Skinner, irritated.

"You saved the world, Scully," says Mulder.

"Yeah. You're right. I did," says Scully, sarcastically.

"What kind of drugs is he on?" asks Frohike.

"I want some," says Langly.

Exasperated, Mulder tries to explain what happened to all of them on the *Queen Anne.* Scully explains that all they found was Mulder in the water, his boat broken into a million pieces.

"And as for the *Queen Anne,*" she says, "It was nothing more than a ghost ship."

"No, no, no, Scully," he replies. "We were on that ship—in 1939."

His visitors smile ruefully, are half amused and half annoyed by these ravings. Skinner promises to kick his butt—but good—when he gets better. All but Scully leave the room.

"I would have never seen you again," says Mulder, with feeling. "But you believed me."

Scully leans forward and whispers, with mock tenderness, "In your dreams, Mulder. I want you to close your eyes, and I want you to think to yourself: 'There's no place like home. There's no place like home.'"

She turns to leave.

"Hey, Scully?" says Mulder.

"Yes?" she says.

Her partner gazes tenderly into her eyes.

"I love you," he says, meaning every word of it.

"Oh, brother," murmurs Scully, rolling her eyes and turning to leave.

His eyes follow her lovingly as she leaves the room. He reaches up, feels the nasty cut under his left eye, and smiles.

Author's note: If you are a film director, cinematographer, or other individual with a better-than-usual knowledge of the technicalities of moviemaking, please skip to the non-italicized portion of this back story. If not, please read the following three paragraphs:

Nearly every motion picture and filmed TV drama is photographed in basically the same way. A single camera shoots a single scene numerous times from various different angles; afterward, short snippets of the best "takes" shot from several or all of these angles are edited together into the version of the scene we see on the screen. Typically, the director and cameraman begin with a straightforward, wide-angle "master" shot, then move in for close-ups, over-the-shoulder shots, "two-shots" (of two individuals interacting in the picture frame), etc. Between each camera "setup" the scenery and people being filmed must be laboriously relit, and for editing purposes the action and dialogue must be identical no matter where the camera is pointed. In this method, rehearsal time can be minimized, and "coverage"—the number of options available for the editor and/or the director—are maximized.

There is another way to make a movie. This is to shoot it in single, fluid takes—limited in length only by the amount of film in the camera—with the cameraman following the action as it unfolds before him. Ideally, the very long takes can simply be pasted together to form the finished edit; in effect the film is edited as soon as it passes behind the camera lens. In this method, planning and rehearsal time is maximized (one blown line, sloppy camera move, or dropped prop usually means that the entire scene must be restarted from the beginning) and the number of postproduction options—for a nervous movie producer say, or network executive—are minimal.

For obvious reasons this method is used very rarely: most notably by Alfred Hitchcock in his 1948 thriller Rope. *Two more recent movies, Martin Scorsese's* Goodfellas *and Brian De Palma's* Snake Eyes, *contained lengthy segments filmed this way. However, doing an hour of episodic television in this manner is absolutely unheard of. Until now.*

The most ambitious—and audacious—episode of the sixth season. A tour de force of innovative camera techniques and editing, imaginative storytelling and intricate plotting, period costuming and scenic design, high-energy acting and high-wire directing.

And perhaps it was nearly as noteworthy for an interesting bit of backstage irony: In its very early stages, writer/director/series creator Chris Carter envisioned the widely acclaimed "Triangle" (6X03) as an innovative way to, among other things, save money.

"To save film," corrects Carter, eyes glinting mischievously.

He adds:

"Last season, while filming *The Red and the Black*

[5X14], I hit the dubious mark of shooting more film doing an episode than any director had ever done before on *The X-Files*—except one, Kim Manners. So everybody decided to get together and present me with a funny-looking second-place trophy.

"It was at that point that I had an idea. I asked, 'How much does one of our big film magazines hold?' Someone told me that each one holds about twelve minutes worth. Then I said, 'Wouldn't it be great if we could just use one magazine, do one shot, for each of the show's four acts?' Everybody laughed, 'Ha ha ha!' But then I realized this is a chance to do what Hitchcock did in *Rope*, which was to film continuous action, or at least try to make it look like that.

"And then I thought I've always wanted to do a Devil's Triangle episode. And now that we'd moved down to Los Angeles, I had the perfect place to do it. So all these things fell together and became 'Triangle.'"

Well, not quite yet. With the shock of boarding the *X-Files* express train having barely set in, individual staffers had to adjust to an entirely new way of making motion pictures, with cavernous new pitfalls to avoid and problems to solve.

It meant that six or seven hours of preparation and rehearsal were often followed by the filming of a single pressure-packed scene. For director of photography Bill Roe, in particular, it meant that much of what he knew about movie lighting was useless. Since the camera would be pointing in all directions, the usual banks of lights and reflectors couldn't be set up out of camera range, and nearly all of the light available

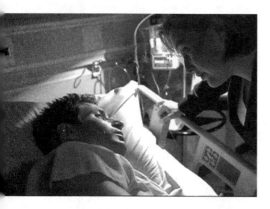

to him was from the *real* lights dressing the interior sets. "It helped that a lot of the episode was intentionally dark and gloomy," says producer Paul Rabwin. "And Bill and Chris used the dark shadows and doorways, when the camera focused on them, as optional editing points—just like Hitchcock did."

For Steadicam operator Dave Luckenback, who executed most of the minutes-long, intricately choreographed camera moves in the episode, it meant a week and a half of extraordinarily intense physical and mental effort. For the actors—from Duchovny and Anderson down to the extras in the crowd scenes—it meant the realization that mistakes would be costly

and retakes precious. For many of the behind-the-scenes crew members, who were used to the hurry-up-and-wait rhythms of even the briskest filmmaking, it meant a new appreciation of the term "real time."

For example, during the first half hour of "Triangle," as Scully moves frantically through the FBI Building searching for answers, she enters the elevator several times to travel to another floor. Since the elevator was merely a four-walled set with a grip-powered sliding door, it meant that the "other floor" was in reality a single set being frantically redressed while Anderson was saying her lines—and being filmed and recorded, of course—in the elevator.

Several times during the shooting of this scene the elevator doors opened right on schedule—to reveal a mortified crew member clutching a prop or pushing a piece of furniture.

To all of this add the stomach-clenching fact that 6X03 was one of the most logistically complex episodes in the series's history. This stems from Chris Carter's early decision to forego creating the fictional *Queen Anne* on his sound stages and use a *real* pre-World War II British ocean liner instead.

As was widely reported at the time, much of "Triangle" was filmed on the *Queen Mary*, the legendary retired Cunard liner now moored permanently in Long Beach, California, as a floating hotel and museum. Altogether, *The X-Files*'s first and second units spent a total of eleven days filming on the historic seventy-five year-old ship.

Co-executive producer Michael Watkins's expression brightens when he recalls how at various times swarms of L.A.–based crew members accomplished the job of blacking out an entire side of the ship (without disturbing the hotel guests who were asleep in their cabins); floodlighting its parking lot and erecting circus tents to house hordes of extras, caterers, and other temporary personnel; and, for the scenes in which rain lashes the *Queen Anne*'s deck, constructing a latticework of sprinkler pipes hooked up to portable water pumps powered by four semi-trailer-borne diesel generators.

"We had to get enough power to lift water hundreds of feet above the ground to make it rain on the bridge of the *Queen Mary*," he says, softly, "which leaked."

To keep the sights and lights of Long Beach out of Dave Luckenback's viewfinder, rigging grip Damon Doherty (son of key grip Tom Doherty) blacked out the *Queen Mary*'s bridge by means of a wraparound scaffolding erected fifty-five feet above deck level. Also, for the scenes in which Mulder is rescued and dives back into the ocean, special-effects "green screens"—one 30 feet by 40 feet, the other 20 feet by 80 feet—were hung precariously over the giant ship's side.

When Chris Carter decided that the *Queen Mary*'s corridors had been renovated too recently to be usable, production designer Corey Kaplan had the portions of it that were to be filmed stripped to the bare walls and floors, then completely recarpeted and redecorated in authentic late–1930s style. The ship's ballroom was given the same treatment, with the added bonus that a present-day derelict version had to be designed and constructed in the same space, as well.

Among the highlights of set decorator Tim Stepeck's week was a desperate search for a genuine, canvas-covered pre–World War II ship's life ring—and someone to reproduce a couple of them by the time they were needed on camera. Property master Tom Day provided the Cigarette-Smoking Man with his historically accurate Nazi SS cigarette lighter. He also commissioned the construction of the (nonworkable) short-wave radio in the Captain's cabin.

"We couldn't use a real one," Day says, "because David and Chris Owens would be bumping into it when they had their fight. But we made sure that the tuning window lit up and was attached to a rheostat—not just for authenticity, but also because the way they were filming they could use as much light as we could get."

Costume designer Christine Peters supervised the clothing of dozens of German soldiers (renting their uniforms from two large Hollywood costume houses); British merchant sailors (with ex-*Titanic* costumes from the Fox wardrobe department); and ship's passengers (with genuine period apparel).

Makeup department head Cheri Montesanto-Medcalf did "tons of research," then hired ten or so extra helpers to apply old-fashioned pancake makeup to most of the extras and supporting players. Hair department head Dena Green was just as busy, arranging the mass application of Brylcreem to crew-cut Nazis on one hand and hot marcelling irons to the curls of sophisticated ladies on the other.

While writing the music for "Triangle," composer Mark Snow listened for inspiration to the records of drummer Gene Krupa and the music of Big Band–era superstars like Glenn Miller, Tommy Dorsey, and Harry James. He readily concedes that the episode's most memorable composition—the bouncy instrumental played during the split-screen chase scene—was kickstarted by John Williams's earlier retro swing tune composed for the fight scene in the movie *1941*.

"So my piece is the third generation of the same inspiration," he says, laughing.

Among many other tasks, producer Paul Rabwin supervised the recording of a special arrangement of "Jeepers Creepers"; then hired an actor who spoke BBC-accented English to record the exact wording of the 1939 radio bulletin of the declaration of war between German and England.

With his computer, visual effects producer Bill Millar replaced the green screen hung over the side of the *Queen Mary* during filming with the angry gray-blue Atlantic Ocean eventually seen by viewers. He also helped plan, calibrate, execute, and tweak the excruciatingly complicated shot where 1939 Mulder and 1998 Scully appear to cross over each other during the split-screen sequence. "It's the work I'm proudest of all season," he says.

Many others involved had similarly strong feelings. "Parts of it were excruciating," says Gillian Anderson. "But parts of it were exhilarating. By that I especially mean the scenes where I was running through the FBI. It was like live theater. We were taking risks, doing things differently, learning. You just *go here* and *do this*. I was resonating on a whole different level."

✕

As many viewers and TV critics noted, Chris Carter inserted numerous affectionate references to *The Wizard of Oz* into "Triangle." The classic movie was released in 1939, the same year much of the action of 6X03 takes place. As did Dorothy Gale, Fox Mulder confronts familiar faces from the "real" world—renamed but with similar character traits—in his "dream" world. Mulder's motorboat was named *The Lady Garland* after Judy Garland, who played Dorothy. The band performing in the *Queen Anne*'s ballroom is "Almira Gulch and the Lollipop Guild"—after the mean Kansas spinster who turned into the Wicked Witch of the West, and one of Oz's more prominent Munchkin reception committees, respectively. Captain Harburg was named after E. Y. "Yip" Harburg, the talented lyricist who wrote the words to all the songs in the film. And, of course, in the final scene of "Triangle," Mulder discovered that there is indeed no place like home.

✕

Alone among the regular *X-Files* cast members in "Triangle," Mitch Pileggi really does speak German. "I attended college in Munich for two years in the early '70s," he explains.

✕

"Thor's Hammer" was not the name of America's pre–World War II atomic research product. "Um, I'm afraid it was called something deceptive and uninspiring, like 'The Office for Research on Alternative Metals,'" says researcher Lee Smith, who had a long talk by phone with the historian of the U.S. Department of Energy in Washington. Another piece of historical license: Scully could not have been an agent of the O.S.S. in 1939. The Office of Strategic Services, direct forerunner of the C.I.A., was started after the U.S. entered the war.

✕

Chris Owens's girlfriend, recent law school graduate Tara Parker, spent a day playing one of the evening-gowned dancers in the *Queen Anne*'s ballroom. "That night, David lent us his suite on the *Queen Mary*," recalls Owens. "It was incredibly generous of him. We had a wonderful time."

✕

"Triangle" was broadcast in "letterbox format" because Chris Carter filmed it in the same height-to-width ratio used for big-screen motion pictures. His reason: to get more action into each frame, especially during the split-screen sequences.

✕

The tagline of this episode is "Die Wahrheit ist Irgendwo Da Drauben." Rough translation: "The Truth Is Out There." **041**

After a close encounter near Area 51, Mulder becomes trapped in the body of another man—who, unbeknownst to Scully, assumes her partner's identity.

DREAMLAND

6⊗04

EPISODE: 6X04
FIRST AIRED: November 29, 1998
EDITOR: Heather MacDougall
WRITTEN BY: Vince Gilligan, John Shiban, and Frank Spotnitz
DIRECTED BY: Michael Watkins

GUEST STARS:
Michael McKean (Morris Fletcher)
Nora Dunn (Joanne Fletcher)
Dara Hollingsworth (Christine Fletcher)
Tyler Binkley (Terry Fletcher)
James Pickens, Jr. (AD Kersh)
Michael Buchman Silver (Howard Grodin)
John Mahon (General Wegman)
Scott Allan Campbell (Jeff Smoodge)
Julia Vera (Mrs. Lana Chee)
Christopher Stapleton (Captain Robert McDonough)
Eddie Jackson (Copilot)
Ted White (Attendant)
Laura Leigh Hughes (Kersh's Assistant)
Freeman Michaels (Guard)
Cesar Lopapa (Soldier)

PRINCIPAL SETTINGS:
Groom Lake and Lincoln County, Nevada; Washington, D.C.

On Highway 375 in rural Nevada, two headlights stab through the darkness. Mulder and Scully, driving through the night, pass Milepost 134—several miles from a top-secret military base. In the passenger seat, Scully appears considerably less than thrilled to be there.

"So, Mulder," she says. "This supposed clandestine source who's contacted you? How do we know he's not just another crackpot whose encyclopedic knowledge of extraterrestrial life isn't derived exclusively through reruns of *Star Trek*?"

Mulder laughs. "Because of where this particular crackpot works," he says. "Groom Lake, Area 51, where the military has conducted—"

"—for the past fifty years, classified experiments involving extraterrestrial technology," recites Scully in a bored monotone.

Mulder shoots her a dirty look.

"It's all our questions!" he insists. "The proof that we've suspected but never been able to hold in our hand. That proof is *here*."

Scully, not even remotely convinced, frowns.

"Mulder, it's the dim hope of finding that proof that's kept us in this car—or one very much like it—more nights than I care to remember. Driving hundreds, if not thousands of miles, through neighborhoods and cities and towns, where people are buying homes, and playing with their kids and their dogs. In short, living their lives. While we just keep driving."

"What is your point?" says Mulder, feigning puzzlement.

Says Scully, "Don't you ever just want to *stop?* Get out of the damn car? Settle down and live something approaching a normal life?"

"This *is* a normal life," replies Mulder, not totally facetiously.

Scully turns away in frustration. She glances into her sideview mirror and sees the bright lights of a fast-approaching vehicle. She warns her partner and he spots several other vehicles—Jeep Cherokees—racing behind and alongside them.

Directly ahead is a three-Jeep roadblock. Boxed in, Mulder brakes to a stop. Rifle-toting soldiers pour onto the blacktop and order the agents out of their car. They do so—and spot a black-suited figure, smoking a cigarette, walking toward them. It is not the Cigarette-Smoking Man, but a world-weary bureaucratic type in his forties. He asks for Mulder's and Scully's identification; when they show him their FBI ID he is less than overly impressed. Oozing scorn, he tells them they'll have to turn their car around and leave immediately.

"Why?" asks Mulder. "It's a public highway."

"It also borders on a U.S. government testing ground," says the Man in Black. "What's your business here?"

Silence.

"What are you doing out here in the middle of the night?"

Asks Mulder, "What are *you* doing out here?"

Says Scully, sardonically, "Hiding top-secret test flights? Using technology from UFOs?"

The Man in Black rolls his eyes—in fact, his whole head—and sarcastically confides to them the top-secret information that flying saucers don't exist. Scully has seen enough; she tells Mulder that it's time to leave.

At that moment a bright light rises over a nearby ridge. It hovers, then passes slowly over the awestruck assemblage. When it is directly, blindingly overhead, a distortion of light and space passes through Mulder. The wedge-shaped object rises, wobbles over another ridge, and is gone.

"Come on, Mulder, let's go," says Scully, stunned.

Mulder is also stunned—for different reasons. He is standing where the Man in Black was just a second ago—and he is wearing the government official's clothing. Wearing *Mulder's* clothing and standing in *his* spot is the Man in Black—whom Scully takes by the hand and leads to her car.

Several moments later Mulder comes to his senses and shouts for Scully and the stranger to stop. They don't.

"Sir? Open fire?" asks a soldier.

"No! No, let them go! Let them go," says Mulder. The soldier asks for further orders. Thinking furiously, Mulder begins to realize that everyone is mistaking him for the man whose clothes he is wearing and vice versa.

"I want to get out of here," he says, finally.

He enters one of the Jeeps and slumps into the front seat. In the back seat is a lean and hungry-looking guy in his thirties, dressed exactly the same as Mulder.

"Morris, what do you think you're doing?" asks the man, whose name is Howard Grodin.

"They didn't know anything," says Mulder, improvising madly.

"They were FBI agents—obviously here to meet someone. Very possibly an informant," says Howard, annoyed. "You just sent away our best hope of finding out who."

Another government clone in the back seat—this one is named Jeff Smoodge; he is pudgier and more easygoing—speaks up.

"We can't just disappear a couple of FBI agents, Howard," he says. "We'll get their own people to deal with them. That's what Morris was thinking.

"Right, Morry?"

They drive off and enter Area 51: a large, floodlit compound surrounded by razor wire and filled with mysterious, triangular-looking aircraft. Inside the administration building a stern-faced MP asks Mulder for his identification. After a few moments of confusion he searches his suit pockets and pulls out a photo ID. It bears the name "Fletcher, Morris"; it's for a project called "Majestic"; and on it is a photo of the man who's just left with Scully.

This satisfies the guard. Mulder looks at a security monitor showing "his" face. Looking back at him is Morris Fletcher.

Preceded by his two new associates, Mulder spots a white-haired general in his office, speaking frantically into his phone. This gets everyone's attention.

"Something must be up. I'm gonna check it out," says Howard, moving off.

"Kiss-ass," sneers Jeff, running his ID card through a scanner and entering an office.

Mulder spots an office door with Morris Fletcher's name on it, runs the ID through the scanner, and enters. Behind the desk is a wall of pictures: Fletcher posing, Zelig-like, with such notables as Ronald Reagan, George Bush, Newt Gingrich, and Saddam Hussein.

"Scully," he whispers, picking up the desk phone and dialing.

At a gas station somewhere nearby, Morris Fletcher halts the rental car in the self-service lane.

"Are you all right, Mulder?" says Scully. "You haven't said a word since we left those men on the highway."

"I'm fine," says Fletcher, calmly. "Gas cap's on your side."

It hovers, **THEN PASSES SLOWLY OVER THE AWESTRUCK ASSEMBLAGE. WHEN IT IS DIRECTLY, BLINDINGLY OVERHEAD, A DISTORTION OF LIGHT AND SPACE PASSES THROUGH MULDER.**

A baffled Scully gets out and begins to refuel the car. Inside the sedan, her cell phone rings, but Fletcher is too engrossed in tuning the car radio to answer it.

At Area 51, Jeff bursts into Fletcher's office.

"Bastards!" he yells.

Mulder quickly drops the receiver into the cradle.

At the gas station, Scully picks up her cell phone just in time to hear him hang up.

"Oh, Dana?" asks Fletcher. "You wanna pick me up a pack of Morleys, please?"

Says Scully, "Since when do you smoke?"

"You're not gonna be a Nazi about it, are ya?" replies Fletcher, exasperated.

At Area 51, a pissed-off Smoodge reveals that a trace of outgoing calls has revealed that somebody is leaking information to the FBI.

"He called the FBI this morning—from Wegman's office," he says. "He used the guest phone from Wegman's office! He's rubbing our noses in it!"

Mulder nods vigorously. A little too vigorously.

"In what?" he says.

"In the fact that he works in this building!" says Smoodge. "That he has access to everything, all our work! And we don't know who he is."

The phone rings. Mulder stares into space, hoping Jeff will ignore it. No dice.

"Morris? Aren't you going to answer that?"

Mulder picks up.

"What are you doing there?" demands a woman's voice, shrilly.

"I'm just trying to work that out," says Mulder, weakly.

On the other side of the connection is an angry, fortyish housewife in a bathrobe. On her desk sits a family portrait of herself, Morris, and two teenage kids.

"It's midnight! I've been waiting up!" she says.

"I—didn't know."

"What do you mean you didn't know? You said you'd call. Morris, you always forget. Well, this time, don't forget the milk!"

Click.

"The wife?" asks Jeff, sympathetically.

Mulder nods. Jeff mimes cracking a whip—complete with sound effect.

"C'mon, man," he says. "Let's go home."

Later that night Jeff delivers Mulder to a darkened two-story house in a generic suburban cul-de-sac. Reluctantly, Mulder enters the front door, looks around, and picks up the phone.

"Base operator," says a woman. "Would you like an outside line, Mr. Fletcher?"

"No, thank you. Good night," he says, hanging up.

He creeps up the stairs, cracks the bedroom door,

and sees his "wife" sleeping in "their" bed. He backs away quickly, settles into an easy chair in the family room downstairs, turns on the TV, channel surfs until he comes to a soft-core porn channel, and hunkers down for the night.

At 2:04 that morning a government-issue Jeep hurtles toward what looks like an airplane crash site. The white-haired general—his name is Wegman—gets out. Kiss-ass Howard meets him among the debris and silver-suited crash personnel.

"It was a routine test flight, sir," says Howard. "The craft suddenly lost altitude at 23:17 hours over Highway 375."

"What happened?"

"We haven't yet determined that, sir. We have recovered the flight data recorder. And the two pilots."

"Alive?"

Howard pauses. Looking troubled, he leads Wegman over to the copilot. The young crew-cut airman is fused with a rock. His hand protrudes; the rock melded with flesh. Part of his face bulges out of the stone. His eyes are open and his lips are quivering. Wegman gapes in horror.

Says Howard, "The other man's alive, but—"

"But what?"

"We're not sure yet."

They walk to a nearby chair where the pilot, an Air Force captain, sits trembling and mumbling.

"What happened, Captain?" asks Wegman.

The pilot looks up—confusion and terror on his face—and, in a pleading voice, speaks unintelligibly in an unknown language.

At FBI headquarters in Washington the next morning, Fletcher arrives at Kersh's office, late for a meeting with Scully and the assistant director. His excuse: that he got lost on the way to work.

Kersh dresses the two agents down for conducting a completely unauthorized investigation and for trespassing on a top-secret military installation.

Fletcher offers up an explanation. "Agent Scully and I were contacted by a confidential source," he says.

"What source?" asks Kersh.

"Oh, if I had the name I'd give it to you," says Fletcher, breezily. "Some whistle-blower working inside this so-called 'Area 51.' Said he had some 'big deal' information."

Fletcher chuckles ruefully.

"I gotta tell ya," he says, "this whole thing was just a gigantic mistake on our part."

Scully stares straight ahead in shock. Kersh tells her and "Mulder" that all X-File–related investigations are now off limits to them.

"Sir, you are absolutely right," says Fletcher, oozing sincerity. "And on behalf of Agent Scully and myself, I'd like to apologize for our blatant disregard

of your direct order. You have our word—we will never, ever do that again."

A few moments later Fletcher sashays out into the hallway with Scully in hot pursuit.

"Mulder. *Mulder!*" she hisses.

"What?" says Fletcher, smiling beatifically.

"What was that about?"

"What was what about?"

"'I'd give you his name if I had it'?" mimes Scully, incredulously. "Whatever happened to protecting our contacts? Protecting our work?"

"He asked," explains Fletcher, calmly and somewhat distractedly.

Fletcher reenters Kersh's outer office, walks over to Kersh's assistant, whispers something in her ear, and gets a broad smile in return. He walks back to Scully—who stares at him as if he's an alien specimen.

"Mulder, you are acting bizarre!" she says.

Fletcher leans toward her, leering crookedly.

"Jealous?" he says.

Scully is stunned into speechlessness. Fletcher gives her a cheeky swat on the behind, then takes off down the hall.

In the Fletcher family room in Nevada, somebody shakes Mulder, still on the recliner, awake.

"Scully?" he says groggily.

It's morning. Standing over Mulder is his "wife"—whose name is Joanne. She clicks off the TV, still showing adult fare, and scowls. She kicks the recliner's footrest downward, propelling Mulder bolt upright.

"I can't believe you. I just can't believe you. And who is Scully?"

"Good morning?" says Mulder, hopefully.

No chance. She reams out her "husband" for letting her sleep alone; for not even pretending they have a happy marriage; and for spending the night watching premium cable filth.

"What if Chris or Terry had come down here first and seen their father being a pervert?" she asks, shrilly. "Did that ever occur to you?"

Mulder hauls himself to his feet, searches his suit pockets frantically, and asks Joanne with servile longing where he might find his car keys. Down the stairs walks a teenage girl, attractive but sullen, wearing way too much makeup.

"Morning, Dad," she says.

"Morning—ah, Terry," guesses Mulder.

Wrong guess. Bursting into tears, Chris runs back upstairs, passing her younger brother on the way down.

"Yo, Dad," he says.

"Hey, Terry."

"Not *Terry.*"

Mulder just stares, completely lost. "Chris?" he says, hopefully.

"*Terrence,*" says the boy. "Terry's for wusses."

After a few more exchanges of this sort—wife Joanne snarls at him for forgetting to buy milk; daughter Chris contemptuously drops his car keys at his feet—Mulder manages to make it almost out of the breakfast nook.

"Morris!" snarls Joanne. "What about Chris?"

He reluctantly turns back.

Says Chris, "You said you'd give me an answer today!"

Mulder goes blank.

"Her nose," says Joanne, angrily. "You said you'd give her an answer about her nose."

Mulder squints at the girl.

"I think—I think she's a little young for plastic surgery. Don't you think?" he says.

Wrong again. Chris crumples into anguished, racking sobs. Joanne is even more incensed.

"Oh, for God's sake, Morris!" she says. "A nose ring! She says she wants a nose ring!"

Chris rises tearfully from the breakfast table. "I hate you! I wish you were dead!" she says to Mulder on her way out.

Almost home free now, all Mulder has to do is get past Joanne—who asks him accusingly if what he's really trying to do is tell her he wants a divorce and insists he change his crumpled clothes before leaving. He trudges upstairs and looks into Fletcher's closet, which contains six identical black suits.

"Ladies and gentlemen," he says, "Mr. Johnny Cash."

He strips down to T-shirt, full-length black socks, and boxer shorts, and glances at a full-length mirror on the closet door. Morris Fletcher, in an identical outfit, glances back at him. He breathes on and fogs up the mirror; waggles his butt; hops on one foot; does the electric boogaloo—and his strange reflection does exactly as he does. Joanne interrupts this little exhibition by handing him a phone. It's Jeff Smoodge, back at the base, asking him where the hell he's been.

"Just running a little late," says Mulder.

"Well, get your ass down here toot sweet," says Jeff. "We got something big going down."

"Big as in what?" asks Mulder.

"Big as in 'I can't say anything more on the phone.' Just get down here."

At Area 51, General Wegman, Jeff, and Howard are still observing the Air Force captain—who is still speaking the same strange language as before.

"It seems he's praying, sir," says Howard. "We've identified the language. A native American dialect—Hopi, to be exact."

He adds that the pilot is named McDonough who now claims to be Mrs. Lana Chee, a seventy-five-year-old Hopi woman from a nearby Indian reservation. He leads Wegman to a glass booth nearby.

> ## "I CAN'T BELIEVE YOU. I JUST CAN'T BELIEVE YOU. AND WHO IS SCULLY?"—Joanne Fletcher

"LADIES AND GENTLEMEN,
MR. JOHNNY CASH"—Mulder

Inside, an elderly Hopi woman sits ramrod-straight. At the sight of the general, she leaps to her feet, stands at attention, and salutes.

"What's your name?" asks Wegman, swallowing hard.

"Captain Robert McDonough, sir!" barks Mrs. Chee. "I apologize for my present condition and appearing out of uniform, sir!"

Says Wegman, "Um, do you know what happened last night, Captain?"

"Sir! We launched from base at 2300 hours and headed south. At approximately 23:15 we lost power in the right rear quadrant. No warning lights came up on the panel. All systems checked out in pre-flight."

Mrs. Chee shakes her head.

"She just wasn't in the mood to fly, sir," she says.

At FBI headquarters Scully sits in the bullpen and watches, disbelieving, as Fletcher, sitting at the desk next to her, plays a rousing game of computer golf on his PC. Her phone rings. It's Mulder, calling from a rusty phone booth at a desert gas station.

"Scully, it's me," he says.

"I'm sorry, who is this?"

"It's me, Mulder. I'm sorry I couldn't call you sooner. Look, something really weird happened last night when that UFO passed over us."

"UFO?"

"You don't remember?" says Mulder, piecing it all together. "You don't remember. Look, the man that you're with—that's not me. His name is Morris Fletcher. He's an Area 51 employee."

"Morris Fletcher?"

"That's right," says Mulder. "Everyone here seems to think that I'm him, but I'm not. I'm me. I'm Mulder. As long as they think that I'm him I have access. But I need your help."

Scully cradles the phone and motions for Fletcher to pick up. He listens in while Mulder asks Scully to head for Nevada to join him.

"How can I get in touch with you?" she asks.

"You won't," says Mulder. "I'll get in touch with you."

Everyone hangs up. Baffled, Scully asks "Mulder" if that was his confidential source. Fletcher shrugs; Scully tells him she'll run a trace.

"Ah, no," says Fletcher, rising. "No, I think we should notify El Jefe ASAP. We don't want our collective asses chewed out all over again."

Says Scully, even more baffled, "Mulder, are you sure that's the best thing to do?"

"Look, little lady," says Fletcher, firmly, "I think it's about time you got your panties on straight. We're federal officers—we go by the book."

At a desert gas station minimart, Mulder buys a bag of sunflower seeds, plunking down two bucks and leaving eleven cents—his change—as a tip for the unshaven attendant. He exits, climbs into Fletcher's car, and drives away.

Inside the minimart, the attendant hears a low rumble. The store's glass display cases begin to vibrate; the cans on the shelves begin to shake, clatter loudly, and fall to the floor. The attendant stares at the front door, terrified. The storefront implodes with a loud crash.

Stopped at a red light on his way back to the base, Mulder spots a convoy of government Jeeps headed in the opposite direction. Jeff is driving the tail-end vehicle; he stops alongside Mulder and rolls down his window.

"Turn around, big guy," he says to Mulder. "We got trouble."

At the wrecked gas station a squad of soldiers search the grounds. One of them yells that he's discovered a gas spill. Disregarding this, Mulder runs into the minimart. As Howard and the others yell at him to get out, he searches for the attendant. He finds the man semiconscious, and in pain—with his torso and upper body fused into the floor.

"It's happened again," says Howard. "Let's get out of here."

"We've got to help this man," says Mulder.

"We've got to help ourselves," replies Howard. "Whatever caused this could come back."

"We can't just leave him here," says Mulder. "This man needs a doctor!"

A soldier draws his automatic and shoots the attendant in the head.

"Not anymore," says Howard. "Burn it."

Mulder recoils in shock. He staggers outside with the rest of the team while a soldier lights a small road flare.

"Come on, Morry," says Jeff, sympathetically. "That guy was dead long before we found him."

The soldier drops the lit flare into a pool of gas, then runs away. The flame zips across to the gas pumps—and the station explodes in a giant ball of orange flame.

That day Scully enters Mulder's apartment building in Arlington. As she approaches his door she hears giggling—and spots Kersh's assistant, hair tousled, leaving the apartment. Scully watches, lets the smiling woman pass, takes a deep breath, and knocks.

"Can't get enough, huh?" says Fletcher, merrily.

"It's me," says Scully, disgustedly.

The door swings open—revealing Fletcher, mouth smeared with lipstick, smiling, and taking a drag on a Morley.

"Oh—hey, Dana!" he says, winking lasciviously. "Just a little lunch break. Heh heh. What's up?"

Scully enters Mulder's apartment and tells him that she's traced the "anonymous" call to a phone booth near Groom Lake.

"And?" says Fletcher, less than impressed.

"*And* I'm thinking it was your source," says Scully, impatiently, "although I don't know why he'd impersonate you."

"Maybe so," says Fletcher, casually.

"You don't think we should follow up on this?" asks Scully.

"Are you out of your pretty little mind?" says Fletcher, scornfully.

Scully explodes. "Am I out of my mind!?" she says. "Mulder, *you* are out of *your* mind! What is up with you? I'm thinking about having you examined for mental illness, or drug use—or maybe a massive head injury! This is an X-File! Your life's work! Your crusade!"

Fletcher is unmoved.

"As I understand it," he says, condescendingly, "we're off the X-Files."

Furious, Scully stares at him, then storms out, slamming the door behind her. Fletcher turns toward a mirror, looking at the real Fox Mulder for a moment.

"Bitch," say both men, simultaneously.

In a forensics lab at Area 51, Howard shows Wegman a strange apparition—a lizard fused into a rock, found ten miles east of the gas station. While Jeff and Mulder watch, he walks to a map and points out the nearby crash site and the spot where the Indian woman was found.

Mulder points to another nearby mark—this one alongside Highway 375—on the map. "What's that?" he asks.

"That, we believe," says Howard, "is ground zero."

He holds up a battered black box. "Once we analyze the flight data recorder, we hope to confirm it's where the warp began."

"Warp?" says Mulder.

"Beam me up, Scotty," mutters Jeff.

"It's a tear in the space-time continuum," says Howard. "An anomaly created by the malfunction of the aircraft, which was operating in gravity-pulse mode before it went down."

Says Wegman, "We've been flying these things since '53. I've never heard of anything like this."

Adds Mulder, deep in thought, "According to quantum physics, it's possible."

Says Howard, "Anti-gravity systems utilize bends in space and time for propulsion. A sudden shift in a craft's trajectory could create the kind of distortion we're witnessing here—a lizard and a rock existing in the same time and space."

Jeff puts his index finger at ground zero. "If this is where your so-called, uh, warp began, we would have all seen it. The three of us were out on Highway 375 at the time, sir, intercepting two FBI agents."

Says Howard, "The fact that none of us remember seeing it is evidence that my theory is correct."

Mulder nods slightly. "Lost time," he says.

Says Howard, "Lost time is a common symptom of close proximity to anti-gravity propulsion systems."

"Then how come," says Jeff, "my head isn't stuck in a rock? Or Morry's?"

Says Howard, "That's one question I haven't been able to answer. It is possible we suffered consequences from our exposure that we're not fully aware of."

"What do we do about it?" asks Mulder.

Howard sizes Mulder up keenly. "Well, that's your department," he says. "Keep it out of the papers, make sure the witnesses disappear."

"Well, yeah," says Mulder. "But I mean—how do we reverse it? How do we get the lizard out of the rock?"

"Who says we can?" says Howard, chillingly.

That night Scully drives—alone—along Route 375. She reaches the roadside lot where the gas station used to be, climbs out, and shines her flashlight into the wrecked interior. She spots a dime and a penny fused together, forming a four-sided coin. She examines this strange discovery curiously.

The next morning Mulder wakes up again on Fletcher's recliner—and gets another state-of-the-marriage address from Joanne.

"Why don't you just say it, Morris? You aren't attracted to me anymore. I disgust you, don't I? That, and you mumble someone named Scully in your sleep. Who is Scully, Morris? Is it another woman?"

Mulder stands. "Does 'Scully' sound like a woman's name to you?"

"Who is Scully? Tell me!"

Smoothly, Mulder invokes the top-secret nature of "his" job.

"My point is," he says, "that there are a lot of things you don't know about me. And I'm sorry. I've been under a lot of pressure lately. Up is down, black is white. I don't know where I stand anymore. I don't even know who I am, really, anymore.

"I just know for sure that I'm not the man you married. I'm just not. And I'm sorry. I'm truly sorry."

Joanne gazes up at him, and softens. "Oh, God, Morris. I didn't know." She embraces him tenderly. "They have that pill now," she says, embracing him. "There's other ways to be intimate. We can make this work."

The doorbell rings. Joanne loosens her grip, dabs her eyes, and opens the door.

"Yes?" she says, smiling through the tears.

"Hi, my name is Dana Scully," says the visitor. "I'm looking for Morris Fletcher."

Joanne freezes, scowls, summons her husband, and slaps him smartly across the face. "You son of a bitch!" she says, pushing past him into the house.

"I'm sorry," says the shocked Scully. "Uh, Morris Fletcher?"

"Scully—it's me. It's Mulder," says Mulder, grabbing her shoulder and walking her into the front yard.

Says Scully, "Uh, you're the man from the other night. From Area 51?"

"Liar!" shouts Joanne from inside the house.

"You phoned me," continues Scully. "Would you mind telling me what this is all about?"

"I'm *Mulder*," insists Mulder. "I'm really Mulder. I switched bodies, places, identities with this man Morris Fletcher. The man that you think is Mulder—but he's not!"

Scully looks at him as if he's insane.

"Of course you don't believe me," says Mulder. "Why was I expecting anything different?"

He thinks for a moment. "All right! Your full name is Dana Katherine Scully. Your badge number is—hell, I don't know your badge number. Your mother's name is Margaret, your brother's name is Bill Jr., he's in the Navy and he hates me."

Scully simply stares at him. Mulder tries harder.

"Lately for lunch you've been having this little six-ounce cup of yogurt. Plain yogurt, into which you stir some bee pollen, because you're on some kind of bee pollen kick, even though I tell you you're a scientist and you should know better."

"Cheater!" yells Joanne, throwing Fletcher's clothes out the front door.

Scully shakes her head and tells Mulder that she's not convinced—that anyone could have gotten those details about her. Mulder promises that he'll provide scientific proof of what happened on Highway 375.

"I'm calling the police!" shouts Joanne.

"Goodbye, Mr. Fletcher," says Scully, turning to leave.

"I will prove it to you, Scully," Mulder yells after her. "Tonight. I'll prove everything. Okay?"

Scully gets into her car and drives away. In another car parked nearby sits Fletcher, watching.

Later that day the phone rings in Howard's office at Area 51. On the other end is Fletcher, calling from his moving car.

"Mr. Grodin?" says Fletcher. "This is Special Agent Fox Mulder with the Federal Bureau of Investigation. How are you this morning?"

"How did you get this number?" demands Howard.

"Well, frankly, that's what I wanted to talk to you about," says Fletcher. "Sir, I'm obligated to inform you that you have a security leak in your facility. A man with whom you have worked very closely has contacted my office on several occasions, and offered me access to highly classified information."

Howard struggles to restrain his excitement. "Would you happen to have a name for this man?" he asks.

"Why, yes," says Fletcher. "Yes, I would."

Some time later Mulder enters the empty forensics lab, finds the flight data recorder, and places it in a paper bag. He leaves. From a catwalk above, Howard watches him unobserved.

Later that day Scully is driving on a desert road. Her cell phone rings; it is Kersh.

"You're in Nevada again," says the Assistant Director, coldly.

"Sir, I, um—"

"Do not speak, Agent. Listen. Your partner has already apprised me of his conversations with the Air Force—and his fervent desire to save you from making a fatal career mistake. Therefore, you will now follow my instructions to the letter."

That night Mulder pulls into Ahearn's Service Station, which includes a minimart, in Lincoln County, Nevada. He is carrying the brown paper bag. Waiting in a far aisle is Scully. He walks quickly over to her.

The cashier ducks behind his counter. Mulder notes this—and a split second later the storefront explodes in

a blaze of light. A squad of soldiers rush inside, seize Mulder, and handcuff him.

"Scully? You?" he says.

Fletcher enters from a back door and stands silently by Scully's side.

"You son of a bitch!" shouts Mulder. "You orchestrated this whole thing! He's not me, Scully! Would I do this? Scully?"

The soldiers drag him to the door.

"You bastard! Tell them the truth! Scully! He's not me! He's not me! Scully!"

To be continued . . .

"YOU BASTARD! TELL THEM THE TRUTH! SCULLY! HE'S NOT ME! HE'S NOT ME! SCULLY!"–Mulder

BACK STORY/6X04

From 1976 to 1983, a young writer/actor named Michael McKean played a popular character—the screwball greaser named Lenny Kosnowski—on *Laverne & Shirley*, one of the most highly rated TV series of its day. Like numerous sitcom stars before him, he could have easily kept the good times rolling: playing Lenny—or variations of him—in countless revivals, reunions, and spinoffs.

Except that he didn't.

"You know what?" says McKean, over lunch at a West Los Angeles restaurant. "You don't become typecast by the first role your career breaks with. You get typecast by the *second* role, if it's identical, or even close to, the first one that put your face in front of the public. After the series ended, I got lots of offers to play goofy best friends. I turned them all down. I told everybody who would listen: 'I've already *done* that.'"

Instead, McKean became one of the most versatile and unobtrusively talented comic actors in Hollywood— a poorly publicized fact that discerning fans and industry insiders have long realized. He has, worked steadily, he says proudly, for twenty-six years—in movie after movie and TV series after TV series, playing foils and bumblers and evil bosses to perfection—all the while carving out successful side careers as a writer, composer, and *Saturday Night Live* ensemble sketch player.

As it turns out, in fact, McKean was also the perfect— if somewhat belated (see p. 064)—choice to play the opportunistic Area 51 *apparatchik* Morris Fletcher in this season's "Dreamland/Dreamland II" two-parter.

Series regulars and staffers were almost unanimously bowled over by his response to the technical and creative demands of this complicated part. As for McKean, he has watched the show for six years and feels that Fletcher— one of the most interesting new *X-Files* characters of the past several seasons—is a valuable addition to his portfolio.

So what was special about Morris?

"It's that I had the chance to play Fox Mulder, *and* get the little FBI name tag to prove it. Fletcher got to go around convincing everyone he looked like David Duchovny. What a huge break! That for me was one of the overriding keys to the character.

"The other important thing I realized was that for all his black suits and top-secret clearances, Morris was really a consummate bureaucrat. He was frustrated with his little office and his bosses and the limits of his job. He knew that by trading places with Mulder he'd have access to all the FBI stuff that he was not privy to. He could shut down anything he wanted to. It was a great opportunity.

"And he was also, for all that, a genuine human being. There was this great scene at the Inn when he sees his real wife in distress, and realizes that because he's now unknown to her he can't walk over and comfort her. It was a really nice, sad moment, and I hinged the rest of the show on it."

Like many other newcomers to the *X-Files* universe, McKean was impressed by the long hours and intense pace of the cast and crew. Like most of them he was less than thrilled to spend his days and nights at the desolate "Dreamland"/"Dreamland II" locations.

But it would also be accurate to say that Michael McKean has ranged as widely, careerwise, as almost anyone in the movie or television business. Born in New York City in 1947, he went to college at NYU and Carnegie Tech, where he met David Lander, the actor/writer who

would play Squiggy to his Lenny on *Laverne & Shirley* and become his lifelong friend and collaborator.

In 1970 McKean and Lander moved to Los Angeles, where they joined satirist/actor Harry Shearer, among others, in a cutting-edge improvisational comedy group called The Credibility Gap. (Robert Goodwin, executive producer for *The X-Files*'s first five seasons in Vancouver, was also a member).

In 1976 McKean and Landers joined the writing staff of *Laverne & Shirley*; they promptly wrote themselves into Garry Marshall's ABC hit. Although McKean's salary didn't come close to matching those of contemporary sitcom stars, it did allow him to get married, start a family, and take a good look at the pleasures and tortures of mainstream show business fame.

"I became, well, sort of famous," says McKean. "Because I didn't wear my hair greased back except when I was doing the show, I was generally incognito on the street. So it was kind of interesting. I mean, I'd occasionally get recognized—just enough so that my ego was stroked, but not so much that it was a nightmare."

After *Laverne & Shirley* left the air, McKean took supporting roles in comedy films like *Used Cars* and *Young Doctors in Love*. In 1984 he was instrumental in several senses of the word in the creation of the seminal rock "mockumentary" *This Is Spinal Tap*. He not only acted in the movie but also co-wrote the script and the music.

From 1991 to 1996 he appeared regularly—as a rapacious Australian media magnate—on the HBO series *Dream On*. During the 1994–95 TV season he put in a stint at *Saturday Night Live* with a cast that included Norm MacDonald, Chris Elliott, and Janeane Garafolo. One of the guest hosts that year was David Duchovny. "It was during May 1995: David's first appearance on *SNL*, and my last," says McKean. "I thought David was a very funny man. I also liked his show a lot.

"So I went up to him, of course, and said I'd love to do an *X-Files* someday. He said he thought it was a great idea."

After that, says McKean, scarcely three and a half years passed before his manager passed along an invitation to audition for the two-parter.

"I said to her: 'What do I have to do?' And then I did it, and they liked it, and they even asked me to come back."

Indeed, in "Three of a Kind" (6X19), McKean does a short but memorable cameo reappearance (see page 247) of his "Dreamland" persona.

"I was delighted to do it," says McKean, who took a short break from filming a pilot—in Vancouver, of all places—to fly to L.A. to film his scene.

"I only had one script demand," he adds. "It was that Morris Fletcher not die."

6⊗05

DREAMLAND II

EPISODE: 6X05
FIRST AIRED: December 6, 1998
EDITOR: Lynne Willingham
WRITTEN BY: Vince Gilligan, John Shiban, and Frank Spotnitz
DIRECTED BY: Kim Manners

GUEST STARS:
Michael McKean (Morris Fletcher)
Nora Dunn (Joanne Fletcher)
Dara Hollingsworth (Christine Fletcher)
Tyler Binkley (Terry Fletcher)
James Pickens, Jr. (AD Kersh)
Michael Buchman Silver (Howard Grodin)
John Mahon (General Wegman)
Scott Allan Campbell (Jeff Smoodge)
Julia Vera (Mrs. Lana Chee)
Laura Leigh Hughes (Kersh's Assistant)
Tom Braidwood (Frohike)
Dean Hagland (Langly)
Bruce Harwood (Byers)
Andrew Sikking (Soldier)
Chris Ufland (Sam)
Mike Rad (Randy)
Lisa Joann Thompson (Kelly)

PRINCIPAL SETTINGS:
Groom Lake and Lincoln County, Nevada; Washington, D.C.; Arlington, Virginia

While Mulder learns how he's switched bodies with Morris Fletcher, Scully discovers the true identity of her "partner." But this knowledge leads only to an unsolvable—and tragic—dilemma.

The action picks up where it left off in 6X04: with Mulder, still trapped in Morris Fletcher's body but shouting out his true identity, being led from Scully's ambush by a squad of soldiers. Outside the minimart, Morris Fletcher—quite happy to be "Special Agent Fox Mulder"—sidles up to Scully.

"You hate me now, right?" he says, unsure of Scully's reaction. "Dana, I'm sorry I narked on you to Kersh. But I—I was scared you were going to lose your job."

She stares at him evenly. "You did the right thing, Mulder," she says.

"I did?" says Fletcher.

"I've been telling you for years you should play more by the book, haven't I?"

Fletcher shrugs and smiles, relieved. "Hey," he says. "It's the new me."

At Area 51, Mulder, in leg irons, is led into a security area. He's tossed into a Plexiglas cell next to the one occupied by Mrs. Lana Chee, the elderly Hopi woman now inhabited by Air Force Captain Robert McDonough, pilot of the crashed UFO.

Mrs. Chee chuckles bitterly. "You ain't goin' nowhere, Mibby," she says. "You and me have had our asses officially disappeared. Looks like we're up fudge creek."

"Who are you?" asks Mulder, confused.

"Call sign's Maverick," she says. "Not like I'm gonna be hot-sticking it anytime soon."

"Are you all right, ma'am?" asks Mulder.

"Ma'am?" says the old lady, disgustedly. "Kiss my ass, you desk monkey!"

At FBI headquarters Fletcher is at his desk, sinking a tricky uphill putt on a PC golf game.

"*I* am Tiger Woods," he crows.

Scully enters—and announces that Kersh has given her a two-week suspension, without pay, for insubordination. She empties the contents of her desk drawer into a cardboard box. Fletcher shakes his head in insincere dismay.

"Hey, Dana?" he says. "You think a home-cooked meal might ease the pain a little? Say, my place? Eight o'clock?"

Scully gives him a barely perceptible nod, then leaves. Fletcher returns to his computer.

"I think she likes me, Tiger," he says.

At Area 51, Mrs. Chee lies on her bunk and—oozing insufferable fighter jock machismo—recites at length the tale of one of his many aerial adventures. Fed up, Mulder tries to stop the torture.

"Hey! Grandma Top Gun! Will you shut the hell up!"

Mrs. Chee glares, stands, and flicks her lighted cigarette into Mulder's lap.

"You're *my* bitch now, pencil-neck!" she says.

They square off—at the same moment an MP arrives to take Mulder to a meeting in the office of General Wegman, Fletcher's boss. Also present are two of Fletcher's Area 51 colleagues, Howard Grodin and Jeff Smoodge. The flight data recorder that Mulder stole in 6X04 sits on Wegman's desk.

"Son, you've got a set on you, I'll say that much," says Wegman.

Says Jeff, "You had us fooled. Why didn't you tell us what you were doing from the start?"

Mulder is, of course, baffled.

"Meaning?" he says.

"It's the wrong one," says Wegman. "You replaced the flight data recorder. This one's from—?"

"A scrapped F-111, sir. It's junk," says Howard.

Howard turns to Mulder. "You gave the FBI the wrong flight data recorder. Why?"

Asks Jeff, "Morry, if you were running a scam on the FBI, why didn't you let us in on it?"

Mulder thinks fast.

"I didn't know if I could trust you," he says, slowly.

His colleagues' faces crumble.

He adds, "We have a security leak, gentlemen. And for all I knew it was one of you. That's why I decided I had to approach Agent Scully alone to find out who her contact is. Unfortunately, her partner"—Mulder screws up his face in disgust "—Agent *Mulder*, screwed everything up."

"So why didn't you tell us everything afterward?" asks Howard, accusingly.

"I knew you wouldn't believe it until you figured it out for yourself," replies Mulder.

"So the real flight recorder is safe?" asks Howard.

"Oh, yeah. Absolutely," says Mulder, breezily.

"And you will bring it back?"

Mulder laughs. "Of course!"

The general laughs along with him. "By God," he says, "You *do* have a set on you!"

Wegman then frowns, turns, and reams out Howard Grodin for falsely accusing Morris Fletcher. He tells the unhappy Man in Black that he's wired Washington recommending censure for his actions.

Back in Arlington, Virginia, somebody unlocks the door to Mulder's apartment. It's Fletcher, carrying two bags of groceries. He sets them down in the kitchen and pulls out two large candles.

"Mood lighting for the bedroom," he says.

He glances around the apartment, puzzled.

"No bedroom," he says.

He tries to open a closed hallway door—one that may or may not have been evident during the past five years. The door sticks in its frame. He yanks it open, and an avalanche of useless junk—old files, cardboard boxes, skin magazines—slides out onto the floor.

Fletcher shakes his head scornfully.

"This guy hasn't been laid in ten years," he says.

In Nevada, Mulder parks Fletcher's car, gets out, and walks warily toward the Fletcher residence. All of Fletcher's belongings are dumped on the front lawn. Another car, a large gold sedan, parks down the street behind him.

Fletcher's daughter strides down the driveway, pretending she doesn't see her father. She has a shiny gold nose ring (see 6X04) prominently looped through one nostril.

"Hey, Chris. Uh—the nose thing," says Mulder, reaching out affectionately to touch the new ornament.

"Ouch! As if!" says Chris, disgustedly, before striding away.

Terry, the Fletchers' twelve-year-old son, jogs down the driveway after her.

"Terry! Buddy! Hey, *Terrence*, how's it going?" asks Mulder.

"Mom says she's taking out a restraining order on you," says the boy, who doesn't stop, either.

Mulder nods, waves, and dejectedly enters the

"SO MAYBE I LIKE TO READ
THE *NEW YORK TIMES* BACKWARDS.
DO YOU HATE IT?"—Morris Fletcher

house. From the family room, he peers through the window blinds at the men surveilling him from the gold car.

Fletcher's wife, Joanne, appears in the kitchen doorway.

"What are you doing back?" she asks, testily. "Your stuff is all outside. Take it and get out."

Wearily, Mulder turns to her. "Ma'am, listen to me," he says. "There's something I've got to tell you."

"I've heard enough from you for one lifetime, Morris!" she says. "Go tell it to that tramp of yours, that Scully whatshername."

"Dana Scully. Special Agent Dana Scully," says Mulder.

"Special *tramp* Dana Scully!" yells Joanne.

"She's my partner, Joanne."

"*I'm* supposed to be your partner!"

Mulder sighs, bites the bullet, and declares forthrightly that he is not Morris Fletcher, but Special Agent Fox Mulder.

"YOU KNOW WHAT WOULD REALLY BE FUN?"
–Scully

"I am not your husband," says Mulder. "We are complete strangers and I have a whole other life that I'm desperately trying to get back to!"

Joanne stares at him, stonefaced.

"You know, Morris," she says, finally, "most men, when they have a mid-life crisis, they go out and buy themselves a sports car. They don't run around calling themselves 'Fox'!"

Mulder drags her to the window and points out the two men surveilling him.

Says Mulder, patiently, "I don't know if your husband ever told you this," he says, "but your husband has a very dangerous job. And those two men in that car, like you, think that I'm him. Only, they don't trust me. So one false move and I'm history. Which means that your husband will also be history, because I won't be able to get back and set things the way they're supposed to be.

"Do you understand what I'm saying to you?"

Joanne closes her eyes and nods.

"Morris," she says, starting softly, "if you don't like the man you've become, I don't blame you one bit. But this flight from reality isn't the answer.

"Accept who you are—however repulsive that may be!"

That evening Scully knocks on Mulder's door.

"Perfect timing!" says Fletcher, wearing a festive chef's apron over his slacks and dress shirt.

Scully scans the premises, astonished. Apartment 42 is tastefully redecorated and neat as a pin.

"You like, huh?" says Fletcher. "I just thought it was time to stop living like a frat boy. C'mon and see the rest of the place."

He steers her toward the bedroom. All of Mulder's junk is gone. At the center of it all rests a large, brand-new bed.

"I didn't even know you had a bedroom," says Scully.

"Oh, yeah!" says Fletcher. "Yeah, gotta have a place to lounge around reading the *New York Times*, you know?"

He urges Scully to check out the bed. Humoring him, she sits down. It gurgles and undulates—it's clear that she's on a waterbed. Fletcher plunks himself down, sending them both sprawling to their backs. They look up—there's a large mirror on the ceiling.

"So maybe I like to read the *New York Times* backwards," says Morris, suavely. "Do you hate it?"

Scully thinks for a moment. "No, I don't hate it," she says.

"Well, all right then!" says Fletcher, hauling himself to his feet. "Don't go away, then!"

He scoots to the kitchen, plunks a large bottle into an ice bucket, hugs the bucket to his chest, and scoops up two champagne flutes. Warbling "Let's Get It On" sotto voce, he sashays back to the bedroom, where Scully waits expectantly.

He hands her a glass, strips the foil off the champagne bottle, and struggles with the cork.

Says Scully, "You know what would really be fun?"

She pulls out her handcuffs. Fletcher quivers with excitement.

"Oh, yeah!" he says. "Me first?"

"You first," says Scully.

Fletcher handcuffs himself to the headboard and looks up. Scully has her pistol out and trained at Fletcher.

"You're not Mulder," she says, sternly.

"*What*? Baby—"

"Baby me and you'll be peeing through a catheter," says Scully. "Your name is Morris Fletcher. How do we return things to normal?"

"How should I know?" snorts Fletcher.

He adds, "I wouldn't do it even if I could. You saw my wife—you think I wanna go back to that? Two kids who'd probably kill me in my sleep for the insurance money, a four-hundred-thousand-dollar mortgage on a

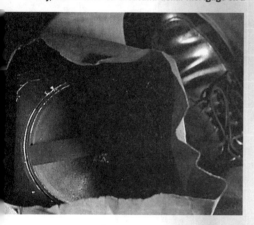

house that just appraised at two-twenty-six—and my job.

"Ye gods! You think being a Man in Black is all voodoo mind control? You should see the paperwork! As far as I'm concerned, this thing is a gift from heaven.

"Besides—no one's going to believe you. So you might just as well get used to me being here."

Still aiming her gun, Scully moves closer.

"Or, I just shoot you—baby!" she says.

Fletcher shouts frantically that he has no idea how to change things back. Under threat of death, he also claims that he doesn't know who Mulder's Area 51 informant was.

At that moment Mulder's phone rings. The answering machine picks up—and after the sound of the tone a man's voice is heard. It is the Area 51 informant, asking Mulder to please pick up.

At the Fletcher house late that afternoon a dis-

consolate Mulder monitors the surveillance team through the front window. Joanne enters the family room lugging a pair of suitcases.

"For God's sake, Morris!" she says. "First you couldn't wait to get away from me, and now you won't leave the house."

Mulder considers this thoughtfully. "You're right," he says. "We should get out of the house. And go someplace with a lot of people."

Joanne looks at him skeptically. "Someplace with a lot of people? In Rachel, Nevada?"

Mulder smiles, reaches out, and strokes her hair tenderly. "What do you say?" he asks.

That night Scully and Fletcher arrive at the Little A'le'Inn, a UFO-themed roadhouse in Rachel.

Scully, holding her pistol in her lap, reviews their plan: Fletcher will go in alone to meet their confidential source, who will be wearing a Buffalo Bills cap. She warns Fletcher if Fletcher tries to slip out the back door, she will hunt him down and shoot him. Fletcher winces.

"Can't we start over? You know, do that thing with the handcuffs?"

Scully cocks the pistol menacingly. Morris gets out of the car, enters the crowded night spot, and looks around. He doesn't notice Mulder and Joanne having an intense conversation at the bar. He does spot the man in a back booth wearing a Buffalo Bills cap. It is General Wegman, in civilian clothes.

Fletcher can't believe his eyes. "*You're* the guy?" he says.

Wegman hauls Fletcher down into the booth. The general's "FBI contact" seems delighted and amused by this turn of events.

"Well, I'll be damned!" says Fletcher.

At the front door the two men who've been surveilling Mulder enter. At the bar, Mulder looks up and notices them.

"Whoa!" he says to Joanne. "Ooh, God! That beer went right through me. I gotta—I'll be right back."

He heads toward the men's room—and leaves the Inn through the back door. In their back booth, Fletcher and Wegman huddle.

"You sabotaged a UFO?" asks Fletcher, incredulously.

"Keep your voice down," growls Wegman. "I didn't intend for it to crash, Agent Mulder. I just meant to disable the stealth module so you could see it."

Outside in the parking lot Mulder sneaks along the lines of empty vehicles, trying their doors. An unlocked door swings open—and to his surprise, he sees Scully sitting inside. He slips into the passenger seat.

"Mulder?" says Scully. "Is that really you?"

"What are you doing here?" asks Mulder.

Says Scully, "I'm trying to figure out a way to help you."

Inside, alone at the bar, Joanne grows impatient. In the back booth, Fletcher is still blown away by Wegman's revelation.

"What are you, like, disgruntled?" he says.

"You make me sound like some postal clerk," says Wegman, with a frown. "What you came for is on the floor by your feet."

Fletcher looks down. Inside a brown paper bag is a flight data recorder.

An irritated Joanne walks through the back door into the parking lot. "Morris?" she says.

She peers down the row of cars—and sees Mulder talking to Scully. She storms back inside and plops back down on her bar stool.

Fletcher, carrying the flight data recorder, rises from his seat. He gives Wegman a smart-ass salute and heads toward the front door. On his way out he spots his wife, in tears. He stops and looks at her with what might be regret—but then sees Jeff Smoodge talking to the two members of the surveillance team.

He ducks his head and skulks away.

Jeff walks over to the bar. "Joanne? How's it going?" he says solicitously. "Listen, have you seen Morris?"

Joanne glares over Jeff's shoulder at Mulder, reentering the Inn. "You bet I've seen him!" she says.

She stands, walks briskly over to Mulder, tosses her glass of white wine in his face, and returns to the bar.

"What the hell was that, Morry?" asks Jeff.

Says Mulder, "I guess I make a lousy husband."

Jeff promises he'll smooth things over. Mulder nods, then heads to the rest room to clean up. He glances into the mirror over the sink and sees himself—actually, Fletcher—standing behind him. Fletcher is holding the flight data recorder. Mulder turns to face the Man in Black, who looks very nervous. Mulder's eyes narrow.

"So you're the guy who wants my life?" he says. "I assume that includes all the ass-kickings?"

Mulder calmly closes the rest room door—then grabs Fletcher by the shirt collar, lifts him off his feet, and shakes him.

"Wait!" croaks Fletcher. "You don't want to do this! Jeff's outside! If he sees us together we're both dead! Especially when he sees this!"

Fletcher shows Mulder the flight data recorder. Reluctantly, Mulder refrains from slugging him.

"You take that to Scully right now!" he says.

Fletcher shakes his head. "You must have some sort of waxy buildup!" he says. "I said Jeff's here. No way I'm gonna go out there until he leaves."

He adds, "You sneak it past him—you're his buddy."

"His buddy?" shouts Mulder, giving Fletcher another shake. "He doesn't trust me as far as he could throw me. You saw to that!"

At the back booth Wegman drinks up, stands, and heads for the front door. He spots Jeff talking to Joanne and curses, does an about-face, enters the men's room, and paces nervously. Mulder and Fletcher peek at him, Kilroy-style, over the top on one of the stalls. Wegman stares back at them, thoroughly flummoxed.

Scully enters the Inn through the back door—just in time to see Wegman steam out of the men's room. On his way to the front door Wegman rounds up Jeff and the surveillance guys and orders them to follow him. At the far end of the parking lot he spots someone carrying a familiar brown bag. To Wegman, he looks a lot like Mulder—actually, Fletcher—carrying the flight data recorder.

"There! Detain that man!" he shouts.

That man is Fletcher—actually, Mulder. "Hey, guys!" he says.

They grab hold of his arms, look inside the bag, and see a six-pack of beer bottles. At that moment Scully peels out of the other end of the parking lot. Fletcher is sitting beside her, holding the flight data recorder.

"Suckers," he says, with a mean chuckle.

Early the next morning Scully and Fletcher arrive at the Lone Gunmen's office. They interrupt an ample breakfast of *huevos rancheros*.

"Who crashed?" asks Langly, eyeing the flight data recorder curiously.

She tells them that that's what she wants them to find out. She adds that the recorder came from Groom Lake. The Gunmen exchange a glance: They've hit paydirt.

"Dreamland," says Frohike.

"The Aurora spy plane," says Langly.

"Black world," adds Frohike. "Top, top secret. A Skunkworks special."

Fletcher—who's been thumbing through a copy of

The Lone Gunman, the Lone Gunmen's newsletter—snorts derisively.

The Gunmen stare at the man they think is Mulder, puzzled.

Says Fletcher, "You guys like that name? I was either gonna go with 'Aurora' or 'Borealis.'"

Says Frohike, "What the hell's he talking about?"

Scully swallows hard and explains that it's not Mulder they're looking at. Fletcher explains who he is and how he switched identities with Mulder. The Gunmen laugh, thinking he's joking. But Scully keeps frowning.

Frohike stares incredulously at Fletcher. Fletcher stares right back.

"Trust me, little man," says Fletcher. "I ain't him."

The Man in Black laughs delightedly. "I love you guys, I really do. You're the Lone Gunmen, aren't you? You guys are my heroes—I mean, look at this crap you print!"

He holds up the newsletter. The headline reads: SADDAM TESTS MANDROID ARMY IN IRAQI DESERT.

Says Fletcher, "I mean, look at this. There is no Saddam Hussein. This guy's name is John Gillnitz. We found him doing dinner theater in Tulsa. Did a mean *King and I.* Plays good ethnics."

Says Langly, "You're trying to say that Saddam Hussein is a government plant?"

Says Fletcher, "I'm saying I *invented* the guy! We set him up in '79. He rattles his saber every time we need a good distraction. If you boys only knew how many of your stories I dreamed up while sitting on the pot—"

"What stories?" demands Frohike.

"I'm sorry, Melvin. That's classified."

"It's Frohike, you punkass!" yells Melvin. "What the hell'd you do with Mulder?"

"Shut up, all of you!" says Scully, pulling the digital tape out of the flight data recorder. "If you want Mulder back, get me those results."

Later that day, Mulder—identifying himself loudly as Fletcher—knocks on the door to General Wegman's office. Wegman, busy shredding documents, beckons him in. Mulder closes the door behind him.

Says the general, "We shouldn't be seen together—not after last night. Fletcher. Mulder. Whoever you are."

Mulder explains that Scully will be there tonight with her analysis of the crash data. Wegman replies, sadly, that the information will come too late for him to save himself—because the real Fletcher now knows that he's the source of the leak.

Mulder asks him why he decided to turn whistle-blower. Wegman sighs.

"There comes a time when you look back instead of forward—see the sum of your life," he says.

"My entire career has been spent hiding the truth from the American people. Destroying, in a way, that which was most precious to me."

Mulder nods. "What is the truth?" he asks.

Wegman shakes his head. "You mean you don't know the truth?" he asks. "What is going on here at Area 51? What are these black budget projects? We just fly these birds—they don't tell us what makes them go. They engineer 'em all up in Utah."

Mulder looks back at him, floored. "Well, if you don't know, why did you call me?"

Wegman smiles ruefully. "I've seen your file," says Wegman. "You've chased flying saucers for years!"

He leans forward eagerly.

"Do aliens *really* exist, Agent Mulder?"

At the Lone Gunmen's office the data from the flight data recorder, de-encrypted, spills out on to a computer screen. In addition to the usual airspeed and flight control information there are some additional parameters: including "Tachyon Flux" and "Gravitational Displacement."

"Aurora, my ass," says Frohike. "What have you guys been flying out there?"

Scully tells the Gunmen to begin their analysis.

Fletcher simply waggles his eyebrows in amusement. Grinning delightedly, he holds up another *Lone Gunman.* The headline reads: MONICA: MINX OR MANDROID?

"Hey! This is one of mine!" he says, proudly.

At 9:28 that night, on a dirt road in the desert near Area 51, three scraggly, flashlight-carrying individuals in their early twenties—Sam and Randy and Randy's girlfriend, Kelly—approach a lone white mailbox standing in the middle of nowhere.

"Far out!" says Sam. "The black mailbox!"

"Dude? That's a white mailbox," says Randy.

"No! They painted it white—to hide it," replies Sam, looking into black night above him. "This is *the* black mailbox. The best place to see Freedom Mountain, and the UFOs over Dreamland, man.

"I know a guy who saw five in one night. He said they danced in the sky."

Sam continues to scan the heavens—oblivious to Kelly and Randy, who are making out furiously behind him.

There is a low rumbling sound in the distance.

"You guys hear that?" asks Sam. "What the hell—?"

A time warp ripples over the desert toward their position, then passes directly through them.

"Co-o-o-o-l!" says Sam. "Did you guys see that?"

He turns to face his friends—whose heads are now fused into one grotesque mass. Kelly and Randy whimper and struggle to disentangle themselves feebly. Sam is frozen in fear at the sight.

Nearby, Scully and Fletcher pull up to an abandoned

desert building. Scully gets out and joins Mulder, standing next to his car.

"You don't look very happy," says Mulder. "Don't tell me I'm going to have to put two kids through school?"

Scully is indeed very sad. She tells her partner that she's just gotten off the phone with Frohike—who told her that there was an anomalous event the night of the crash.

"And how do I get back?" asks Mulder.

"Well, that's just it," says Scully. "It's all about random moments in time, about a series of variables approaching an event horizon. Even if we could re-create this moment, if we could sabotage another craft—Mulder, if we were off, if the event were off by one millisecond—"

"I might end up with my head in a rock," says Mulder.

"Something like that, yeah," whispers Scully.

Mulder turns and gazes toward Fletcher. Scully tells him that her "partner" is AD Kersh's new golden boy, assigned to return the stolen flight data recorder to Area 51.

Adds Scully, "The son of a bitch confesses to Kersh even more than I do to my priest. I'm just tagging along for the ride."

Says Mulder, "What do you mean, 'just tagging along'?"

"I'm out of the Bureau, Mulder," she says. "I've been censured and relieved of my position."

Mulder fervently tries to convince her that a complete explanation will enable her to get her job back. Scully shakes her head.

"I'd kiss you if you weren't so damn ugly," she says.

A car horn, honking loudly, interrupts them. It's Fletcher. Mulder stares at the man inhabiting his body.

"If I shoot him, is it murder or suicide?" he says.

"Neither," says Scully, "if I do it first."

She squeezes his hand and walks slowly back to her car. Mulder stops her, gives her a fistful of sunflower seeds, then takes a few back for himself.

In another part of the desert a hysterical Sam flags down a car on the highway and pounds on the driver's tinted window. Inside is Howard, who coolly agrees to accompany Sam to the spot where his friends have been fused. They reach Randy and Kelly—who are snuggled together on a blanket, appearing perfectly normal.

Sam turns to Howard, bewildered. "I swear, man. They were messed up," he says.

"I believe you," says Howard.

The next day Scully and Fletcher cruise down the highway, homeward. Fletcher announces a thrilling discovery: that he'd been able to cadge a free motel room and a six-pack the previous night simply by flashing Mulder's FBI badge.

"Listen, Dana," he says. "After we return this flight recorder, what do you say I have a word with the big man? See if I can get you your job back."

Scully says nothing.

"We could have lots of fun together once you got to know me," he adds. "You know that, Danes?"

Scully eyes him venomously. "I've still got my gun," she says.

Fletcher gives up—and at that moment something at the side of the road catches Scully's attention. It is the gas station that was exploded in 6X04. Scully orders Fletcher to stop and back up. She sees a man emerge from the minimart. It is the attendant looking alive and well, just as he had been before being fused into the floor, then executed.

At Area 51 Jeff escorts Captain McDonough—still babbling in Hopi—to the security zone where Mrs. Chee is being held. Two burly MPs grab her by the elbows and pull her from her cell.

At the Fletcher home Mulder is loading Morris's possessions into a U-Haul trailer. The rental sedan carrying Scully and Fletcher pulls into the driveway. As angry as ever, Joanne pushes Fletcher's recliner out the front door. She glares at the Other Woman: Scully.

"You got a lot of gall coming here, sister!" she shouts.

Says Mulder, "Joanne, I told you. I'm not your husband. This man is."

Mulder points to Fletcher. Joanne turns to face him.

"You come here to watch my family fall apart? You getting some kind of kick out of that?"

Scully quietly pulls Mulder aside.

"Home wrecker!" screams Joanne.

Fletcher, obviously distressed, walks up to her. He takes a deep breath.

"Joanne, what he said about me being your husband, it's true."

"Get the hell off my porch!"

Fletcher sighs. "We got married on June 13, 1978. It rained that day. You got mad at me at the reception because I said I couldn't see the cake behind your fat ass.

"Remember our first apartment? That dump in Pentagon City? You'd turn the air conditioner on and the lights would go out. And how when you were pregnant I tickled your kneecaps to make you laugh?"

Joanne stares at him, stunned.

Says Fletcher, tearfully, "Remember the night Chrissy was born? I held her in my arms, red-faced and screaming?"

Joanne, softening, looks into Fletcher's eyes. "That was the only time I saw you cry," she says. "Oh, my God! Morris, is that you?"

Mulder and Scully interrupt the reunion.

"SO THIS IS TIME SNAPPING BACKWARD."

—Morris Fletcher

Says Scully, "Mrs. Fletcher, we have reason to believe that whatever event caused this to happen may be in the process of reversing."

Says Mulder, "We've got to get back to that highway. Back to the exact spot where this all began. It may be our only chance."

Two government Jeeps pull up; out spill a squad of soldiers, led by Jeff. One soldier seizes the flight data recorder from the rental car.

"Sorry, Morris," says Jeff. "A traitor's a traitor."

That night, in the back seat of Jeff's Jeep, Mulder, Scully, and Fletcher ride down Highway 375 near Area 51. The Jeep stops at a roadblock. Howard, with a larger squad of soldiers, is in charge.

"What are you doing?" demands Jeff.

Says Howard, "I'm cleaning up a mess."

"What are you talking about?"

"About an hour ago I put Captain McDonough and Mrs. Chee back where they belong. Now it's their turn."

Says Mulder, "The warp that started this is snapping back like a rubber band."

"Only, we have to be in its path when it happens," says Scully.

Mulder asks Howard why he's doing this. He tells the agent that he wants his spotless career record back. Fletcher figures it all out.

"So this is time snapping backward," he says.

Mulder nods. "It'll be like the last few days never happened. We won't remember any of this."

Fletcher has another revelation. "Well, in that case, Dana," he says, giving her a pat on the rump for punctuation, "it's been real."

There is a low rumbling noise in the distance. Everyone looks skyward; a time warp passes through Mulder's body.

A split-second later everything is as it was at the beginning of 6X04: Mulder stands, in his clothing, on his side of the confrontation. Fletcher stands, in his clothing, on the other.

"Come on, Mulder," says Scully, softly. "Let's go."

Mulder and Fletcher—the real ones—stand and stare at each other for a long moment. Fletcher lights a cigarette. Then both get into their respective vehicles and drive away.

The next night—or what we might as well call the next night—Mulder trudges down the hallway of his apartment building. His cell phone rings.

"Mulder, it's me," says Scully, in her FBI office.

"I just wanted to let you know that we slipped under Kersh's radar. That little field trip to Nevada went unnoticed. I'm sorry that your confidential source didn't pan out."

Says Mulder, "I guess you were right, Scully. Just another crackpot who watches too much *Star Trek*."

He unlocks his apartment door. "Hey, Scully? I know it's not your 'normal life,' but thanks for going out there with me."

He hangs up and enters his apartment.

In her office, Scully opens a desk drawer. She notices something strange: a dime and penny fused together, forming a four-sided coin.

In Mulder's building the apartment door reopens. Mulder emerges into the hall, astonished. He's seen something very strange, also.

BACK STORY/6X05

In Hollywood parlance, certain projects are "star-driven." In an interesting variation to this, "Dreamland" and "Dreamland II"—two of the funniest and most labor-intensive episodes in *X-Files* history—were nearly star-driven to distraction.

"Did you hear the story how all of this happened?" asks co-executive producer Vince Gilligan, one of the three writers, with executive producer Frank Spotnitz and producer John Shiban, of 6X04 and 6X05.

"It started last season," he adds. "We knew that Chris wanted more comedy this season. We knew that David Duchovny was good friends with Gary Shandling, and we loved Gary Shandling and all the episodes he did with David on *The Larry Sanders Show.* And we thought it would be really cool to have an *X-Files* episode with David Duchovny—as Mulder—and Shandling together. We didn't know for sure whether Shandling would do it, but we thought he'd probably do it—well, let's say we *hoped* he would do it.

"It seemed a sort of funny way to work—casting the show first and then writing the show to fit—but we got into it. And then we thought: 'Wouldn't it be neat if Shandling played a Man in Black? Wouldn't it be great if he was Mulder's Area 51 contact?'

"From there the idea of them changing bodies blossomed pretty quickly, and it was a fun show to write because my girlfriend Holly and I had just moved into a new house, and I remember setting up the laptop with a second monitor so all three of us could work together. It was a nice experience; the last time during the season that we could do that. And the writing went fairly quickly and easily."

By midsummer 1998 the easy part was over. After much doubt and delay, it was learned that—you guessed it—Gary Shandling would not be guest-starring on *The X-Files* those two weeks. "He was in the middle of filming a movie, *Town and Country,* with Warren Beatty," explains Gilligan. "But we still wanted a big name for the role."

"We went through lists and lists of people," recalls casting director Rick Millikan.

Adds Gilligan: "Michael McKean (see page 052) was at the top of our list from the beginning. Looking back, he should have been, because he did a great job, and in

hindsight there's no one else who would have done it as well as he did." All concerned agree that the ex–*Saturday Night Live* cast member won the role with a triumphant audition—held, not atypically for *The X-Files*, a breathtakingly brief time before shooting was scheduled to start.

As is also customary on particularly ambitious *X-Files* episodes, all that was left for the rest of the cast and crew to do was face their own creative and logistical nightmares, hurdles, and cliffhangers.

Gillian Anderson, for one, found the two-parter's Fletcher-Mulder bodyswitch alternately fun and difficult to deal with. Not so much because it was hard to keep the characters' identities straight but because it was hard to act with her long-time partner as if she and the actor—and his character—were nearly strangers.

Anderson says, "I found it easy to treat McKean like Mulder—after all, I've been dealing with Mulder for five and a half seasons. But the other way around? Treating David like McKean's character? That was a challenge. I have this intense history with David. There's a lot of energy and chemistry between us; and I had to work hard to not fall into those patterns while I was dealing with him as if I didn't know him. In the end I think we pulled it off. But it was very tricky, very interesting."

In order to simulate the arid environment surrounding the real Area 51, much of "Dreamland" and "Dreamland II"

was filmed at "Club Ed," a small movie ranch owned by a fellow named Ed Waldhaus on the outskirts of Lancaster, a high desert community some eighty miles—and a solid two and a half hours of driving—from the Fox Studios.

The scenery was ideal, but little else was: daytime temperatures soared to 110 degrees; nights were, by contrast, chilly; wind, dust, and even rainstorms frequently interrupted filming; and cast and crew members had to choose between making a daily soul-consuming commute to Los Angeles or spending their nights in thin-walled motel rooms listening to the plaintive wails of passing freight trains. Shuttling supplies and personnel from the studio to Club Ed was a logistical nightmare. Since Lancaster is well outside the thirty-mile "zone" surrounding Los Angeles, significant amounts of overtime, meal and lodging allowances, and per diem expenses had to be added to an already thinly stretched budget.

For obvious reasons, the scraggly desert gas station—a significant location in both episodes—could not be rented. It had to be built from scratch: a grand collaboration of the construction, art, and special effects departments.

Set decorator Tim Stepeck located a gas station in Los Angeles about to go out of business, bought up its gas pumps and other fittings, and shipped them off to

Lancaster. The fixtures and other merchandise inside the store were obtained from restaurant supply houses, cooperative food manufacturers, and the simple expedient of loading up shopping carts with canned goods and groceries from discount supermarkets. Schedules were juggled so that both Michael Watkins and Rob Bowman could direct scenes for their respective episodes.

The last scene filmed there, of course, was of the gas station exploding up—it had been rigged to do so in a spectacular manner throughout the construction process. Then all remnants of the gas station were removed and the roadside site restored to its previous desolate state. "I think they shot maybe two days there," says Tomasick, shaking his head and smiling. "Then, it was if the whole thing never even existed."

By contrast, Area 51 was "built" by visual effects producer Bill Millar and his associates, who created the secret base's aircraft—B-2 Stealth bombers and F-117A Stealth fighters as well as alien antigravity craft—on their Macintosh computers. "The only 'practical' part was the base's front gate, which we shot at a fence at the San Bernardino county line one hundred and twenty miles out of Los Angeles," says Vulich. "We opened and closed the fence and drove the white Cherokee through it. All the rest is matte paintings and make-believe."

To create the illusions in 6X04 and 6X05 of gravity-warped individuals fused into rocks and floors, special effects makeup supervisor John Vulich made extensive molds of the affected actors' body parts; stuck their faces, arms, and torsos into specially constructed holes in the set; then attached silicon body pieces to "feather" the pertinent parts of their body onto the solid surface. And the Gila monster with its head stuck inside a rock?

"Well, for that one," says Vulich, "we actually had the insane idea of getting a real Gila Monster and putting it into a fake rock—probably the opposite of what you would think we would do. We made a little clamshell fiberglass rock, padded it so it wouldn't hurt the creature, glued on a little appliance that blended into his neck, and put it on him.

"He didn't seem to mind it, although, because of his life cycle or something, he didn't seem to get really animated until two or three in the morning. After that we took everything off him and he rode home with his trainer in his little cage."

Another example of creative initiative: In order to obtain the scenes of soft-core pornography Mulder watches while marooned in the Fletchers' living room, producer Paul Rabwin contacted an X-rated movie producer of his acquaintance and contracted for several not-so-risqué outtakes to be made during the filming of his next porn video. And, yes, Rabwin says he knows the name of the movie these actors were making—but he isn't telling.

Of all the scenes in this two-parter, though, the most highly praised and commented-upon is the one where Mulder encounters his own reflection—as Fletcher—in Morris's bedroom closet mirror. Film and TV buffs recognized immediately that this was a loving near-recreation of the famous mirror scene between Groucho and Harpo Marx in the classic 1933 comedy *Duck Soup*—which was subsequently reenacted by Harpo and Lucille Ball in a famous 1955 episode of *I Love Lucy*. The scene was inserted, say the episode's three writers, as soon as the delicious possibilities of the Mulder/Fletcher identity switch were realized.

But how to film it?

During initial production meetings the obvious solution was suggested: that it be pulled off primarily with the help of special effects. "But that would have been very expensive, and I think it's the human touch, the little imperfections, that really make the scene work," says Kim Manners, who directed the tour de force. In the end, only one small touch—the circle of fog on the mirror as Mulder blows onto it—was inserted electronically.

David Duchovny and Michael McKean volunteered immediately to do the scene the old fashioned way. They both watched tapes of *Duck Soup,* then worked with a specially hired choreographer every day, more or less, for a week and a half.

There was, of course, no mirror on the set, but actually two mirror-image sets of the same bedroom, facing across from each other. In rehearsals and during filming, Duchovny and McKean synchronized their movements with an electronic metronome, clicking away in the background, but erased from the final mix.

There are no cuts in the insanely complicated scene—it would have to be done in one complete take from beginning to end. Producers and crew members watched the two actors, several reports reveal, with a mixture of delight, incredulity, and terror.

"They got it on Take Twelve!" recalls Manners, happily. "The Marx Brothers," he adds, "would have been proud."

John Gillnitz—the name of the actor whom Fletcher in "Dreamland II" asserts is impersonating Saddam Hussein—is actually an amalgam of the names of the three writers of the episode: John Shiban, Vince Gilligan, and Frank Spotnitz.

The "mandroid army" scoffed at by Fletcher in 6X05 is a sly flashback to "Jose Chung's From Outer Space" (3X20).

The Little A'Le'Inn is an actual cafe off Highway 375—the "Extraterrestrial Highway"—in Rachel, Nevada. Alas, it is a much smaller and less creatively decorated place than depicted in 6X05.

Lana Chee, the seventy-five-year-old Hopi woman inhabited by the personality of a young hot-shot Air Force pilot, was played by Julia Vera, a fifty-eight-year-old actress of Hopi ancestry, who wore elaborate facial appliances to age herself for the role. She was also fitted with special clouded contact lenses to complete the illusion. Nearly blinded, she took five tries before she could flick her cigarette butt into Mulder's lap. Vera credits her winning the role partly to the speech patterns she learned during a stint in the U.S. Army.

Construction supervisor Duke Tomasick was a Los Angeles City firefighter before entering the film business. He worked on the movie *Demolition Man* as well as the series *Brooklyn South, Civil Wars,* and *Doogie Howser, MD.*

According to director Kim Manners, there are two noticeable mistakes in the mirror scene between David Duchovny and Michael McKean. The first: "I believe it's when they're bending over and shaking their asses. Michael McKean's hand is on what would be the left leg of his underwear and he's pulling it down just a little bit. David's isn't." And the second mistake? "That's my secret."

One of the signature backstage moments of the entire sixth season occurred during a particularly bleak morning at the distant Lancaster location during the filming of the two-parter. David Duchovny emerged from his trailer and said, "When is this show moving back to Los Angeles?" Within days, dozens of *X-Files* insiders were wearing T-shirts emblazoned with the exact same question.

TERMS OF ENDEARMENT

In a "normal" middle-class community, a mother is accused of murdering her late-term fetus. Mulder, however, suspects an even more shocking crime.

EPISODE: 6X06
FIRST AIRED: January 3, 1999
EDITOR: Louise A. Innes
WRITTEN BY: David Amann
DIRECTED BY: Rob Bowman

GUEST STARS:
Bruce Campbell (Wayne Weinsider)
Lisa Jane Persky (Laura Weinsider)
Grace Phillips (Betsy Monroe)
Chris Owens (Agent Jeffrey Spender)
Michael Milhoan (Deputy Arky Stevens)
Michael Rothhaar (Dr. Couvillion)
Lenora May (Kim Britton)
Jimmy Staszkiel (Mr. Ginsberg)
Karen Stone (Nurse)
Matthew Butcher (EMT)

PRINCIPAL SETTINGS:
Hollins and Roanoke, Virginia;
Washington, D.C.

Two expectant parents, Laura and Wayne Weinsider, sit in the consulting room of their ob/gyn, Dr. Couvillion. He shows them an ultrasound picture of their future child—and points out a disturbing anomaly. He also urges them not to become alarmed or to jump to any conclusions.

"We see a development," he says. "An abnormal bony formation involving the upper vertebrae. And something growing here, on the plates of the skull."

Wayne Weinsider, an ordinary-looking man in his late thirties, grimaces and closes his eyes. Terribly upset, he leaves the room. Laura, a plain but sincere-looking woman of the same age, follows him into the hallway. She repeats what the doctor told her and urges him to wait and hope for the best.

"I just want it to be normal," says Wayne, in obvious emotional turmoil.

The couple return to their cottage in suburban Virginia. That night Wayne locks the front door and walks upstairs, bringing his very pregnant wife, who is already in bed, a glass of milk. He lies down beside her, turns off the light, and they snuggle.

"I love you, Laura, no matter what," he says, with a tinge of sadness. "You know that, Poopydoo?"

"I know," says Laura, smiling. "Good night, Wayne."

"'Night, Laura," says her husband. "Sweet dreams."

A few minutes later a fiery light explodes the darkness illuminating Laura, who wakes and turns over with fright. At the foot of the bed is a horned demonic figure, silhouetted against a wall of fire.

She sits bolt upright. "Wayne! *Wayne!*" she screams.

Laura turns toward her husband. He is gone. The fiery demon grabs her feet and pulls her toward him.

"No! Please! What are you doing? *Stop!*" screams Laura.

Hot, smoky breath comes out of the creature's mouth. The demon spreads the pregnant woman's legs apart and reaches down. Laura struggles for her life, calling her husband's name. She bites the demon on one of his bony shoulders. He pushes her away. She screams again.

"Wayne! Where are you!? *Don't let him take my baby!*"

The demon reaches down again and this time rises with a demon baby in his arms. He holds the misshapen, wriggling infant above his head, as if offering it to the demon gods.

"Wayne! *Wayne!*" pleads Laura.

"Laura?" says Wayne, waking.

He switches on the bedside lamp and shakes his wife awake. As she emerges from her nightmare, he comforts her.

"Oh, Wayne, it was terrible!" says Laura, between sobs. "They were trying to steal our baby!"

Wayne looks down and compassion slowly turns to shock. His hands are now bright red. Seeing this, Laura throws back the covers. Her nightgown is covered with blood and she is no longer pregnant. Her anguished wail cuts through the dark night.

At FBI headquarters in Washington, a rotund lawman from Hollins, Virginia, explains that the case he's working on is stranger than anything he's encountered.

"But given the victim's statement," says the officer, "the unusually vivid detail—well, I just have to take Laura's word about her baby being abducted. I hear you specialize in these types of cases."

Seated at Fox Mulder's desk, Jeffrey Spender nods gravely.

"You've come to the right place, Deputy, uh—"

He looks down at a case report.

"—Stevens. Now, this woman making these claims, she's your sister?"

"Yes, sir," says Stevens. "I've heard about the things people are saying about her—not to my face, of course—but real mean and awful things about what Laura's part is in all of this."

Spender shakes his head sympathetically. He asks Stevens about the ultrasound; the lawman repeats the fact that nothing conclusive was found.

"Okay, Deputy," says Spender. "We're gonna put this right into our priority caseload."

Stevens is extremely gratified by this response. Certain that the matter is in good hands, he thanks Spender and leaves. The moment he clears the door Spender inserts the case report right into his paper shredder.

Sometime afterward Stevens stops his patrol car in front of the Weinsider house.

"I know this went right into your caseload," he says, "but I never imagined you'd get here so soon, Agent, um—"

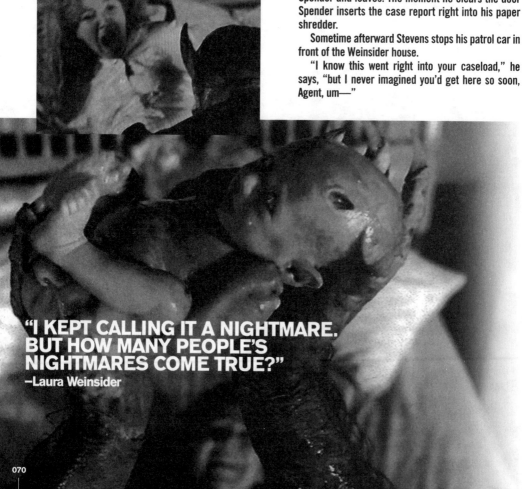

"I KEPT CALLING IT A NIGHTMARE. BUT HOW MANY PEOPLE'S NIGHTMARES COME TRUE?"
—Laura Weinsider

"Mulder. Fox Mulder," says the helpful-looking man sitting in the front seat next to him. "Though I ask you not to make that known to anybody. The FBI likes to keep our work on these cases very hush-hush."

Fox Mulder holds the shredded case report, now painstakingly Scotch-taped together. Stevens nods gravely and asks him to thank Agent Spender. Mulder promises to do so in his next progress report, then lifts the door handle, exits. Moments later he's in the Weinsiders' living room, facing the anguished couple.

"I kept calling it a nightmare," says Laura, sitting beside her husband. "But how many people's nightmares come true?"

Mulder nods. "Not many," he says.

He asks Laura if the baby stolen from her in her dream was normal.

"No," she whispers tearfully. "It was some sort of monster with horns and a tail. Will you excuse me?"

She leaves the room, leaving Mulder with Wayne, who looks almost as traumatized as Laura.

"My wife appears resilient," says Wayne, "but I know she's suffered ever since the doctor told us about the complications."

Mulder nods sympathetically. "Um, you were right there in bed with your wife the whole time, Mr. Weinsider?"

"Wayne. Yes, I woke her up," replies Wayne.

"But according to your wife's statement," says Mulder, "at one point she reached over for you in the bed and you weren't there."

Wayne appears puzzled. "Well, it was a dream."

Mulder nods again, curtly.

"I have to use your phone, Wayne," he says.

At the headquarters of the U.S. Department of Agriculture in Washington, Scully sits at a tiny desk and interviews, extremely politely, a prospective federal employee. His name is Mr. Ginsberg. He is a long-haired, bloodshot-eyed, wild-bearded veteran of the sixties.

Asks Scully, "Do you, or have you ever, smoked marijuana?"

"Nope. Nosiree," Mr. Ginsberg replies.

"Have you consorted with people who have, now or in the past?"

Mr. Ginsberg sighs, blinks, and thinks hard.

"No," he says, finally. "I really don't think so."

Scully stares at him in disbelief and pure boredom. Her cell phone rings. It's Mulder, calling to tell her he won't be coming in to work today. Annoyed, Scully asks him where he's calling from.

"Before I tell you," says Mulder, a tad sheepishly, "I'm going to ask you to keep an open mind."

Mulder tells her he's in Roanoke County investigating what some citizens are calling a demon baby snatching.

"You're in Virginia!" says Scully, accusingly.

Replies Mulder, "Look, I want you to take a look at this woman's charts. Strange in-utero deformities were detected. I'm going to courier them to you, all right?"

"Mulder, we are supposed to be doing background checks, not chasing down X-Files."

"Look, Scully," says Mulder, "Spender just round-filed this case. It's unconscionable."

"And what do you call rooting through his trash?"

"Well, like that's any different from the assignment we're stuck with?"

"We, Mulder? I'm stuck with. You're not here." Mulder shrugs.

"Scully, this is a classic case of demon fetal harvest—what they called in the Middle Ages *atum nocturnem*—the impregnation of an unwitting woman by a dark lord of the underworld—"

"As host for his demon seed," says Scully, skeptically. "I saw *Rosemary's Baby* on cable the other night, Mulder."

"Yeah, but this is the real deal," says Mulder. "You check that woman's charts and you'll get hard evidence. Check her prenatal ultrasound."

As Mulder says this an electronic baby monitor is broadcasting everything he says to Wayne Weinsider, listening in from the bedroom.

At 10:56 that night Laura Weinsider, in her bathrobe, enters her bedroom.

"Wayne, have you seen my nightgown?" she says.

But Wayne does not answer. Laura walks downstairs, calling for him. A red glow through the window catches her eye; someone is burning something in a backyard incinerator. In the backyard Wayne reaches into a pile of leaves on the ground and pulls out a cloth-wrapped parcel. Laura exits a back door and walks hesitatingly toward him.

"Wayne?" she says, fearfully.

As Laura nears the glowing incinerator she gazes into the flames. Something the size of a newborn infant is burning. She gasps and turns. Standing behind her, his face beaded with sweat, is Wayne.

He asks her what she's doing there. Still rattled, Laura asks her husband the same.

"Burning leaves," says Wayne.

"At this time of night?"

"Well, you asked me to rake up the yard," he replies. "It was in the job jar. Hey, come on! You're making me feel weird."

Laura shakes her head.

"Come to bed, Wayne, *please*," she says.

"I will, honey," says Wayne. "I just wanted to—I just wanted everything to look perfect when you woke up. I'll be right in."

He kisses his wife. Laura turns and walks slowly back to the house. Wayne turns back toward the incinerator. He stares into the flames, weeping.

His eyes glow faintly, like an animal's. Or a demon's.

At 6:57 the next morning Mulder—sleeping in the front seat of his car, parked across the street from the Weinsiders' house—is woken by his ringing cell phone. It is Scully, in her FBI office. She's been up all night examining Laura Weinsider's medical records.

"The prenatal birth defects you spoke of?" she says. "They're all here. But they're subtle. They look to be discrete bony deformities—spurs on the superior aspect of the scapula and small protuberances on the skull adjacent to the coronal suture."

"Protuberances?" says Mulder. "You mean, like horns?"

He casually draws a set of horns on a photo of Wayne Weinsider. In Washington, Scully replies that the protuberances could merely be vestigial features or an expression of a recessive gene.

"Something that could be passed along by the father?" asks Mulder.

"No," says Scully. "I wouldn't look to the father as any kind of dark force here, Mulder. I think it's the mother. And Virginia law on third trimester abortions requires you to put her under arrest."

She adds, "Labor was induced, Mulder. In the mother's blood there was found a significant trace of an herb called mandrake—it's a poison that's been known to facilitate self-abortion. It's also been known to be used as an hallucinogenic."

Mulder watches as Wayne leaves the house and gets into his car. Scully adds that she phoned Dr. Couvillion, who told her of Wayne's distress and Laura's contrasting calmness at the news of the possible birth defect.

"Mulder, I suggest you proceed very carefully," she says. "This could be very emotional for everybody concerned."

Mulder gets out of his car and heads for the Weinsiders' door.

Someone knocks on the door of a very similar cottage and it is opened by an attractive, late-thirtyish woman named Betsy. Standing on the front porch, facing her, is Wayne.

"Sorry. I forgot my key," says Wayne, sheepishly.

"Well, where have you been?" asks Betsy.

Says Wayne, "Well, I told you I was going to be on the road until Tuesday, Poopydoo."

Says Betsy plaintively, "I was just so worried, Wayne. We're so close now,"

Betsy smiles now, relieved. It appears she is about eight months pregnant. Wayne puts down his briefcase and gives her a tender kiss on the lips.

"I wouldn't let anything happen to you," he says. "Not to our little bundle of joy."

Inside the Weinsider cottage later that day, Mulder confers with Laura and Deputy Stevens; several uniformed cops are also present. Angrily, Stevens protests that his sister has never used mandrake or any other dangerous drug.

Wayne enters the house and Laura tells him, in tears, that she's been accused of killing their baby.

"Who's accusing you?" asks Wayne.

"Who do you think?" says Stevens, angrily. "I don't know where you've been, Wayne, but I seem to be the only one keeping the dogs from the door!"

"Well, a man's got to make a living," protests Wayne, defensively.

Mulder steps between them.

"Wayne? Mr. Weinsider?" he says, evenly. "I don't want to arrest Laura. I'm sure you'd hate like the devil for that to happen."

Mulder's eyes lock on to Wayne. Wayne seems shaken.

Adds Mulder, "So why don't you tell Deputy Stevens that it's okay to search the premises so we can clear up any misunderstanding about who's responsible for what happened here."

Sometime later Mulder and the police are deep into a search of the house and grounds. Wayne is watching them closely. Laura turns to him.

"I know there's nothing they're going to find, Wayne," she says. "But why do I feel guilty, anyway?"

Wayne chokes back tears, then tells her he has to divulge a secret to her. He swallows hard and closes his eyes.

"On the night that you lost the baby," he says haltingly, "I had gotten up because I couldn't sleep. And when I came back to bed you had our little baby in your hands. You were in some kind of trance. I couldn't get you to wake up! You kept chanting, over and over—*zasas, zazas, nastanda, zazas*—"

"Wayne!" says Laura, shocked.

"—and all I could do was take our little son, our little baby, and wrap him up so no one could ever learn the truth."

"Oh, my God!"

"And the other night, when you saw me outside, and I was burning the leaves—"

"No! No! *No!*"

"—I was just doing it to protect you. I knew I could never bring back our little boy, our precious little Wayne, Jr., but I couldn't bear losing you."

Wayne turns abruptly away from his distraught wife. There is a commotion outside; uniformed police are excitedly gathering around the incinerator.

A few minutes later Laura, still almost hysterical, sits across the kitchen table from her brother.

"I don't know what to tell you," she says, sobbing. "All I can think—when they told me that something was wrong, that there was a problem, was that this thing growing inside me was evil.

"I kept thinking that maybe there was something I

"I KEPT THINKING THAT MAYBE THERE WAS SOMETHING I DID WRONG, AND THIS WAS MY PUNISHMENT. TOLD WAYNE THAT EVERYTHING WAS GOING TO BE OKAY, BUT I LIED."

Laura Weinsider

did wrong, and this was my punishment. I told Wayne that everything was going to be okay, but I lied."

Standing nearby, Mulder turns his attention to Wayne, who is sitting in the living room, head in hands. Stevens advises his sister not to say anything more until he reads her her rights and takes her to the station house. Wayne remains seated on the couch while his wife is led away.

"You're gonna be okay," he says, finally. "I'm gonna get the best attorney!"

Mulder follows Laura, walking past Weinsider and gazing at him with contempt.

"I know what you are," he says, with chilling certainty.

Later that day Wayne speeds happily down a nearby road in his Camaro convertible. On the radio, playing a little too loud, is Garbage's "I'm Only Happy When It Rains." He dials Betsy on his cell phone and tells her he's on his way home. She tells him that he's late and that she's going to leave for her sonogram without him. Wayne protests vehemently.

"I want to be there, honey!" he says. "I don't want to be the kind of husband who isn't there every step of the way. It's not just a sonogram, honey. It's a picture of the expression of our beautiful love."

Phone held to his ear, Wayne stops at a red light. Someone pulls up next to him. It's Mulder, leaning out the driver's window of his rental car.

"Hey, Wayne!" says Mulder, grinning slightly. "Where ya goin'?"

"What?"

"Who ya talkin' to?"

"Wayne, who are you talking to?" asks Betsy, via the cell phone.

Says Mulder, "You seem like you're in an awful big hurry."

"Wayne?" says Betsy.

"I'm late for an appointment," says Wayne, annoyed.

"Appointment with who?" says Mulder.

"A business client," says Wayne.

Exasperated, Betsy hangs up. So does Wayne.

Mulder grins. "You're in the insurance business, aren't you? That must take you out on the road an awful lot, huh?"

Annoyed, Wayne tells Mulder that he's an insurance medical technician—not that it's any of his business.

"So, where's our appointment?" asks Mulder, breezily. "How far do we have to go?"

"What?"

"Come on, Wayne," he says. "I'll race ya."

The traffic light turns green. Wayne revs his engine and speeds off. Mulder spots him a few seconds, then happily pulls alongside.

. A few minutes later Wayne knocks on somebody's

front door. It's opened by a housewife named Kim Britton. Wayne announces that he's there—several days early—to draw some blood for her insurance physical.

She reluctantly invites him in. In the living room, Wayne prepares his medical equipment. Three tow-headed young boys race through, heading for the front door.

"Slow down, monsters!" shouts their mother.

Wayne gazes at them wistfully. "I love kids," he says, beginning to draw blood. "I've got a baby on the way myself. Seems like I've been trying forever."

He draws his hypodermic needle from Kim's arm and gazes at a family portrait on her wall.

"You don't know how lucky you are," he says. "Two cells, with all that can go wrong, and there they are. Perfect."

Wayne bends forward to place the blood sample in his case on the floor. On the back of his neck, just above his shirt collar, are several rounded spikes protruding from his upper vertebrae. Kim sees them and frowns worriedly. Wayne straightens up and asks her if she's feeling faint.

"No," she says, smiling nervously. "I'm okay."

A car horn sounds outside. It is Mulder, standing next to the convertible, waving jauntily.

"Can I use your phone?" Wayne asks the puzzled woman.

Under Mulder's approving gaze, Kim's three sons bounce noisily around the interior of Wayne's convertible. Wayne leaves the Britton house, chases the boys away angrily, slips behind the wheel. At this moment Scully phones her partner with the news that Weinsider has called AD Kersh, complaining that Mulder is harassing him.

"Leave me alone!" says Weinsider, before roaring off.

Scully is still on the line.

"Mulder?" she says. "I've got to tell Kersh something. What do you want me to say?"

"Tell him I'm down here doing a background check on somebody," says Mulder.

At the Roanoke County Jail that night, Laura Weinsider paces nervously. Wayne Weinsider is let into her holding cell, looking none too eager to be there.

"I got a message you need to see me, Laura," he says, coldly. "What is it?"

"I'm afraid," says Laura, looking at him searchingly.

Wayne is unmoved.

"Well, I've been meeting with attorneys," he says. "And given the circumstances, and your emotional state, they feel confident of an acquittal. If that's what you're worried about, Laura."

"No, Wayne," says Laura, staring at her husband. "I've been thinking," she replies. "About your story.

About how it doesn't make sense. You said you wrapped the baby up to hide it, but what they found in the fire was wrapped in the nightgown I had on when I woke up from my nightmare."

"But that's not possible," says Wayne. "You must be mistaken."

Laura shakes her head slowly.

"And I keep thinking about the face of that terrible creature at the end of my bed. And I remember something that I didn't tell anybody—not even you."

Wayne moves toward her, taking her in his arms.

"Laura, you're scaring me," he says, soothingly. "No matter what you believe, I only have one desire: to protect you, to put all this behind us."

As he says this, Laura pulls up his shirt collar and spots the bite mark on his neck. Her face becomes a mask of fear. Wayne realizes what she's done.

"Why'd you go and do that, Laura?" he asks, voice cracking. "You've got to know that I love you and I just wish you could've been the one."

He grasps Laura's hands tightly. He breathes in deeply, and sucks a ghostly vapor from her mouth into his own.

Several long minutes later Wayne watches anxiously as paramedics work frantically to revive Laura.

"She just collapsed," he says. "It was like she died right in my arms."

The paramedics place defibrillator paddles on Laura's chest. They shock her once, then twice.

"We've got a heartbeat," says one of the medical workers.

"What?" says Wayne, startled.

Later that night Wayne parks his car in Betsy's garage, sprints to the front door, and enters. Betsy is waiting impatiently in the living room. She brushes aside his apologies and tells him that she went to the doctor's office alone.

"Did you get the sonogram?" asks Wayne. "Did you bring it back home?"

Betsy—her face somewhat clouded—lifts a folder from the coffee table.

"Is there a problem?" asks Wayne, apprehensively.

"The doctor found something," says Betsy evenly. "She doesn't know yet, but there's some kind of bony growth on the baby's spine and skull. It may just be a stage of development. The doctor really just wants to wait and see."

The news hits Wayne like a sledgehammer. "Okay. Sure," he says, overwhelmed.

He moves toward his wife on the sofa, and looks into her eyes. "Whatever happens, you know I love you," he says. "No matter what."

Betsy glows when she hears this. Wayne offers to get her a glass of warm milk before they go to bed.

At 10:02 P.M. Mulder rushes into the ICU ward at

WAYNE BENDS FORWARD TO PLACE THE BLOOD SAMPLE IN HIS CASE ON THE FLOOR. ON THE BACK OF HIS NECK, JUST ABOVE HIS SHIRT COLLAR, ARE SEVERAL ROUNDED SPIKES PROTRUDING FROM HIS UPPER VERTEBRAE.

Roanoke County General Hospital. Scully is waiting for him there.

She says, "Mulder, you ask me to come down here, and then you're nowhere to be found."

Says Mulder, "I was down in the basement at County Records, doing a background check."

"Mulder, it's me," replies Scully. "That's your cover story, remember?"

Mulder insists he has indeed been doing a background check: on the man who put Laura Weinsider into a coma. Scully protests that there isn't a shred of medical evidence that Laura was the victim of foul play.

"Perfect," says Mulder. "Not a shred of evidence is exactly the evidence I hoped you'd find."

Mulder hands Scully a file. It has a name on it.

"'Ivan Veles,'" she reads. "'Born in Czechoslovakia, 1956. Married twice, widowed twice. No children. Prosecuted twice for murder of wives Gisele and Helga, acquitted twice on lack of evidence.'"

She looks up.

"Who is Ivan Veles?"

"Wayne Weinsider," says Mulder. "He's a Czech national, emigrated 1994. He's also known as Bud Hasselhof; also known as Gordy Boytano. There's more. Read on."

Scully does.

"'In Slavic society the name Veles is synonymous with the devil. From the Lithuanian root Vele: a horned demon who sucks the souls of innocents.'

"Mulder, you're not suggesting that he is, himself, a devil, are you?'

"I'm not suggesting anything," says Mulder. "I think the facts speak for themselves."

In Betsy's kitchen that night Wayne heats some milk on the stove, pours it carefully into a glass tumbler, and walks upstairs. Betsy is already in bed.

"This'll put you to sleep on a cloud," says Wayne. "Your troubles will melt away."

He hands Betsy the milk. She smiles and sighs.

"Sometimes I remember why I married you," she says.

In the Weinsiders' backyard several cops dig holes with shovels, by flashlight. Scully and Mulder join Deputy Stevens at the site. A technician fires a shell into the ground, triggering through a subterranean mapping device. The results appear on a nearby computer monitor.

"Over here!" shouts a policeman, excitedly.

At the far corner of the yard a few moments later Scully pulls on some latex gloves and reaches down into the earth. Mulder leans down to speak to her.

"You're going to find discrete osteopathic deformities to the upper vertebrae," he says. "Two bony protrusions between the parietal and occipital lobes of the skull."

Scully smoothes the dirt away from a tiny skull—

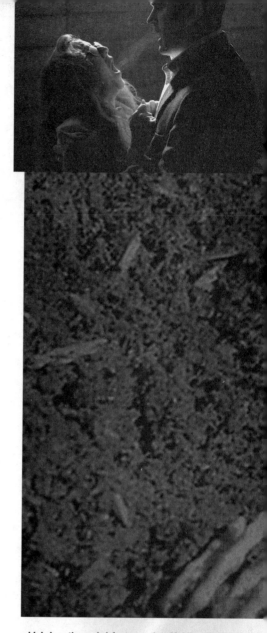

which has the weird features that Mulder predicted.

"Good lord!" says Stevens, shocked.

"Put out an A.P.B. for your brother-in-law," Mulder tells him. "He's not going to come back here."

Both Scully and Stevens are confused. As the deputy hurries away, Mulder explains.

Says Mulder, "He's done this to other women here, Scully," he says. "Just like he did in Czechoslovakia. My guess is that the baby we just dug up belonged to another one of Wayne's 'wives.'"

"What are you saying?" asks Scully. "That he's trying to propagate? He's trying to breed?"

Says Mulder, "He's exercising his biological imperative, and he'll do anything or say anything he has to to succeed."

"Maybe you didn't hear me," she says, brusquely.

Betsy pulls Wayne's face toward hers. He is no longer a demon, just plain Wayne, looking a little disheveled and surprised.

"I said—what are you doing, Wayne?"

Later that night Mulder and Scully drive through the night; Mulder talking on his cell phone and taking down an address. He does a 180-degree power turn and heads in the opposite direction, and tells Scully that Wayne's employer has a second home address for him.

"You think he's got a second wife?" asks Scully.

"Think about it, Scully," says Mulder. "He meets or screens prospective women through his work—that's probably why he came to this country in the first place; bigger gene pool, more women—then he plants as many seeds as he can. Let's just hope he hasn't been able to harvest any more of them."

A car hurtles past them in the opposite direction, then lurches to a halt. Its driver gets out: Betsy. There is blood on her hands and nightgown. She staggers toward the agents.

"He took my baby!" she sobs. "He took my baby! Wayne! Wayne! He took my baby!"

A few minutes later, when Mulder and Scully arrive at Betsy's house, it is already surrounded by police. Guns and flashlights drawn, they enter the front door. Inside, the only light is from a television set playing a family reunion scene from the movie *The Man in the Gray Flannel Suit*. In the backyard, Wayne is feverishly digging a shallow grave.

"Wayne!" shouts Mulder. "It's over."

Wayne turns to face him.

"A normal life. A family. That's all I ever wanted."

"Where's the baby, Wayne?" asks Mulder.

"How could she do this to them?" says Wayne.

"Put the shovel down!" shouts Mulder. "Your lies won't work anymore."

"My lies? What about her lies?"

Wayne keeps digging. Scully eyes him warily.

She says, "Whatever the truth, Mr. Weinsider, you can't hope to bury it now."

Replies Wayne, "I'm not burying anything. I'm digging it up. Don't you understand? She took it! Betsy took it!"

Mulder looks at him intently. "You can't blame anyone else this time!" he says. "Like you did with Laura."

Wayne stops digging and faces Mulder.

"Don't you see? Betsy isn't like Laura. Betsy is—"

Two shots ring out in quick succession. Wayne falls—blasted backward by Deputy Stevens's bullets. The lawmen rush to where he fell. Scully yells for the paramedics.

"I just wanted what everyone wanted," moans Wayne, weakly.

In the I.C.U. at Roanoke County General sometime

"But it doesn't make sense, Mulder. If he's trying to breed, then why would he be snatching his own babies and burying them in his backyard?"

"Because they're demons," says Mulder. "And he wants a normal child."

In the middle of the night Betsy Monroe sleeps soundly. A fiery light explodes the darkness—illuminating Betsy, who wakes and sits up abruptly. At the foot of her bed is a horned demonic figure, silhouetted against a wall of fire. The fiery creature grabs her feet, pulling her toward him.

"Wayne! Wayne! What are you doing?" she screams.

Betsy leans forward and grabs the demon by the throat.

later, Laura Weinsider still lies unconscious. In an identical state, strapped onto a gurney, Wayne is rolled into the space beside her.

Deputy Stevens arrives, angrily demanding that Wayne be moved away from his sister. Mulder tells him to calm down. Stevens casts a hateful look at his brother-in-law.

"The son of a bitch had better live," he says. "So I can beat the truth out of him. Find out how he did it. And why he did it."

Replies Mulder, grimly, "I think the why is directly related to the how. I think we need to have a talk with this other wife of his."

Mulder leads the fuming deputy away. At that moment Wayne's heartbeat becomes erratic and he begins to convulse wildly.

A ghostly vapor spews forth from his mouth, crosses the room, and enters Laura's. She starts to convulse as well. Alarms go off in the I.C.U. Doctors and nurses rush in and try to revive Wayne with no success.

At Betsy's house the next morning Scully kneels alongside a backyard excavation.

Mulder arrives, and walks over to his partner.

"How many?" he asks.

"Four total," says his partner. "All here for some time. Maybe years. All normal, though, Mulder. No osteological deformities. And Betsy's baby isn't here. There are no fresh graves."

Says Mulder, quietly, "I know."

Scully stares at him. "What do you think he did with it?"

"I don't think he did anything with it," says Mulder.

"But she was recently pregnant. I saw her records, her sonograms, in the house."

Mulder nods.

"Showing the same defects," he says. "These weren't Wayne's babies, Scully."

He adds, "I think Wayne realized something last night. That's why he was out here, digging. He realized that he'd met someone even more evil than he was. Who would sacrifice what he desperately wanted for himself."

"Betsy?" says Scully.

Mulder nods again.

"It was no coincidence that she ran into us last night," he says. "We were taken in by her just like Wayne was. By a woman who would say anything, do anything to get what she wanted. Was even more driven than he was."

"Driven to what?"

"To have," says Mulder, "what only Wayne could give her."

The next day Betsy Monroe, at the wheel of Wayne's Camaro, drives along a rural two-lane. The car radio blasts out Garbage's "I'm Only Happy When It Rains."

She glances tenderly at the bundled-up baby in the seat alongside her; its tiny, gruesomely clawed hand clenched idly into a fist.

In a state of total bliss the baby's mother faces forward again—her eyes glowing faintly red—and accelerates down the open road.

BACK STORY/6X06

"Terms of Endearment" is a solid stand-alone episode; a smooth melding of the series's characters, attitudes, and plotlines with a familiar horror subgenre. It also marks a series first: the mid-production withdrawal of a guest actor for religious reasons.

It happened on the day director Rob Bowman was shooting the birth of Wayne and Laura Weinsider's demon child. After several hours spent setting up the cameras, lights, set, and special fire effects, several technical rehearsals were held using a rubber doll. Watching the final run-through was the mother of the real baby hired to do the scene—who promptly gasped, clutched her child, conversed feverishly with the on-set social worker and studio nurse, and retreated to her dressing room.

'Then she told us 'The X-Files is my favorite show, but we can't do this. It has to do with the devil, and I'm a devout Catholic,'" reports second-unit production manager Harry Bring. "Then she asked 'Is this going to cause a problem?'"

No problem. Bowman and Bring assured her that they understood her dilemma completely, presented her with an X-Files movie poster, walked her and her baby to the soundstage door—then contacted the parents of two more infant "actors" on call for just such an unforeseen occasion. After forty-five minutes, and the arrival of a substitute child, the cursed birth proceeded uneventfully.

Indeed, for all of its hellish underpinnings, 6X06 is remembered as a fairly nontraumatic feat to pull off. It was the first X-Files written by executive story editor David Amann, who had previously written two network TV movies (The Man Who Wouldn't Die and Dead Air) and spent two years on the staff of CBS's Chicago Hope.

The thirty-nine-year old Amann is not a noticeably high-strung individual, and unlike other first-timers he recalls that the pitching, boarding, and writing process went no more or less easily than he expected. Amann adds that the process gave him an accelerated course in X-Files script construction, especially on how to come up with a satisfactory mix of the scientific and the paranormal, and integrate an interesting Mulder-Scully argument—"Escalating throughout the whole hour," he says—into the central mystery.

"It was about the fifth or sixth idea I suggested," he says. "I had this idea for doing a kind of Rosemary's Baby in reverse—not from the point of view of the hapless woman unwittingly impregnated, but from the point of view of the devil, who has his own needs and ambitions. Chris seemed to really like this.

"Afterward there were more boards and drafts and rewrites than I can remember, to be honest, but I do remember a lot of sessions with Daniel (Arkin) and Jeffrey (Bell), a lot of feedback from Frank and John and Vince, and finally we hit upon a version that everybody seemed to agree was good."

Earlier versions, recall several participants in the process, were heavier on pure shock value and lighter on humor and human interest. At one point Laura Weinsider gave birth to a serpent, not a humanoid. (Rob Bowman, for one, remembers feeling much relief when that aspect of the story was changed.)

"Actually," adds Amann, "I think the biggest problem was one that Chris solved. Up until a pretty late version of the script it was a bit linear in its storytelling. You had this guy who wanted a normal baby from his wife, didn't get it, killed her, then moved on to his second wife. And there was a certain inevitability to the idea that the wife was going to meet the same end.

"Then Chris had the idea: 'What if the second woman wants the exact opposite of what the guy wanted?' And that's what really made the whole story work well."

As is usually the case on The X-Files, an early choice was made to spend as little time as possible focusing on the "scary monster"—in this case the scary demon—and concentrate instead on the human side of the equation. Accordingly, the casting process was an intense one. It yielded one very interesting result.

Bruce Campbell, who played the devilishly vulnerable Wayne, is not only a veteran of several well-regarded Sam Raimi horror flicks (and a particular favorite of Rob Bowman, who's worked with him in the past), but had the title role in The Adventures of Brisco County, Jr., a whimsical western series that aired briefly on the Fox network in 1993.

Also, Lisa Jane Persky, who played Laura, is a character actress with impressive movie credits (The Big Easy, When Harry Met Sally, Coneheads), who had long been on the top of casting director Rick Millikan's wish list. Grace Phillips is a striking leading lady type, who was a contestant in Robert Redford's film Quiz Show and a regular on the first season of Steven Bochco's Murder One.

To play the part of the Monroe and Weinsider cottages and environs, locations manager Ilt Jones and his staff found several desirable residences in and around Pasadena, the most East Coast–like part of the Los Angeles metropolitan area. Wayne's car was a Chevrolet Camaro Z28 convertible, downgraded from a BMW Z3 at one point during the rewrite process (and loaned gratis by General Motors, which apparently had no qualms about seeing their vehicles driven onscreen by a relative of Satan). Researcher Lee Smith authenticated the show's police uniforms, buildings, and insignia by contacting Roanoke magazine—and quickly reaching a rabid X-Files fan in the advertising department who volunteered to rush outside, take dozens of pertinent photographs of policemen, police cars, and police stations in the area and post them immediately on her web site.

In keeping with the comparatively low-stress nature of this episode's production, some creative low-tech methods were employed during key scenes. Instead of computer-generating the flames in the childbirth scenes in postproduction, for example, special-effects gas burners were brought to the sound stage, placed well away from the fireproofed bed and bedding provided by set decorator Tim Stepeck, and shot through a very long lens to make it seem as though the fire was dancing only inches from the characters.

To produce the tell-tale sonogram of the in utero demon child in the episode's first scene, property master Tom Day modified a videotape of a completely normal prenatal test borrowed from a crew member whose wife was pregnant. To create a suitably creepy soundscape for crucial passages of 6X06, composer Mark Snow dipped heavily into the dolorous Gregorian chants he has stored on his computer.

And finally, to show the burnt skeletal remains of the Weinsider baby, special makeup effects supervisor John Vulich at first thought rather uneasily about trying to obtain—for $3,000, he estimates—one of the only two or three fetal skeletons for rent by medical supply houses in the United States. "Then my office manager, Donovan Brown, said, 'Why don't we just build our own from one of those human skeleton kits?'

"At first it sounded dumb," he adds. "But then we got two or three of those adult skeleton models, cut a foot or so off a leg here and shortened an arm there, glued them together to a plaster model of a fetal skull we found, and put together something that worked wonderfully."

Ⓧ

Although it was the sixth show filmed this season, "Terms of Endearment" was the seventh aired. The reason: an elaborate shuffling of the production schedule to get Chris Carter's "How The Ghosts Stole Christmas" (6X08) on the air on December 13, 1998, the final original-episode air date before the end of the holiday season.

Ⓧ

Shortly after 6X06 aired in January 1999, actor Chris Owens began noticing interesting reactions from people who recognized him on the streets of Los Angeles. "People kept looking at me with expressions that I guess were saying: 'You destroyed evidence! What a prick you are, Spender!' One day, somebody actually waved his finger at me and just said, 'Paper shredder!'"

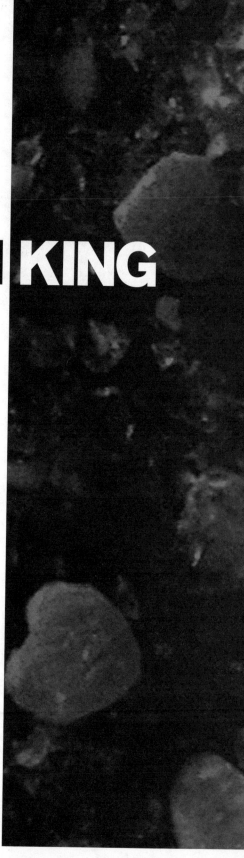

6(X)07

THE RAIN KING

In rural Kansas, thousands of **drought-stricken citizens** are being forced to enrich the town drunk—who seems able, through mystical means, to control the weather.

EPISODE: 6X07
FIRST AIRED: January 10, 1999
EDITOR: Heather MacDougall
WRITTEN BY: Jeffrey Bell
DIRECTED BY: Kim Manners

GUEST STARS:
Clayton Rohner (Daryl Mootz)
David Manis (Holman Hardt)
Victoria Jackson (Sheila Fontaine)
Dirk Blocker (Mayor Gilmore)
Francesca Ingrassia (Cindy Culpepper)
Sharon Madden (Motel Manager)
Tom McFadden (Doctor)
Dan Gifford (Local News Anchor)
Brian D. Johnson (Chainsaw Man)

PRINCIPAL SETTINGS:
Kroner, Kansas; Wymore, Nebraska

On February 14 in Kroner, Kansas, a pleasingly plump late-thirtyish woman named Sheila Fontaine signs a Valentine's Day card, seals it with a kiss, and places it carefully next to a gift package wrapped in red paper with white hearts.

She lights a red scented candle, grabs a chocolate from a heart-shaped box, and settles onto her couch to watch a local news program. A TV weatherman named Holman Hardt forecasts no respite for a long winter drought.

The front door bursts open and Sheila greets the man who enters—an ill-shaven, dubious-looking, debatably handsome guy named Daryl Mootz—enthusiastically.

"Sheila, we got a really big problem here," whines Daryl.

He holds up a local newspaper. On an inside page is a large notice announcing the upcoming marriage of Daryl and Sheila. Daryl complains that they'd agreed to keep their engagement secret. Sheila—who's wearing a red satin peignoir and dressing gown—kisses him.

"I know," he says, "but I just wanted everybody in town to know why I've been so happy the last few months."

Daryl pulls away angrily.

"I know business has been slow," says Sheila, "but we can't stop living just because it hasn't rained in a spell."

"Maybe we should just call off the engagement," says Daryl.

"Don't do this!" says Sheila. *"Not today!* It'll rain soon—I can feel it."

Daryl shakes his head. "I just need time to think," he says.

He glances down at the half-empty box of chocolates.

"Oh, look at that!" he says. "And you wonder why your ass is so big!"

He storms out, swaggers to his old Mustang, and drives away.

Depressed, Sheila switches on her stereo. The Carpenters' "Rainy Days and Mondays" is playing.

It's playing on Daryl's car radio, too. Daryl grabs a beer from a cooler, pops the top, and takes a long swig.

Sheila grabs another piece of chocolate. Two tears splash onto her coffee table.

Down the road, raindrops splash onto Daryl's windshield. He whoops with pleasure and hits the wipers. The rain, however, quickly turns into hail and after a few seconds a torrent of Ping-Pong ball–sized ice pellets shatter his windshield. Unable to see, Daryl skids off the slick highway and slams into a telephone pole. Dazed, Daryl cracks open his door—and a giant

hailstone smacks him on the head, knocking him unconscious. The hailstone bounces to the pavement. It and every one of its companions are in the shape of a frozen heart.

Six months later a small Cessna lands at Kroner's dusty unpaved airstrip. Mulder and Scully emerge. Their welcoming party consists of a ruddy-faced, middle-aged man and a small girl wearing a red, white, and blue leotard.

"Don't look at me," says Scully, to her partner. "This was your idea."

The little girl clicks on a boom box, starting a sprightly march tune, and begins twirling a baton energetically. The man—Kroner's mayor, Jim Gilmore—steps forward and shakes Mulder's hand.

"If I'd known you were bringin' the missus," he says, smiling, "I'd have arranged for fancier accommodations."

After this little awkwardness is cleared up, he turns to face the performing girl.

"Okay, Rhonda, that's enough!" he shouts. "You go find your momma!"

His expression becomes more serious. At Scully's prompting, he describes the crisis that has prompted him to contact the FBI.

"Well, it's all around us," he says. "Runted crops, field fires, bankruptcies. This drought is destroying people's lives. And it's wrong for a single man to prosper at the expense of others."

"A single man?" asks Scully.

"Daryl Mootz," says Gilmore. "He's a local fella, charging people for rain."

He produces a brochure advertising a company called "Rain King, Inc." A full-length photo of Daryl, who's wearing a crown on his head, is on the cover.

"You mean cloud seeding?" asks Scully.

"The hell I do," says Gilmore. "I mean he shows up at a farm, does his dog and pony act, and the heavens weep."

Scully shoots Mulder a dirty look, then turns back to the mayor.

"Sir, if this man Mootz could, in fact, somehow produce rain, then what's the crime?"

Says Gilmore, "I believe Daryl's actually causing the drought, so he can charge people for the rain."

A few minutes later the agents drive through Kroner's tiny, deserted-looking business district. They park, get out, and start walking.

"C'mon, Scully," says Mulder, defensively. "You're acting as if I intentionally misled you."

He tells her that over the last thirty years Kroner has suffered more tornadoes, hailstorms, and heatwaves than any other town in the country.

Scully is unimpressed. Mulder is not discouraged.

He says, "Well, if that's true—if Daryl Mootz is controlling the weather for profit—then that is a crime, and that should be investigated."

They enter a storefront office—the headquarters of Rain King, Inc. Behind a large desk, talking on the phone, sits a local blonde bombshell named Cindy Culpepper. Mulder flashes his ID and tells her they're looking for Daryl Mootz. She holds up one finger and mouths, "One sec."

She speaks into the phone.

"Yes, ma'am. Appendix C, that's right. I need a six-pack of beer, a carton of Morley Lights, and a big ol' bowl of jelly beans. And can you pick out the green ones? 'Cause he don't like the green ones. You're welcome!"

She hangs up the phone.

"Now, what can I do for the FBI?" says Cindy, with a wide smile.

"We want to see the King," says Mulder, with more than a hint of Elvis in his delivery.

Cindy's smile shrinks. She tells them that Mr. Mootz is out on business and unavailable: He's currently making rain in the nearby town of Wymore, Nebraska. At Mulder's request—but even more testily—she hands over a list of her boss's clients.

"What are you investigatin' Daryl for?" she asks. "He's a hero in this community."

"So you actually believe that he makes it rain?" asks Scully.

"I know it to be fact!" says Cindy. "He saved my daddy's farm. How dare you people?"

A nearby big-screen TV set catches Mulder's eye. On it, weatherman Holman Hardt is holding forth. His radar map indicates a large green blob nearing Wymore.

"See?" says Cindy, triumphantly. "Daryl's makin' that rain!"

At 12:41 P.M. Mulder and Scully arrive at the studio of the local TV station, KPJK Channel Five. They're greeted enthusiastically by Sheila Fontaine—who mistakes them for the farm couple who've just won the "Watch the Weather and Win" contest. She introduces them happily—as the Gundersons—to Holman Hardt.

After this little misunderstanding is cleared up, the weatherman escorts the agents back to his office. Mulder takes a seat next to his partner.

"Well, from what I've read about Kroner," he says, "you've had more than your fair share of unusual weather."

Hardt smiles and nods.

He says, "To you, Kroner must seem small and simple. But through the eyes of meteorology—low pressure systems, storm fronts, tornado watches—Kroner is sophisticated, complex. And, well, sexy."

Frowning, Scully asks the weatherman whether he agrees with the mayor and thinks that Daryl Mootz somehow caused the drought.

"Of course not," says Hardt. "A huge high pressure system is the primary culprit. There's no credible evidence that suggests that Daryl, or any man, can be held accountable for our predicament."

"Thank you," says Scully, turning to Mulder. "Can we go now?"

Mulder keeps his eyes on Hardt.

"What about the rain?" he asks.

"That's a more clouded issue," says Hardt, "if you'll excuse my pun."

Mulder pulls the rainmaker's client list from his pocket. "Now, I have a list of over forty names here. People in four different counties who claim that Daryl Mootz has made it rain for them."

Hardt smiles sheepishly. "Now, I went to high school with Daryl—uh, different social circles—and frankly he's about the last man I would give credit to for anything—"

"I hear a big 'but' coming," says Scully.

"Daryl appears to be the real deal," says Holman. "I can't explain it, but where he wanders, showers follow."

That afternoon the agents arrive at the Monroe Farm nearby. About a dozen anxious farm folk are standing under an awning tent. Then what they've been waiting for arrives: It's Daryl Mootz, who steps out of his shiny new Suburban, wearing one red lizardskin cowboy boot. His other leg has been amputated just below the knee.

He takes a pair of crutches from Cindy, and hobbles over to his clients. He pulls an iced beer from a waiting bucket, settles down into a comfortable chair, takes a big swig, and watches as Cindy opens a large suitcase proudly presenting for his inspection a prosthetic leg fitted with a tan cowboy boot.

"That is the wrong damn boot now, isn't it, hon?" he says, irritation mixed with more than a hint of arrogance.

Cindy scurries back with a red lizardskin prosthetic, and Mootz greets the FBI agents sarcastically. Scully returns his sentiments in kind. Mootz straps on his false foot, casts his bleary eyes on Mulder, and starts speaking loud enough for the assembled farmers to hear.

"If you're wonderin', did I ask for this gift? No, sir, I did not," he declaims. "No, sir, I did not. No more than I asked to lose this here limb. But I should have expected it, and I'll tell you why: Because I come from a long line of healin' people. I'm a spiritual man in touch with the really real. The unseen real."

"FBI, MY LORD! I DON'T THINK I'LL BE ABLE TO SLEEP TONIGHT, KNOWING THEY'RE POKING AROUND."
–Sheila Fontaine

Mootz pulls himself to his feet. Cindy switches on a boom box and a spacey, bouncy soft-rock tune starts to play. Daryl starts moving enthusiastically, if spastically, to the music: Elaine Benes meeting the Karate Kid.

"I am one-sixty-fourth Cherokee," he announces, "and I can summon up my ancestors to bring water to this thirsty land! Yeah!"

Disgusted, Scully walks away into a parched field. Her partner follows her and she asks him why they are wasting their time watching all this.

"Well, this is not without historical precedent," says Mulder. "The Old West was full of traveling men who claimed to be rainmakers. The Pueblo Indians even had a rain dance."

"Mulder, that is not a rain dance," says Scully. "I mean, look at him, Mulder. Does that look like a man capable of controlling the weather?"

Her final word is punctuated by a loud clap of thunder. It starts to rain heavily, bordering on torrentially. The Monroes hug each other, ecstatic. Mulder and Scully, caught in the downpour, stand and watch in drenched amazement.

Inside the KPJK studio Sheila Fontaine approaches Holman Hardt, who is working at a computer at the anchor desk, and confirms their date for their twenty-year high school reunion that Friday night. Sheila wonders wistfully where the past two decades have gone—evoking a soulful stare from Holman—and asks him what Mulder and Scully wanted.

"Oh, they were asking questions about Daryl," says Hardt. "About making it rain."

Sheila frowns unhappily at this news. "I just wish they'd go back to where they came from and leave him alone," she says.

Holman glances up at her incredulously.

"You don't still love him, do you?" he says.

Her strained silence is her answer.

"I can't believe you still care about him after the way he treated you," Holman says. "He never loved you, Sheila. All he cared about was your money, and as soon as he got some of his own, he left."

MULDER HEARS A DESPERATE MOOING SOUND–AND SOMETHING BIG AND DARK PLUMMETS THROUGH THE CEILING WITH A THUNDERING CRASH, COLLAPSES HIS BED, AND EXPIRES.

"I know," says Sheila. "But I think he used to love me."

Holman considers this notion, then forces himself to speak. "There are other men who'll love you more," he says, with feeling.

His words fall on deaf ears. Sheila's mind is wandering.

"FBI, my lord!" says Sheila. "I don't think I'll be able to sleep tonight, knowing they're poking around."

At the Cool View Motor Court that night Scully is wakened at 3:08 A.M. by a screen door flapping in a fresh breeze. She rolls over and goes back to sleep.

In an adjoining room Mulder lies wide awake, munching on sunflower seeds and reading news clippings about wild weather. Metal blinds rattle loudly in his open window, and he gets out of bed to shut it. He looks out into a pasture next to the hotel and sees a small herd of spotted cows. Without warning, one of them is sucked up almost directly into the darkened sky.

Astonished, Mulder cranes his neck to see where it's going, makes some quick mental calculations, and dives to one side of his room. He hears a desperate mooing sound—and something big and dark plummets through the ceiling with a thundering crash, collapses his bed, and expires.

The next morning Scully gazes up at a cow-sized hole in the motel roof. A workman holding a chain saw gets her attention.

"Ma'am, unless you want to get covered in hamburger," he says, "I reckon you should step outside."

He yanks the starter cord and the saw roars to life. The motel manager tells Scully that she's moved her "boyfriend's" things into her room. The agent tartly sets her right. She walks over to Mulder, who is sitting on the tailgate of a police vehicle in the motel parking lot, being tended to by the middle-aged town doctor.

Says Mulder, "Scully, I don't think it's coincidence that a cow gets hurled at me just as we're down here investigating the weather."

"Mulder, did they check you for head trauma?" asks Scully.

"Scully, I'm telling you that cow had my name on it."

Holman Hardt arrives at the motel. He rushes over to Mulder, tells him he feels terrible about his ordeal, and asks whether there's anything he can do to help.

"Perhaps there is," says Scully. "Mr. Hardt, would you please reassure Agent Mulder that this cow incident was in fact a natural phenomenon."

"With pleasure," replies the weatherman, voice still shaky with concern. "It's my belief that a mini-twister picked that poor creature up, lifted it about twelve thousand feet where the air cooled, and—I'm just grateful you weren't hurt any worse."

At this moment a distraught Sheila brushes past her friend—who tries frantically to stop her—and approaches the agents.

"It's my fault," she says. "I did it."

In Scully's motel room a few minutes later—as the doctor bandages Mulder's arm—Sheila, weeping copiously, elaborates.

"I murdered that poor cow!" she says. "This isn't the first time something like this has happened."

She narrates a series of brief flashbacks:

"The night of my senior prom a tornado demolished our high school. And then, on my wedding day, a day I'd always dreamed about, the ceremony was outdoors on the Fourth of July weekend. It snowed six inches. Then three years later my husband ran off with some gal from the phone company, and on the day our divorce was finalized, I stepped out of the courthouse and you know how you can see shapes in those big fluffy clouds? Well, I swear that every cloud in that big blue sky was a face laughing at me. And that was about ten years ago, and that was the last time it happened until last night."

The agents take a moment or two to absorb all this.

"What's your connection to Daryl Mootz?" asks Mulder, finally.

Sheila tells them of their brief engagement and the freak Valentine's Day hailstorm and car crash that cost Daryl his leg.

Mulder nods. "And ever since then the rain's been following him," he says.

This announcement makes Sheila's face crumble all over again.

"Am I under arrest?" she asks.

"No!" says Mulder, emphatically. "I can tell you without a doubt that you're not responsible for any of that weather."

"You're sure?" she asks, hopefully.

"Yeah, yeah. I'm sure. Scully? Have any doubts?"

"No. None," says his bewildered partner.

Sheila takes Mulder's hand and kisses it. "I really want to believe you," she says. "Thanks."

Sheila leaves, touching Holman's shoulder on her way out. When she's gone, the doctor speaks for the first time.

"That hailstorm didn't cause Daryl's car crash," he says.

"What are you talking about?" asks Mulder.

Says the doctor, "Sure, the weather was bad. But Daryl was drunk and he was driving way too fast."

This news astonishes Hardt.

"Drunk?" he says. "I never heard that."

The doctor replies somberly. "We all felt that Daryl losing his leg was punishment enough," he says.

At the Monroe's farm, Daryl Mootz sits under the protective canopy as the downpour continues into a second day. Cindy gives him a supportive shoulder massage.

Says Daryl, "People don't realize how hard a work this is. I mean, sure it looks like I'm just sittin' here, but my powers of concentration are—oh yeah, right there, owww! Now, what was I sayin'?"

Cindy leans over and gives him a kiss.

"Powers of concentration," she says.

"Yeah, right. Now, my brain's functionin' on somethin' like fourteen different levels, takin' in a whole bunch of variables like wind velocity, and humidity, and—"

"Daryl, you hear that?" says Cindy.

"Hear what?"

Says Cindy, "The rain's stopped."

Daryl looks around him. It is indeed sunny and completely dry.

"Uh-oh," he says, in a tiny voice.

At the Cool View Motel that night Scully enters her room. Mulder is sprawled on her bed, holding a faded

doesn't work the other way around? That the way someone feels can affect the weather? That the weather is somehow an expression of Holman Hardt's feelings? Or better still, the feelings that he's not expressing."

At Holman Hardt's office that night the weatherman delivers a heartfelt declaration of his love for Sheila—to a makeup mirror. His phone rings. It's Sheila, who greets him cheerfully.

"You sound in a good mood," says Hardt, shakily.

"Well, I am, Holman," says Sheila. "And it's all because of you. I wanted to let you know I've been thinking about what you said about Daryl yesterday, and I realized that you were right."

"I was?" says Holman, hopefully.

"Yes, you were. And I am so over him. 'Daryl who?' That's what I say. I realized that I've been chasing the wrong kind of guy. I need someone whom I can talk to. I need someone whom I can feel safe with."

"YOU'RE NOT JUST *A* WEATHERMAN, YOU'RE *THE* WEATHERMA

back issue of the *Kroner Press*. Its front-page headline reads: FLOWER SHOWERS. Scully announces that the next plane out leaves the following morning at ten. Mulder ignores her.

"Scully, look at this," he says. "September 20th, 1991. It rained rose petals for nearly an hour."

"Mulder, we're going home," says Scully. "The rain stopped this afternoon. Daryl Mootz's being sued by about fifty people. There's no case. And you told Sheila herself she's not controlling the weather."

"She's not," says Mulder, pointing to the newspaper. "And neither is Daryl. But check this out. The same day it rained rose petals."

He folds the paper to an inside article.

"'Irene Hardt,' he reads, 'beloved wife and devoted mother, passed away yesterday afternoon. She's survived by one son, Holman Hardt.'"

Mulder adds, "Holman Hardt is manufacturing the weather. Did you see how relieved he was when he learned that Daryl was drunk? I've been doing some checking."

He grabs a file from a nearby table. "Holman Hardt's been hospitalized five times for nervous exhaustion, each time coinciding with a major meteorological event."

Says Scully, "Mulder, it is still a huge leap to say that he's manufacturing the weather."

Replies Mulder, "Most people will admit that the weather plays a significant role in the way they feel, right? There's even that disorder."

"SAD. Seasonal Affective Disorder," says Scully.

"Yeah," says Mulder. "Well, who's to say that it

Holman is stunned and his shock starts to melt into happiness.

"I can't tell you what that means to me," he stammers.

"Holman," says Sheila, "I want to ask you something. And I hope we can keep it our secret for the time being."

"Of course, Sheila. Anything!" breathes Holman.

"Well—what do you think of Agent Mulder?"

Hardt's face freezes in pain and disappointment. Dozens of lightning bolts flash down from the sky, striking the roof of the TV station.

The next morning Mulder arrives at Hardt's office and tells the severely depressed man that he's leaving town.

"But I want you to get some help," he says, "before you kill somebody."

"I don't know what you're talking about," says Hardt, not exactly thrilled to see his rival.

"You know what I'm talking about," says Mulder. "You're not just *a* weatherman, you're *the* weatherman. You're the person that's been affecting the weather."

Hardt blinks, then smiles wryly.

"Agent Mulder, if I could control the weather, don't you think I would make it rain? That I would end this drought?"

"I don't think it works that way," replies Mulder. "I don't think you do it on purpose. I just think that you bottle up your emotions—anger, grief, or love, or whatever—and then as a response it rains or hails, or there's a flying cow!"

He adds to the agonized Hardt that the solution is obvious: that the weather is affected when he expresses—or represses—his deep, secret love for Sheila. Holman shakes his head and sits behind his desk, disconsolate.

He says, "The night of our senior prom I accidentally stumbled on her and her boyfriend in *flagrante delicto*. The next thing you know—"

"And you've never told her the way you feel?" says Mulder.

"How does a frog tell a swan he loves her?" says Holman.

"Well, you'd better tell her," says Mulder, "before you kill somebody."

Hardt asks Mulder for his help in this matter. Mulder shakes his head and says he has to leave town.

His cell phone rings. It's Scully, at the airport, who tells him that Kroner is completely socked in with fog and that they're going nowhere. She asks her partner what he's doing, and he tells her that

Mulder turns to face him stoically, but says nothing.

"I confess I find that shocking," says Holman. "I've seen how you two gaze at one another."

Mulder gazes at Holman for a second, pats the weatherman on the back, and pushes him gently toward Sheila's office.

"This is about you, Holman," he says. "*I'm* here to help you. I'm perfectly happy with my friendship with Agent Scully."

They peer through Sheila's office window and see her calmly working. Mulder straightens Holman's tie.

"Just tell her how you feel," he says.

Hardt gamely heads toward Sheila's office.

"And, Holman!" Mulder calls out after him. "I do not gaze at Scully."

Inside her office Sheila is loading her briefcase for an off-site presentation. Holman nervously makes small talk about that night's reunion, then forces himself to come to the point.

U'RE THE PERSON THAT'S BEEN AFFECTING THE WEATHER."
—Mulder

he's with Holman—giving him dating advice.

Scully is stunned.

"Mulder, when was the last time you went out on a date?"

"I will talk to you later!" says Mulder, peppily, hanging up.

Scully is too shocked to remove the dead phone from her ear.

"The blind leading the blind," she mutters.

At the headquarters of Rain King, Inc., the next morning Cindy adds up Daryl's corporate debt and shows the disastrous total to the despondent rainmaker. Mootz bangs his head rhythmically against the top of his desk.

"Daryl," says Cindy, "you're like one of those tragic rock stars. You know, like Jim Morrison or Kurt Cobain. You shined too bright for too short a time! We'll tell our kids all about it."

This snaps Mootz out of his self-abusive reverie.

"Cindy, you have been real sweet and all," he says, "but I think we can use some time apart."

"What?" says Cindy, angrily. "Are you breakin' up with me?"

"Nothin' personal," says Daryl, already hobbling his way out the door.

At the TV studio Hardt and Mulder are well into their man-to-man chat. Holman appears startled.

"I've been envious of men like you my whole life," says the weatherman. "Based on your physical bearing I assumed you were . . . more experienced. And you spend every day with Agent Scully—a beautiful, enchanting woman. You mean, you two have never, uh . . ."

"I—I love you," he stammers.

"I love you, too," Sheila says too quickly, misunderstanding.

She turns to leave, but sees the hurt look on his face.

"Holman, what's wrong?" she says.

There is a flash of lightning and heavy rain begins to pour down on Kroner. Sheila leaves her office, passing Mulder on her way out.

"Good afternoon, Agent Mulder," says Sheila, excitedly. "See you tonight, Holman."

Sheila goes on her way. Mulder grins mischievously.

"Aw, you did it!" he tells Holman.

"No, *you* did it," says Hardt, in agony. "She said that she loves me, but that she's *in* love with you."

In a corridor nearby Sheila is trying to get past Daryl Mootz, who's had just enough beer to think that yelling is a normal way to communicate.

"Whattaya mean there's somebody else?" he shouts, grabbing her arm. "Just tell me who it is!"

"Let me go!" says Sheila.

Mulder rounds the corner and orders Daryl to stop. Sheila gazes at the agent admiringly. Daryl whirls and squints at Mulder.

"*This* is the guy?" shouts Daryl. "What's he got that I ain't got?"

Mulder shrugs his shoulders sheepishly.

"A job," says Sheila. "A way with words. Intelligence, good looks."

"Good lookin'?" shouts Daryl. "I'll show you good lookin'!"

Daryl takes a wild swing at Mulder, who steps

"PEOPLE DON'T REALIZE HOW HARD A WORK THIS IS. I MEAN, SURE IT LOOKS LIKE I'M JUST SITTIN' HERE, BUT MY POWERS OF CONCEN-TRATION ARE—OH YEAH, RIGHT THERE, OWWW! NOW, WHAT WAS I SAYIN'?"
–Daryl Mootz

back, grabs his arm, and bends it behind the ex–Rain King's back.

"Daryl! Not on the face! Don't you touch his face!" screams Sheila.

Mulder shoves Daryl against the wall and handcuffs him.

"Oh, good!" says Daryl. "Pick on a cripple! You'll hear from my lawyer!"

Sheila walks directly over to Mulder.

"You deserve a big reward!" she says.

She grabs Mulder around the neck and gives him a big juicy kiss on the mouth. At that moment Hardt and Scully, attracted by the commotion, arrive on the scene. Mortified, Holman flees.

Scully stares at her partner for a second.

His lips are smeared with bright red lipstick.

"Mulder, the fog has lifted," she says evenly, "and if you're ready, the plane is waiting."

But Mulder's attention is already elsewhere. He's staring into Holman's office. On the weather radar is a huge, angry-looking rotating red blob.

"What does red mean?" asks Mulder.

"Thunderstorms, I think," says Scully.

"I don't think we'll be able to catch our plane," says Mulder somberly.

That night, at the Kroner High reunion—its theme "Over the Rainbow"—Mulder and Scully rendezvous amongst a gymnasium full of disco-dancing thirtysomethings. It's raining outside; several buckets on the floor catch water dripping through the leaky ceiling.

"Seven inches in the past six hours," reports Scully. "The National Weather Service has issued a flash flood warning for the county. Mulder, are you sure he's here?"

"If she's here, he'll be here," he replies.

Scully spots Holman Hardt at the bar, chatting to a classmate. The agents haul him into a corridor.

"Come on, Holman," says Mulder. "Make it stop."

"This is your fault, not mine," says Hardt. "You were kissing her!"

The lights flicker momentarily. Sheila enters, dressed in a bright red jacket, and heads straight for the trio.

"Oh, look who's here!" she bubbles. "Some of my favorite people. Old friends and new ones."

She smiles adoringly at Mulder.

"You look lovely this evening, Sheila," says Holman.

"And you look very handsome," Sheila replies. "Both of you."

Sheila asks Mulder if he'd like to dance and Scully tactfully suggests that she dance with Holman instead. Holman takes her arm.

"Tell her, Holman," whispers Mulder, as the weatherman escorts her toward the gym.

On the dance floor Hardt—at the ragged edge of his composure—works up the courage to talk to Sheila.

"Um, when I stopped by your office this afternoon, when I said that—"

"When you said that you loved me," prompts Sheila.

"What I meant to say—what I wanted you to understand—is that I'm in love with you. I've loved you since high school."

Sheila immediately stops dancing and hurries away from Holman. Mulder and Scully, standing at the edge of the dance floor, see this.

"I'll build the ark," says Mulder. "You gather the animals."

Distracted, Scully hurries away.

"Just kidding!" says Mulder, calling after her.

In the ladies' room Sheila stands in front of the mirror, checking her makeup. Scully enters and steps up next to her.

"Sheila," she says. "My partner has a theory. And even though I don't share his belief, I feel that given the circumstances you should hear his theory, because it involves you and Holman."

Scully explains Mulder's theory of Holman's emotional effect on the weather. Sheila looks Scully in the eyes and nods slightly.

"You love him, don't you?" she says.

"What?" says Scully.

Says Sheila, "You're jealous that Agent Mulder and I have a special connection, and you're trying to divert me to Holman."

"What?"

At that moment Daryl Mootz, soaking wet and thoroughly drunk, bursts through the entrance to the gym, on crutches. He spots Mulder talking to Holman.

"Where's Sheila?" Daryl demands.

"Where's your leg?" says Mulder.

"Cindy took it. Said I'd have to crawl back to her. Now, where's Sheila?"

In the ladies' room Sheila and Scully are still talking. Sheila appears startled.

"Not even a kiss?" she says.

Scully shakes her head.

Sheila can only shake hers, also.

"Trust me," she says. "The man knows how to kiss."

Sheila adds, "I've just never thought of Holman that way, you know? He's my closest friend. And to not even suspect—"

"Well, it seems to me," says Scully, "that the best relationships, the ones that last, are frequently the ones that are rooted in friendship.

"You know, one day you look at a person and see something more than the night before—like a switch has been flicked somewhere. And the person who was just a friend is suddenly the only person you can imagine yourself with."

As she says this, filthy water begins overflowing from the faucets into the bathroom sinks.

"The storm drains are full," says Scully. "We need to get out of here."

Inside the gym, an irate Daryl is taking wild swings with his crutch at Mulder. One bad miss sends him sprawling to the floor. All the lights short out in a shower of sparks, and the reunion is plunged into darkness. Scully rushes over to tell Mulder she's called the police.

"What happened to Sheila?" Mulder asks.

In the darkened gym Holman sits bereft. Sheila steps over to him. She asks him if all the weather tragedies in her life were caused by him.

He admits everything, and apologizes abjectly.

"Even this rain? Because you love me?" Sheila asks, tenderly.

"Because I love you," says Holman.

Replies Sheila, "That is the most romantic thing I've ever heard."

She grabs Holman around the neck and gives him a passionate kiss on the mouth. Lightning flashes, sparks fly, and lights in the gym come on, as if by magic.

The reunion-goers applaud. Strains of "Over the Rainbow" come over the sound system. Cindy Culpepper rushes in, spots Daryl, and runs over to him.

"I'm sorry, baby!" says Mootz, tearfully.

"Me, too!" says Cindy. "I brought you a leg!"

They kiss—as do all the couples on the dance floor.

Mulder and Scully stand in the center of all this passion.

Says Mulder, "I didn't know reunions could be so—"

"Wet?" says Scully.

Sheila and Holman, holding hands, approach the agents.

"Well, how'd it go?" asks Mulder.

"You should try it some time," replies Holman, beaming.

One year later a smiling Holman Hardt forecasts yet another beautiful day on his weathercast. Sheila watches this from her bedroom as she coos to her newborn baby. Outside the window, birds sing and a rainbow arches into a pastel-blue sky.

BACK STORY/6X07

Long on whimsy and wry humor, *very* short on monsters, evil masterminds, and any real threats to Mulder and Scully, this episode—filmed in the fall but not aired until the second week in January—came in for particularly sharp criticism on the Internet.

"I know it wasn't a favorite online, but I loved it," says executive producer Frank Spotnitz. "I mean, it was a little broader than what we usually do, but it was a very sweet story and everyone was charming in it. It worked for me."

"The Rain King" was the first *X-Files* script assignment for new staff writer Jeffrey Bell. A thirty-eight-year-old former graphic designer and photographer, his only previous screen credit had been *Radio Inside*, a 1994 independent feature starring Elisabeth Shue.

"I hadn't really been that interested in working in television," Bell says, "but I've been a huge, terrific fan of the show, and in the spring of 1998 I had some ideas

SHEILA GRABS HOLMAN AROUND THE NECK AND GIVES HIM A PASSIONATE KISS ON THE MOUTH. LIGHTNING FLASHES, SPARKS FLY, AND LIGHTS IN THE GYM COME ON, AS IF BY MAGIC.

that I thought might be useful or relevant to *The X-Files*. So I asked to come in, then I pitched them three ideas—one of which became 'The Rain King.'

"They bought that one as a freelance script, and over the next couple of months I worked with Frank Spotnitz and John Shiban and Vince Gilligan 'boarding' the story on index cards. In August we went in and pitched the final board to Chris, and when I got home there was a message that they wanted me on staff that year."

According to Bell, many aspects of the story changed during the writing and rewriting process ("I had no idea that the Daryl Mootz character would steal the show like he did," he says), and the relationship between weatherman Holman Hardt and the FBI agents—the true heart of the story—became considerably stronger.

Explains the writer: "Here you have a guy who's affecting the weather because he's repressing his emotions and not expressing his true feelings. And who better to help him than two people whose emotions are repressed and never express their feelings for each other?

"Frank and John were really helpful with this aspect, in bringing Mulder and Scully into the story in a way that

echoed thematically what was going on in the story itself."

Nearly as interesting—albeit invisible to all but a few goggle-eyed insiders—was the relationship between the final script's imaginatively bizarre touches and the efforts needed to bring them to the screen.

For example, the staging of the heart-shaped hailstorm that sends the drunken Daryl Mootz skidding into his disastrous Valentine's Day accident.

To shoot that scene, set on a rural highway in pitch darkness, director Kim Manners and the *X-Files* second unit journeyed up Interstate 5 to a location just right for such an operation.

"It was a *very* lonely road," says Manners, shuddering. "Way up the Grapevine, north of L.A., in the middle of nowhere, and so lightly traveled that the Caltrans highway official said, 'Yeah, sure, we don't care. Nobody goes out there. We can shut it down for you completely.'

"So here we are, in this deserted place way past midnight, freezing cold, with two forty-foot flatbed trucks with huge ice crushing machines on the back of them. And these trucks are rolling down the road, driving alongside my camera car, while the hero car [Daryl's 1966 Mustang] is behind us, getting sprayed with crushed ice by twelve guys on these trucks pointing these big hoses.

"And you know something? Everything worked! Except we had a hell of a time trying to crash that car into a pole. Because I wanted it to slide in at a ninety-degree angle, and the damn thing kept correcting itself and hitting the pole head on. So we keep doing it again and again until finally, with the sun just coming up, I had about three little pieces of film to edit together."

Other behind-the-scenes personnel, while not always subject to the same extreme working conditions, tried just as hard to help "The Rain King" achieve its potential. To create an instant high school reunion, Corey Kaplan's art department decorated a soon-to-be-demolished school gym in nearby Culver City with the appropriate "Over The Rainbow"-themed streamers and posters.

To secure an appropriate location for Kroner, Kansas, locations manager Ilt Jones headed fifty miles north of Los Angeles to the town of Piru. It's a tiny, time-warped community of dusty-looking wood frame houses, one of which—an abandoned meat market that, according to construction coordinator Duke Tomasick, smelled pretty awful—was turned into headquarters for "The Rain King."

In charge of the office's interior was set decorator Tim Stepeck, who installed a series of weird indoor fountains and oversize fake tomato plants—most of which, unfortunately, went unseen in the final cut. To Stepeck's resigned disappointment, most of the cute-as-a-button homemade handicrafts in Sheila Fontaine's apartment didn't make it to the screen, either.

Actor Clayton Rohner was turned into the one-legged version of Daryl Mootz by the team of property master Tom Day and costume designer Christine Peters. Day came up with a properly fitting prosthetic leg and kneepad; Peters custom-made the button-legged pant and painful behind-the-back harness (that attached to his belt loop and pulled his real foot up and out of sight).

The rendition of the Carpenters' song "Rainy Days and Mondays" that plays on both Daryl's and Sheila's radios in the opening scene was actually a cover version— Richard Carpenter not being amenable to licensing the original—sung by vocal artist Sally Stevens, who also warbled "Jeepers Creepers" in "Triangle" (6X03).

But "The Rain King's" most startling piece of cinematic creativity—and the one that producers and crew members get asked about most often—involved lifting that unfortunate cow from its pasture, flying it several thousand feet in the air, and dropping it through the roof

of Fox Mulder's motel room. "Now, *that* was an interesting production meeting," recalls Jeffrey Bell, still wide-eyed at the memory nearly six months later.

Step One: Well before the filming of 6X07 started, Ilt Jones approached the owner of the Sierra Palona Motel, in the Santa Clarita Valley town of Canyon Country, and asked whether he'd like to let some guys from *The X-Files* chop a big hole in his roof—and get a free brand-new roof afterward. That sounded good to the innkeeper.

"The fun part," says Duke Tomasick, "was calling local roofers for estimates and explaining just what kind of damage they'd be repairing for us."

Step Two: Sometime later special effects producer Bill Millar, hired a flock of cows and a cow wrangler, put them in a rented field in the seaside town of Costa Mesa, then photographed them for digital reference. Later, back at his computer, he animated one of these cows to create the astonishing shot of it being sucked upward.

Step Three: Mulder's motel room was reproduced exactly on one of the *X-Files* Fox Studio sound stages, and a 500-pound model cow—"A cow puppet, basically," says Bell—was filmed inside it. All went smooth as milk until Bill Millar arrived.

Says Millar: "I stepped onto the stage just in time to see a brown cow falling through the roof of the set. It was a spectacularly good shot, but it had nothing to do with the script, which said a *black-and-white* cow falls through the ceiling. So I asked everyone why the cow had changed color, and nobody seemed to know anything. All I knew was that I had to go back and re-render my own into a brown one. And in a hurry."

Dirk Blocker, who played the mayor in "The Rain King," is the son of the late Dan Blocker, one of the stars of the classic TV western *Bonanza*.

Victoria Jackson, who played Sheila, was the third *Saturday Night Live* alumnus to appear on *The X-Files* during Season Six. She was in the cast of the NBC show from 1986 through 1992.

Kroner, Kansas, was named for Paul Kroner, writer Jeffrey Bell's college roommate at the University of Cincinnati.

If he had to do it all over again, Kim Manners would go back and make one small but significant change to 6X07. Says the director: "I screwed up big time— which I realized while I was driving along the Ventura Freeway two months later. When that cow dropped through the ceiling I should have had David ad lib, 'Got Milk?' I'm still pissed at myself that I didn't."

6 X 08

On Christmas Eve, Mulder and Scully are trapped in a house haunted by its murder-filled history.
They encounter the mansion's original owners—and struggle to stay alive until midnight.

EPISODE: 6X08
FIRST AIRED: December 13, 1998
EDITOR: Lynne Willingham
WRITTEN BY: Chris Carter
DIRECTED BY: Chris Carter

GUEST STARS:
Edward Asner (Maurice)
Lily Tomlin (Lyda)

PRINCIPAL SETTING:
Somewhere in Maryland

HOW THE GHOSTS STOLE CHRISTMAS

On the night before Christmas Mulder sits in his car, alone. He is parked across the road from a darkened Victorian mansion. Bing Crosby's "Have Yourself a Merry Little Christmas" plays on his car radio. Another car pulls up behind him. In it is Scully.

"I almost gave up on you!" says Mulder, through his open window.

"Sorry," says a frazzled-looking Scully. "The checkout lines were worse than rush hour on 95. If I heard 'Silent Night' one more time I was gonna start taking hostages."

She eyes Mulder balefully. "What are we doing here?" she asks.

Mulder tells her that they're on a stakeout.

"On Christmas Eve?" says Scully.

"It's an important date," says Mulder.

"No kidding."

"Important to why we're here," says Mulder. "Why don't you turn off the car and I'll fill you in on the details?"

Scully closes her eyes in frustration. "Mulder, I've got wrapping to do," she says.

Mulder cranes his neck to peer into the back seat of Scully's car. It is completely filled with neatly wrapped Christmas gifts. Scully sighs, rolls up her window, and joins Mulder in his car. She asks her partner who lives in the house.

"No one," says Mulder.

"Then who are we staking out?"

"The former occupants."

"They've come back?"

"That's the story," says Mulder.

Scully nods.

"I see," she says, looking at the house. "The dark, gothic manor; the omnipresent low fog hugging the thicket of overgrowth. Wait, is that a hound I hear baying out on the moors?"

"No," replies Mulder. "Actually, that was a left-cheek sneak."

"Mulder, tell me you didn't call me out here on Christmas Eve to go ghostbusting with you."

"Technically speaking, they're called apparitions."

"Mulder, call it what you want. I've got holiday cheer to spread. I've got a family roll call under the tree at 6 A.M."

Scully reaches for her door handle, but Mulder, grinning, hits the auto-lock switch. Scully sighs in frustration.

Says Mulder, "I'll make it fast. I'll just give you the details."

He recites them in a hypnotic monotone:

"Christmas, 1917. It was a time of dark, dark despair. American soldiers were dying at an ungodly rate in war-torn Europe while at home, a deadly strain of the flu virus attacked young and old alike. Tragedy was a visitor on every doorstep while a creeping hopelessness set in with every man, woman, and child. It was a time of dark, dark despair—"

"You already said that," says Scully.

Mulder points to the house.

"But at 1501 Larkspur Lane, for a pair of star-crossed lovers, tragedy came not from war or pestilence, not by the boot heel or the bombardier, but by their own innocent hand.

"His name was Maurice. He was a brooding but heroic young man, beloved of Lyda, a sublime beauty with a light that seemed to follow her wherever she went. They were likened to two angels descended from heaven, who the gods could not protect from the horrors being visited upon this cold, gray earth."

"And what happened to them?" asks Scully.

"Driven by a tragic fear of separation, they forged a lovers' pact so they might spend eternity together, not spend one precious Christmas apart."

"They killed themselves?"

"And their ghosts haunt this house every Christmas Eve," intones Mulder, adding, "I just gave myself chills."

Scully smiles despite herself.

"That's a nice story, Mulder, and very well told. But I don't believe it."

"You don't believe in ghosts?"

"That surprises you?" says Scully. "Mulder, if it were any other night I might let you talk me into it. But the halls are decked, and I gotta go."

She steps outside. So does Mulder who starts out alone toward the house. Scully walks toward her locked car, but can't seem to find her car keys anywhere. Reluctantly, she trails after her partner.

Flashlight in hand, Mulder pushes open the double front doors of the mansion, and enters a rather elegant foyer. There is a flash of lightning and another noise behind him. It is Scully, looking a bit nervous.

"Change your mind?" says Mulder.

"Did you take my car keys?" asks Scully.

"No," says Mulder. "Maybe it was a ghost."

There is a knocking noise at the top of a stairway followed by dull, off-key chimes from an old grandfather clock in a corner. A cold wind ruffles their hair. Scully feels it.

"There must be a window open upstairs," she says, a bit too quickly. "You know, the weather report said that there was an eighty percent chance of rain, maybe even a white Christmas."

A strong gust hits the agents. The front doors close behind them. Scully runs desperately to the entrance, grabs the doorknobs, and pulls with all her strength. The locked doors do not give. While Scully struggles, Mulder sweeps the foyer with his flashlight.

"I think the spirits are among us," he says.

Scully tells him to quit trying to scare her and to help her get the doors open.

Mulder ignores her.

"Sounds like there's somebody walking around upstairs," he says. "There—you hear that?"

Scully impatiently tells her partner that she really has to go home.

"There's nothing to be afraid of," says Mulder.

Scully tells him indignantly that she's not afraid. There are more thumping sounds from upstairs.

"Ghosts are benevolent entities, mostly," says Mulder.

Scully checks her watch against the grandfather clock. They both read just past eleven o'clock. Briefly a lightning flash illuminates the figure of a woman, dressed in a flowing robe, standing by a window adjoining the foyer. Scully spots this out of the corner of her eye—but then the apparition is gone.

Mulder climbs the staircase slowly, homing in on the thumping noises.

"Mulder—" says Scully.

"Shhh!" hisses Mulder. "Quiet! What was that?"

Scully frowns up the stairway at Mulder, who's still climbing.

"These are tricks that the mind plays," she insists. "They are ingrained clichés from a thousand different horror movies. When we hear a sound we get a chill; we see a shadow and we allow ourselves to imagine something that an otherwise rational person would discount out of hand."

Mulder disappears from view. Scully starts climbing the stairs after him.

"Mulder, the whole idea of a benevolent entity fits perfectly with what I'm saying. That a spirit would materialize or return for another purpose than to show itself is silly and ridiculous. I mean, what it really shows is how silly and ridiculous we have become in believing such a thing."

Scully joins Mulder on the next floor's landing.

She says, "I mean, that we can ignore all natural laws about the corporeal body; that we witness these spirits in their own shabby outfits, with the same old haircuts and hairstyles, never aging, never in search of more comfortable surroundings. It actually says more about the living than it does about the dead."

Mulder checks several doors leading from the landing. They are locked.

"And, Mulder," says Scully, "It doesn't take an advanced degree in psychology to understand the unconscious yearnings that these imaginings satisfy: the longing for immortality, the hope that there is something beyond this mortal coil; that we might never be long without our loved ones. These are powerful, powerful desires—I mean, they're the very essence of what makes us human. The very essence of Christmas, actually."

There is a loud creaking sound. Behind the agents, a formerly locked door swings open a crack revealing a lighted room on the other side.

Whispers Mulder, "Tell me you're not afraid."

"All right, I'm afraid," says Scully. "But it's an irrational fear."

There is a loud crash of thunder. Scully swallows

hard and moves toward the open door.

"I've got your back," says Mulder, weakly.

Scully pushes open the door and sweeps her flashlight into the adjoining room.

"Mulder, did it ever occur to you that there aren't ghosts here—but that someone might be actually living in this house?"

"No one lives here," says Mulder.

She counters that the house seems to have electrical power—and that the clock downstairs is keeping perfect time. They walk through the door and enter a beautiful two-level room—think Professor Henry Higgins's library—lined with valuable-looking old books from floor to ceiling. It is lit by a crystal chandelier. A fireplace smolders; the fire seems to have just gone out. Mulder looks around.

"Who'd live in a cursed house?" he says.

"Mulder, it's not enough that it's haunted?" says Scully. "It has to be cursed?"

"Every couple that's ever lived here has met a tragic end," replies Mulder. "Three double murders in the last eighty years. All on Christmas Eve."

As he says this every light in the house flickers out. There is another flash of lightning and thunder, and the thumping noises resume. They seem to be coming from the floorboards at their feet, which creak and bend with each thump. Scully checks the door to the library. It's

"YOU DON'T BELIEVE IN GHOSTS?" –Mulder

"THAT SURPRISES YOU?" –Scully

now locked. She turns to see a strange apparition: Mulder, holding his flashlight under his chin, like every kid who's ever gone to summer camp.

"Aaaagh!" Scully screams. "That's not funny!"

Mulder grins and tells her that he thinks there's a hiding space under the floorboards. He takes a fireplace tool and starts to pry up the planks. Scully grabs his arm.

"Mulder, don't," she begs. "Not now."

"Hey!" replies Mulder. "You have a gun, right? Rationally, you've been in much more dangerous situations."

He resumes his task—pulling up a plank and revealing a horribly decayed male body. He pulls up another plank—exposing a female corpse, in the same state, lying behind it. Both have been killed by gunshots. The male corpse is wearing the same outfit as Mulder's and its female companion the same clothes as Scully.

"Oh, Scully," says Mulder, realizing.

"That's us," says Scully, overwhelmed.

The agents shake off their paralysis and run for the door, which is now open. They charge through it and find themselves in another library—in fact, the same room, exactly—that they've just fled.

Mulder retraces his steps, Scully right behind him. The previous room is exactly as they've left it, down to the pried floorboards. They cross this room, pass through another unlocked doorway, and find themselves right back at the skeletal couple's final resting place.

They stand for a moment, then look at each other, frightened out of their minds and completely at a loss.

Mulder speaks first. "All right," he mumbles. "I'm beginning to, uh, get this."

Scully points hopefully to one of the exits.

"You go through that door and I—"

Mulder points hopefully to the other exit.

"I should come out this door."

There is a flash of lightning. Mulder leaves through one door. Scully watches him, hesitates, and goes out through the other. She finds herself in the same library alone.

"Mulder!" she yells.

The door slams shut behind her.

"Scully!" yells Mulder.

He is also in the library, and also alone. He runs back through the door he just walked through and finds an identical library. But no Scully.

Mulder rushes to the far door, which is now locked. He pounds on it and calls his partner's name. No response. He draws his automatic, fires, splinters the doorjamb, grabs the knob, pulls the door open—and comes face-to-face with a floor-to-ceiling brick wall.

"Hey!" says a gruff male voice behind him.

Mulder whirls and points his gun at a middle-aged man standing in the far doorway. It is a grumpy-looking man in his late fifties, dressed casually, as if for gardening or walking the dog, wearing one of those houndstooth *New Yorker* mail-order hats.

"Who are you?" demands Mulder.

"That's a question I should be asking," says the man, "being this is my house you're standing in. This isn't one of those home invasions, is it?"

"No," says Mulder, frowning.

"OH, SCULLY." –Mulder

"THAT'S US." –Scully

"Good," says the man. "Would you like me to show you the door?"

"That's very funny," says Mulder.

"I wasn't making a joke."

Mulder points at the brick wall.

"Have you looked at the door?"

"Uh-huh. I'm looking at it now."

"Tell me what you see."

"I see a door. With the lock shot off it. You gonna pay for that?"

Mulder looks quickly behind him and smiles triumphantly.

"It's a door with a brick wall behind it."

"Okay, sure," says the man condescendingly, as if such a ridiculous assertion isn't even worth checking out.

"You're playing tricks on me," says Mulder.

"If I am, I'm sorry," says the man. "But I don't know any tricks."

"Uh-huh," says Mulder, nodding. "But that's a trick in itself, isn't it? You've been playing tricks on us since we got here."

"Am I to take it that we're not alone?"

Mulder laughs. "Now, that's very funny, coming from a ghost."

Now it's the man's turn to laugh. Uproariously.

"Yeah, yeah!" he says, still chuckling. "The gun had me a little fooled. You're a ghosthunter, huh? And you think I'm a ghost!"

Hands on hips, he sizes up his adversary. "I've seen a lot of strange people come around here, with a lot of strange equipment, but I think that you must be the first I've seen come armed."

"Strange folks?" replies Mulder. "Like those folks under the floorboards—"

He whirls and looks at the spot where he pried up the planks. The floor is now undisturbed; the corpses nowhere to be seen.

"How did you do that?" asks Mulder.

"I didn't do anything. Why don't you have a seat, son?" says the man, not unkindly.

Mulder slumps into an armchair, head in hand. The man gazes sternly down at him.

"You drink? Take drugs? Get high?" he asks.

"No," says Mulder.

"Are you overcome by the impulse to make everyone believe you?"

This rings a bell. Mulder stares silently at his interrogator.

"I'm in the field of mental health," says the man. "I specialize in disorders and manias related to pathological behavior as it pertains to the paranormal. My specialty is in what I call 'soul prospectors.' A cross-axial classification I've codified by extensive interaction with visitors like yourself. I've found you all tend to fall into pretty much the same category: narcissistic overzealous self-righteous egomaniacs."

"That's a category?"

"You kindly think of yourself as single-minded, but you're prone to obsessive compulsiveness, workaholism, antisocialism. Fertile fields for a descent into total wacko breakdown."

Mulder chuckles a bit nervously.

"I don't think that pegs me exactly," he says.

"Really?" says the man. "Raving like a lunatic

about some imaginary brick wall? You've probably convinced yourself you've seen aliens!"

He adds, "You know why you think you see the things you do?"

"Because I *have* seen them?" says Mulder.

"Because you're a lonely man, chasing paramasturbatory illusions that you believe will give your life meaning and significance, which your pathetic social maladjustment makes impossible to find elsewhere. You probably consider yourself passionate, serious, misunderstood. Am I right?"

Mulder thinks for a second.

"Paramasturbatory?" he says.

Says his adversary, "Most people would rather stick their finger in a wall socket than spend a minute with you. Is this the way you spend every Christmas Eve? Alone?"

Wounded, Mulder protests that he's not alone, that he's in the house with his partner.

"Behind the brick wall?" replies the man, sarcastically. "How'd you get her to come with you? Steal her car keys?"

"Or brick wall?"

Mulder gives it a thought, strides toward the doorway, and walks directly into a brick wall.

There is another flash of lightning.

In her copy of the library, a visibly distraught Scully calls Mulder's name. There is no response. The door behind her opens, and the woman in the white robe enters. Seeing her, Scully screams and the woman screams even louder. Scully fumbles for her gun.

"No! Please! I won't hurt you!" insists the woman in white frantically.

"Federal agent! I'm armed!" shouts Scully, pulling out her automatic and aiming it shakily at the woman.

"Please! I'm a little on edge! Don't come any closer! I'm Special Agent Dana Scully, and I, uh, can show you my ID."

The woman clutches her chest and laughs nervously. "Oh, my goodness!" she says. "I thought you were a ghost."

"I can assure you that I'm not," says Scully, pulling herself together. "I got stuck in this room looking for my partner."

The woman smiles and points to her nose. "Oh! The gangly fellow with the, uh, distinguished profile."

"You've seen him?"

"With you. In the foyer. I thought he was a ghost, too."

"That was you?" says Scully.

"I sleepwalk sometimes. I thought maybe I'd dreamed it. But then here you were again."

"I'm sorry," says Scully, still somewhat hyper. "I, uh, it's just that we found bodies."

"Bodies? Where?" asks the woman.

Scully turns around and sees undisturbed floorboards, just like Mulder. The sight raises her anxiety level considerably.

"You look like you saw a ghost," says the woman, her voice becoming slower and deeper. "There are ghosts in this house, you know."

Scully takes another long look at the woman and raises her gun.

"Who are you?" she whispers.

"I live here, thank you very much," the woman replies.

"Where's my partner?"

"Why are you pointing that gun?"

"There were corpses! Right there under the floor!"

The woman laughs mirthlessly and walks to the fireplace. Scully rushes to the door. It's locked.

"I think maybe the ghosts have been playing tricks on you," says the woman.

"I don't believe in ghosts!" says Scully.

She pulls open the door and faces a brick wall.

"Then what are you doing here?" asks the woman.

"It's my partner—"

Mulder grins sheepishly. The eerie analyst bores in for the kill.

"You know why you do it—listen endlessly to her rationalizations," he tells Mulder. "Because you're afraid. Afraid of the loneliness. Am I right?"

Mulder nods curtly and says he just wants to find Scully.

"Good. Easy. Piece of cake," says the man.

He walks to the doorway. The brick wall is gone.

"Brick wall?" says the man, who then points to his head.

"He believes in ghosts?"

"Yeah," says Scully, circling the woman warily, gun still raised.

"Oh, poor child!" says the woman, solicitously. "You must have an awful small life. Spending your Christmas Eve with him, running around chasing things you don't even believe in."

"Don't come any closer!"

"I can see it in your face—the fear," says the woman. "The conflicted yearnings. The subconscious desire to find fulfillment through another. Intimacy through codependency."

"What?"

"Maybe you repress the truth about why you're here. Pretending it's out of duty or loyalty. Unable to admit your dirty little secret: Your only joy in life is proving him wrong."

Scully has been inching backward throughout this.

"You don't know me!" she says. "And you don't live here! This isn't your house!"

"Ha! You wouldn't think so, the way I'm being treated," says the woman.

"Then why is all the furniture covered?"

"We're having the house painted."

"Well, then, where's your Christmas tree?"

"We're Jewish," says the woman. "Boo!"

The door behind Scully opens and the man—Mulder's antagonist—steps inside. Scully turns, aims her gun at him, and demands, her voice quavering, to know what he's done with Mulder.

"Mulder? Is that his name?" says the man with a wry smile. "He'll be along."

Scully waggles her gun, herding the man and woman into the center of the room.

"This violates our civil rights," says the man. "I have friends at the ACLU."

"Put your hands up!" shouts Scully.

They do so. The woman's robe falls open—revealing a large, round, bloody hole clear through the front of her midriff to the back.

Frightened practically into a stupor, Scully walks slowly to the man and pulls off his hat, revealing a large gunshot hole through his head. She immediately faints dead away.

The ghostly pair, neither surprised nor delighted in the least, lower their hands and turn to each other.

"You see what we've resorted to?" says the man, disgustedly. "Gimmicks and cheap tricks. We used to be so good at this."

"We used to have years to drive them mad," says his companion, testily. "Now we get one night."

"This pop psychology approach is crap," he says. "All it does is annoy them. When was the last time we actually haunted anyone?"

She says, "When was the last time we had a good double murder? Not since the house was con-demned. Look, if we let our reputation slip, they're gonna take us off the tourist literature. Last year no one even showed up."

He scowls. "No! Of all days, why did you pick Christmas? Why not Halloween?"

She laughs scornfully.

"Now, who's filled with hopelessness and futility on Halloween? Christmas comes but once a year."

He chuckles a little, won over despite himself.

"These two do seem pretty miserable," he says. "We need to show them just how lonely Christmas can be."

His companion edges in for a kiss. There is a flash of lightning.

"Now, that's the old Yuletide Spirit," she says.

In his own version of the haunted room, Mulder—still groggy from hitting the brick wall—balances himself on a wingback chair and hauls himself up to the library balcony. The white-gowned woman watches him balefully from below, then somehow stands on the balcony above him as he struggles toward his destination. She asks him if he's Agent Mulder and why he's using her chair as a ladder.

"Trying to get out of this room," says Mulder.

"You can't get out that way," she says.

She blocks Mulder's way to the exit door. Mulder pokes her on the shoulder, as if to see if she's a ghost. She is, however, solid. Mulder lifts her up by the shoulders and moves her aside.

"Masher," says the woman, primly.

"Frump," says Mulder, opening the door and finding a brick wall.

Mulder spins around to see the woman descending from the balcony to the library floor on a ladder that hadn't been there earlier.

"I don't know who you're calling a frump, but I don't appreciate that," she says, angrily. "Being manhandled or called names? Certainly not at this hour."

Mulder shines his flashlight down at her.

"You're a ghost!" he says.

"Ha! More names!" she says.

Mulder climbs down the ladder after her. "What happened to the star-crossed lovers?" he asks. "It's you—you're Lyda. And that was Maurice. But you've aged."

The woman ghost takes mock offense. "I hope your partner finds you a lot more charming than I do," she says. "Let's see. Where is it?"

She sashays over to the bookcase, pointing at individual books, which pop out from the shelves just far enough for her to see their titles. She points a dozen or so right back into place before she finds the one she's looking for. It's titled *The Ghosts Who Stole Christmas,* by an author named "R. Grimes."

She turns to Mulder.

"I was young and beautiful once," she says. "Just like your partner."

She plops down into the wing chair and opens the book. "Look at us! Maurice is so handsome. He didn't have a gut."

Lyda points her finger at the fireplace, starting a roaring fire on the spent logs.

She says, "I hope you're not expecting any great advantages to all this. I'm assuming you came here with similar misconceptions."

Says Mulder, "We came here looking for you."

"Oh, yeah?" she says coyly. "You didn't come here to be together for all eternity?"

"No," laughs Mulder.

"Because you're filled with despair and woeful Christmas melancholy?" asks Lyda, coyly.

Mulder says nothing.

"Maybe it was your partner, then. You knew this house was haunted. Maybe you two should have discussed your real feelings before you came out here. I'm speaking from experience."

"What experience?"

"I'm not going to get into semantics. A murder-suicide is all about trust."

"I thought you had a lovers' pact?"

She laughs.

"Poetic allusions aside," she says, "the outcome is pretty much the same."

Lyda pulls open her robe to show Mulder the gaping hole. "I don't show my hole to just anyone," she says.

Mulder recoils in revulsion. "Are you trying to tell me that Scully's going to shoot me? Scully is not going to shoot me."

"Suit yourself," she replies. "But if you shoot first, for her the rest is an act of faith."

"I wouldn't shoot her," says Mulder.

"Maybe she shoots herself."

"I wouldn't let her."

Lyda thinks for a moment. "The bodies under the floor—maybe that was just some kind of Jungian symbolism," she muses. "Or maybe there's a *secret* lovers' pact."

"We're not lovers," says Mulder.

"And this isn't a pure science," she replies. "But you're both so attractive and there's going to be a lot of time to work that out."

Lyda extends her hand. In it is a gun—which Mulder realizes is his own after checking his now-empty holster.

"Go ahead, take it," she says. "Take it. Think of it as the last Christmas you'll spend alone."

A crash of thunder, and she vanishes. Mulder catches his gun in midair, and is rooted to the spot in shock and wonder.

In her room Scully is lying on the floor. She regains consciousness, grabs her gun, stands, and scans the room. Empty. She tries the doors. Locked.

"THESE TWO DO SEEM PRETTY MISERABLE. WE NEED TO SHOW THEM JUST HOW LONELY CHRISTMAS CAN BE."–Maurice

"NOW THAT'S THE OLD YULETIDE SPIRIT."–Lyda

"I locked it," says a familiar voice behind her, "for your own protection."

The male ghost—Maurice—is sitting in the arm-chair. Scully gasps, aims her gun, and orders him to stay away.

"I want you to get me out of here," says Scully. "I am quite capable of pulling this trigger."

"Glad to hear it," Maurice replies calmly. "You may well have to defend yourself against that crazy partner of yours."

"What have you done with him?" says Scully.

"Kept him safe from his own mad devices, at least for now," he says. "Do you have any idea why he brought you here? To this house?"

"Look, all I know is this is all some bad dream," says Scully. "This is all in my head."

"And here you are waving a gun at me. Like your partner."

There is a knock on the door, and Scully hears Mulder calling out to her.

Maurice shakes his head.

"Do you realize how disturbed that man is? How dark and lonely? What he's capable of?"

Scully rushes toward the sound of Mulder's voice.

Maurice reaches into his pocket and pulls out the agent's missing car keys.

"He's got nowhere to go this Christmas," he says. "No one to go with. Did he mention a story about a lovers' pact?"

"Where did you get my car keys?" asks Scully.

Maurice doesn't answer her.

"The man is acting out an unconscious yearning," he says. "A deep-seated terror of being alone."

Mulder knocks and calls out again. Scully calls Mulder's name in reply. She snatches her car keys away and orders Maurice to open the door. The ghost walks to the doorway, and pauses.

"I've seen it happen too many times in this house," he says.

"I don't believe you," says Scully. "Just open the door. Open the door!"

Maurice pulls a key from his pocket, unlocks the door, and Mulder enters.

"Where's Scully?" he asks Maurice.

"Mulder—" says Scully.

Mulder turns. He has a half-crazed expression on his face. He aims his gun at his partner, and fires a shot—then another—into the wall behind her.

"Mulder! What are you doing?" says Scully, terrified.

Mulder fires again.

"Mulder?"

"There's no getting out of here, Scully," he says grimly, advancing. "There's no way home."

Another shot. Scully aims her own gun and scuttles backward, begging her partner to put down his gun.

"It's me or you," says Mulder, looking completely crazed. "You or me. One of us has to do it!"

"Mulder, look! We don't have to do this!"

"Oh, yes, we do!"

"We can get out of here!"

"Even if we could," sneers Mulder, "what's waiting for us? More loneliness! And then three hundred and sixty-five more shopping days till even more loneliness!"

"I don't believe what you're saying!" says Scully, desperately. "Mulder, I don't believe a word of it!"

Mulder's face is a mask of insanity. He fires one shot into Scully's stomach. The agent gasps, looks down at the blood spreading across her shirt front, staggers, and falls. Mulder steps over her, smoking gun in hand.

"Merry Christmas, Scully," he says.

He raises the gun to his own head. A flash of lightning and Lyda, with Maurice behind her, is standing in Mulder's place with his gun to her head.

"And a Happy New Year," she says.

Before she can fire, Maurice rushes in to seize her and as he grabs the gun, he is wrestling Mulder.

"Let me go!" shouts the agent.

"Let me go!" says Lyda, in his place.

A flash of lighting. The door to the room bursts open, Mulder enters and is shocked to see Scully lying on the floor in a pool of blood. Barely conscious, she moans weakly.

"Mulder, is that you?" she says. "I didn't believe it."

"Didn't believe what?" says Mulder.

"I didn't believe that you'd do it, that I would."

Mulder glances down to see a gun pointing at his stomach. It is Scully's.

"Merry Christmas, Mulder," she whispers.

She fires. Shocked, Mulder looks down at his wound, tries to stanch the blood with his hands, and falls backward to the floor.

In another haunted library Maurice and Lyda lie covered with blood in the same positions as Mulder and Scully. Lyda raises her head and cackles maniacally. Without benefit of human intervention an old Victrola starts up. Its tone arm rises, slides over to the start of a 78 rpm record on the turntable, and drops.

Scully opens her eyes and raises her head. As a scratchy version of "Have Yourself a Merry Little Christmas" plays, she drags herself across the floor. At the same moment the wounded Mulder tumbles painfully

down the staircase. Collapsing at the bottom, he drags himself along the floor toward his partner.

"Scully!" he groans.

Scully uses her last drop of strength to aim her gun at him.

"I'm not gonna make it," she says.

"No, you're not," says Mulder. "Not without me, you're not."

Mulder aims his gun at Scully. But he is very weak.

"Are you afraid, Mulder?" asks Scully. "I am."

"I am, too," says Mulder.

There are a few more moments of labored breathing.

"You should have thought of this," groans Mulder.

"You should have," says Scully.

"You shot me first!" replies Mulder.

"I didn't shoot you. You shot me," says his partner.

There are a few more moments of groaning, overlaid with Bing Crosby's crooning. Mulder rolls over, pulls himself to his feet, and tells Scully to get up.

"I can't," says Scully.

"Get up," says Mulder. "We're not shot. It's a trick. It's all in your head."

Mulder stretches out his hand and pulls Scully to her feet. They examine their bloodstained bodies briefly, then rush through the unlocked front door. When they reach the front porch the blood is completely gone. They run for their cars as fast as they can and drive away.

Inside the house the grandfather clock bongs midnight. Maurice and Lyda sit, relaxed and cozy, in front of the fireplace.

"Hear that?" says Lyda. "It's Christmas."

"One for the books," says Maurice.

"We almost had those two, didn't we?" says Lyda.

"Almost had 'em," chuckles Maurice.

She says, "Two such lonely souls!"

He says, "We can't let our failures haunt us."

"You wonder what they were really out here looking for?"

"Hard to say," he replies. "People now—this is just another joyless time of the year."

"Not for us."

"No," says Maurice, reaching out to take his lover's hand. "We haven't forgotten the meaning of Christmas."

Later that Christmas morning an exhausted Mulder sits slumped on the couch in his apartment, watching the Alastair Sim version of *A Christmas Carol* on his TV. There's a knock at his door. It is Scully. She tells Mulder that she couldn't sleep and asks to come inside.

"Aren't you supposed to be opening Christmas gifts with your family?" says Mulder.

Scully turns and stares at her partner. "Mulder, none of that really happened out there tonight. That was all in our heads. Right?"

Mulder nods.

"It must have been," he says.

She says, "Not that my only joy in life is proving you wrong."

He says, "When have you proved me wrong?"

She says, "Well, why else would you want me out there with you?" says Scully.

He says, "You didn't want to be out there?"

Scully says nothing. Mulder closes his eyes.

"Oh," he says. "That's self-righteous and narcissistic of me to say, isn't it?"

"No," she says. "Maybe I did want to be out there with you."

They stare at each other momentarily. Mulder walks to the TV, picks up a wrapped present that was on top of it, and hands it to Scully.

"I knew we decided we weren't going to exchange gifts, but—it's just a little something."

Touched, Scully smiles warmly and reaches into her coat pocket.

"I got you a little something, too," she says.

Mulder and Scully rush delightedly to the couch and open their gifts. In the background, Bing Crosby reaches a heartfelt finish.

BACK STORY/6X08

"How The Ghosts Stole Christmas," written and directed by Chris Carter, is a tense and twisted evocation of the holiday spirit; a masterwork of tight plotting; and a delightfully creepy look into the darker recesses of the Mulder-Scully relationship.

"It's the absolute record holder for fewest dollars spent on a sixth season episode, and also one of the most difficult shows that we've ever done," says Carter, proudly. "We worked very hard on this one, especially toward the end of the shoot. The final day, as I remember, we filmed for nineteen hours straight, from 3 P.M. on a Friday afternoon to 10 A.M. Saturday morning."

Adds Carter: "It's based on an idea about a haunted house that Frank Spotnitz and I had been working on. Actually, the whole episode is about getting to the scene where David and Gillian drag themselves bloodily across the floor, and about keeping all of the action basically on one set and one location."

Did you notice? Amidst the episode's ambitious camera moves, interlocking plot lines, spooky atmospherics, and sophisticated dialogue, 6X08 is told in seamless form *without* several costly X-Files production staples: large numbers of stage sets and out-of-studio locations, for instance; or an extensive list of guest stars and supporting players.

Expenses for budget items like scouting, location rental, wardrobe and transportation were kept to a bare minimum. Nor was the sound, special effects, or other postproduction tasks particularly complicated—at least for *The X-Files*. Of course, there was a price to pay: economizing in this manner put even more of the burden on Carter, the four actors, and several other key staffers. For example:

"Right after the fourth show," recalls production designer Corey Kaplan, "I got a call from Frank and he asked me, 'Do you think we could shoot a whole episode on one stage?' And I answered, 'Well, why don't we do something like *My Dinner With Andre*, where the camera just stays in one room and keeps circling and circling the action? And he said, 'Well that's a good idea, I'll go tell Chris about that.'

"And Frank called back a day later and said, 'Okay, we're going to do it. Chris is inspired. We'll just have the camera circle around one of the sets.' Then I said, pretty naively, I guess, 'Why don't we do it in Scully's apartment? It's one of our permanent sets and we haven't shot anything at all there this season.'

"And that's when he asked me: 'Do you think you could build a mansion?'"

Kaplan gulped, braced herself, and with a month or so head start, designed the most complicated and beautifully detailed stage set of the season. The richly decorated full-scale interior of a two-story Victorian house, complete with enough trap doors, secret passageways, hallways, and stairways, gave full reign to her boss's imagination.

"It had to be bleak, but not too bleak. Decrepit, but not too decrepit. Deserted, but not too deserted," says the designer, still turning the problem over in her mind months later.

Says construction supervisor Duke Tomasick, admiringly: "It was quality work. I don't think I've ever seen better. It was an honor to build it for her."

Also several notches above the ordinary, of course: the casting of Lily Tomlin and Edward Asner as the mansion's long-term tenants.

"The way all that started," says casting director Rick Millikan, "was that Lily Tomlin approached us a couple of seasons ago. Her agent called, actually, and told me that Lily loved *The X-Files* and would love to come on the show some day. So I told Chris, and he had me set up a meeting for Lily with him, and they got together and discussed some ideas for the future.

"Well, two years passed, and then suddenly Chris decided to write this episode for her. Originally, I think, he had Bob Newhart in mind to play her husband. But Bob Newhart didn't want to do it."

Veteran actor Asner—former star of *The Mary Tyler Moore Show* and *Lou Grant*—proved both available in mid-October and capable of wrapping himself around Chris Carter's unusual vision of his character. "Obviously," says Millikan with a contented smile, "It all worked out very nicely."

Yes, but not until some other problems—no more or

less unsolvable than on any "normal" *X-Files* episode—were solved. To create an "ethereal" look for Tomlin's character, makeup department head Cheri Montesanto-Medcalf gave her as radiant and non-threatening a complexion as possible, drawing attention to her eyes to produce a "dreamy" and "mesmerizing" effect. To make her a stylishly dressed Victorian ghost, costume designer Christine Peters rented an antique 1890s nightgown, then constructed several exact copies for Tomlin to wear during filming. ("I just didn't see her flying around the mansion in bell bottoms and *Maude* hat," says Peters.)

To craft the mummified remains of Mulder and Scully, special effects makeup supervisor John Vulich called his predecessor in Vancouver, Toby Lindala, to borrow silicon molds of two plaster skeletons of Mulder and Scully, that were used in previous episodes. "Then," says Vulich, "we poured sculpting clay into the molds, and carved the mummified and emaciated features of the two agents. We were careful not to make the likenesses too recognizable—Chris didn't want their identities apparent to the viewers until a long beat or two later."

To produce the interesting sight of large, round, bloodless bullet holes clear through Ed Asner's head and Lily Tomlin's stomach, special effects producer Bill Millar attached pieces of orange fluorescent cloth to the areas of the actors' bodies to be excised; added an ultraviolet light source to the set lighting; and used the invisibly reflected ultraviolet light as tracking data to place the computerized digital illusion on the actors' bodies in postproduction.

"Yes, that's the same thing they did previously on that movie *Death Becomes Her*," concedes Millar. "But we did it better and with less money."

And, finally, to provide the one and only location in "How The Ghosts Stole Christmas"—the exterior of the haunted mansion—locations manager Ilt Jones traveled back to Piru, the small town where much of "The Rain King" had been filmed. He rented the Piru Mansion: a circa 1890 Queen Anne–style residence built by an eccentric millionaire and now used mainly for weddings, fund-raising events, and dozens of other TV and movie projects.

What could go wrong with such a simple and straightforward arrangement?

"Nothing," says Jones. "Except that one Sunday afternoon I was home relaxing when I got a call from my assistant Francie Metz, who was prepping the mansion for the filming beginning the next day. She said, 'Ilt, I don't mean to alarm you or anything, but the whole hill behind the house is on fire.' I said, *'What?'*

"It seems there was a big-time brush fire in the area. I jumped in my car and broke every speed record to get there. When I arrived the ridges for five miles in each direction were blazing merrily. I'd never seen so many fire engines in my life. Seven or eight of those Super Scooper firefighting planes were bombing the area, and lots of water-dropping helicopters were buzzing overhead also.

"I thought, *Oh, God! This is great. What am I gonna do?* It looked like the fire would be on top of our mansion within minutes. So I sort of pathetically went over to some firemen who were just standing around—smoking cigarettes, I might add—and asked them what we could do to stave off this catastrophe and let me keep my job.

"They said, 'Don't worry about it! We've dug a fire break. It'll be cool.' And sure enough, about an hour later the whole thing fizzed out—about three hundred feet from the house."

Gillian Anderson remembers 6X08 as a "really fun" episode, and says she particularly enjoyed working with Edward Asner. But she also recalls that the vast amounts of fake blood applied to her solidified quickly—and uncomfortably—into a gummy mess.

Composer Mark Snow particularly enjoyed this episode and creating passages of Baroque-style harpsichord music. "I remember ripping off Haydn's 'Toy' Symphony for that," he says, smiling. Another important creative influence: Johnny Mandel's "brilliant" score for the 1982 movie *Deathtrap.*

"R. Grimes," the author listed on the book version of "How The Ghosts Stole Christmas" was named after *X-Files* assistant property master Marty Grimes.

Ilt (short for Illtyd) Jones is a native of Wales and a former semiprofessional rugby player. Before becoming a location manager for TV shows and movies, he learned the geography of Los Angeles by operating a motorcycle messenger service.

For her work on "How The Ghosts Stole Christmas," production designer Corey Kaplan won an award of excellence from the Society of Motion Picture and Television Art Directors.

6(X)09

Separated from Mulder and teamed with another FBI agent, Scully pursues a crime photographer with an uncanny **ability to predict death**—or, perhaps, to cause it.

EPISODE: 6X09
FIRST AIRED: January 24, 1999
EDITOR: Louise A. Innes
WRITTEN BY: Vince Gilligan
DIRECTED BY: Michael Watkins

GUEST STARS:
Geoffrey Lewis (Alfred Fellig)
Richard Ruccolo (Agent Peyton Ritter)
James Pickens, Jr. (AD Kersh)
Matt Gallini (Hood)
Naomi Matsuda (Streetwalker)
Ange Billman (Secretary)
Barry Wiggins (NYPD Detective)
Javier Grajeda (Desk Sergeant)
Dell Yount (Truck Driver)
Nicky Fane (Blue-Collar Man)
Don Fehmel (Ambulance EMT)
Coby Ryan McLaughlin (Young Agent)
Jolyon Resse (Second Young Agent)

PRINCIPAL SETTINGS:
New York City; Washington, D.C.

TITHON

At day's end in a Manhattan skyscraper a young female secretary pushes her mail cart out of the elevator. A graying, nondescript middle-aged man in the elevator car watches her intently.

The secretary pushes bundles of letters through the mail slots of several offices. Sensing someone behind her, she turns and sees the nondescript man, carrying a worn leather satchel, standing alone in the corridor behind her. Nervous now, she distributes several more bundles, then turns and spots the graying man again.

She rings for the elevator and enters it, joining several other occupants. The man enters behind her. The occupants of the elevator car are reflected in the mirrored closed doors: Every one of them—except the nondescript man—are black-and-white; all the color bleached out of them.

The nondescript man stabs an elevator button, gets out at the seventeenth floor, and runs as fast as he can down the emergency stairwell. Inside the elevator a few moments later the lights flicker and it jerks to a stop. The elevator cable breaks and the car plunges downward through the shaft.

Panting for breath, the nondescript man reaches the basement landing. Several seconds later the elevator—its occupants screaming in terror—smashes into the bottom of the shaft. The man smiles with obvious pleasure. He pulls a camera out of his satchel, and turns on the electronic flash attachment. The doors to the elevator open. A single hand twitches into view, followed by a spreading pool of blood. The nondescript man raises the camera and takes several flash photos in rapid succession.

At FBI headquarters in Washington, Mulder and Scully sit at tiny desks in a large bullpen—just as in "Dreamland," 6X04—conducting boring background checks over the phone. Scully hangs up her phone wearily. Mulder leans back in his chair and peers across his desk at her.

"Hey, Scully," he says. "Maybe if we're really lucky, next time they'll let us clean toilet bowls."

"Are you ready to quit?" asks Scully.

"No," says Mulder. "I would make way too many people way too happy."

Scully's phone rings. She listens for a few seconds, tells her caller she's on her way, hangs up, stands, and prepares to leave.

"They're calling me to Kersh's office," she whispers.

"Just you?" says Mulder, surprised.

Scully nods.

"Don't forget your toilet brush," says her partner.

In Kersh's office the assistant director greets Scully

curtly and introduces her to Peyton Ritter, a lean-and-hungry-looking young agent from the FBI's New York office.

Ritter tells Scully that his office had been updating its case filing system. While scanning old crime scene photographs into the computer he'd come across a puzzling photograph. He hands the black-and-white print to Scully; it depicts a nightgown-clad woman sprawled across an apartment floor. The woman's hand grasps an open prescription bottle; white pills lie scattered around her. Scully reads from the case report.

"Margareta Stoller. Age fifty-seven. Cause of death: an overdose of traz—"

Ritter interrupts. "Take a look at when they found her."

"A neighbor called police at 11:14 P.M.," says Scully. "So what's wrong with this picture?" says Ritter.

Scully takes another look at the photo and finds the anomaly: A digital clock next to the body reads 10:29.

"The clock says it's forty-five minutes earlier," says Scully. "Well, a clock can be wrong."

"They certainly can," says Ritter, quickly. "So, I checked the *Post* from the following day. These are straight from their photo files."

He hands Scully another photo of the crime scene—identical, except that the clock now reads 11:52.

"Two different negatives, same photographer," says Ritter. "The guy's name is Alfred Fellig. He's rattled around Manhattan for years, apparently a stringer for the wire services, and an on-call guy for the NYPD."

He hands Scully a New York City press pass application. The attached photo is of the nondescript man from the elevator crash scene.

Says Scully, "And you suspect this man Fellig? You think Mrs. Stoller wasn't a suicide."

Ritter's eyes light up.

"This guy's into taking pictures, right?" he says, excitedly. "So I'm thinking: What if? What if he poisons this woman, then gets his jollies by snapping a few of her dead body, then winds up back in the same apartment an hour later after Midtown North calls him over to do the job."

Scully thinks for a second.

"That's quite a theory," she says.

"Yeah," says Ritter. "Well, the thing of it is, he might have done it on more than one occasion."

He hands Scully three more black-and-white prints. "I've sifted through probably two thousand of his police photos. These had measurable solar shadows. And since we know the location in each case—"

"We can tell the time of day by the shadows," says Scully.

Ritter nods, and tells Scully that the three deaths in the photos—a supposed suicide, a heart attack, and a murder for which a man was convicted—now appear suspicious to him.

"There's no consistent M.O.," says Scully.

"There's no consistent anything," says Ritter, flatly. "I can sure use your help."

Scully, surprised and a little suspicious, says nothing. Kersh asks Ritter to leave the room, then turns to Scully.

"I would say he has a promising career ahead of him," says the AD. "So did you."

Scully struggles to control her reaction. Kersh tells her that with her expertise in forensic pathology she would be a big help to Ritter—and that for her, the work would be more challenging than doing background checks.

Scully seems to agree.

"Agent Mulder and I will begin immediately," she says.

"Agent Mulder is a lost cause," says Kersh. "I'm taking the chance you're not. It's you and Ritter. Do not let me down."

On Pacific Street in Brooklyn a city bus pulls to a stop and a blue-collar type workman gets off. He clutches his chest and walks away. From somewhere down the block Alfred Fellig watches him impassively: The workman is now black-and-white, devoid of color.

The man enters a brownstone apartment building, mops his brow, and, trembling, checks his mailbox. He looks out a lobby window and sees Fellig staring back at him. He groans, cries out, and falls to the floor. Fellig enters the lobby, raises his camera, and snaps black-and-white flash photographs of the dying man.

In the FBI bullpen that day Mulder calls up a succession of similar black-and-white photos on his computer monitor. Scully enters, sits at her desk, and asks him what he's doing.

"Being nosy," Mulder replies. "Eating my heart out. They're sending you on an X-File."

"It's not an X-File," says Scully, packing her briefcase.

"That's not what I'm reading," says Mulder. "I'm thinking murder by telekinesis. I'm thinking maybe a shamanistic 'death touch.' I'm thinking about the Muslim superstition that to photograph a person somehow steals their soul."

He stops and looks at Scully.

"So, they're splitting us up, huh?" he says.

Scully stops and looks at Mulder.

"No," she says. "This is a one-time thing."

"Who told you that?" says Mulder, skeptically. "Obviously, if you do a good job, they won't stick you back here. Right?"

Scully says nothing. She spots Ritter entering the bullpen, then walks over to Mulder's computer, taps

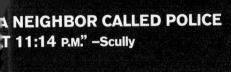

A NEIGHBOR CALLED POLICE
T 11:14 P.M." –Scully

SO WHAT'S WRONG WITH THIS
ICTURE?"–Agent Peyton Ritter

THE CLOCK SAYS IT'S FORTY-
IVE MINUTES EARLIER. WELL,
CLOCK CAN BE WRONG."
Scully

the keyboard, and erases the photos from his screen. Only then does she introduce the two male agents.

"It's a pleasure to meet you, Fox," says Ritter.

"Pleasure to meet you, Peyton," says Mulder.

At 18th Precinct headquarters in Manhattan the next morning, Scully and Ritter question a bored-looking desk sergeant about Alfred Fellig. He tells them that no background check on Fellig has ever been done; that the photographer merely renews his press pass every year. Scully asks the cop when Fellig's original application was filed. A disinterested shrug is his only answer.

In the precinct file room shortly afterward, Scully and Ritter unearth Fellig's renewal forms. Scully finds the oldest one, dated 1964.

"Old-timer," says Ritter. "Anything interesting?"

"Maybe," says Scully.

On a tabletop, she lines up Fellig's applications—a passport-type photo attached to each one—in reverse chronological order. The shots of Fellig are clearly 35 different ones: his suits, the backdrop colors, his hair style all change over the years. At one point the photos go from color to black-and-white. But his middle-aged face doesn't get any younger—not even all the way back to 1964.

Ritter stares at them, not sure what to make of it. He shrugs.

"Guy's a regular Dick Clark," he says. "I don't know what to tell you, Dana. Other than the fact that this guy's always been a geezer, it's looking like a dead end."

That night on Jerome Avenue in the Bronx, a young male figure, clad in a down parka, a stocking cap, and expensive basketball shoes, runs for his life headlong down the street, yelling for help. No one in the darkened, deserted neighborhood answers him.

He stumbles into the side of a passing car; the frightened driver brakes, takes one look at the situation, and speeds off. The fleeing man caroms into a pile of garbage cans and falls heavily. His pursuer pulls out a butterfly knife and drags him, screaming, into a dark corner. The mugger pulls off his victim's shoes—and as he does so hears a peculiar *click-whir* noise above him. He looks up. On a fire escape above, Alfred Fellig is taking pictures.

Fellig calmly walks down a ladder to street level and photographs the corpse. He turns to face the mugger, who is holding his knife in his hand. The mugger stabs Fellig, leaving the knife stuck in his back, yanks the camera from around Fellig's neck, and runs off. Fellig lies motionless for a few seconds, then reaches back, pulls the knife from his back, pulls himself slowly to his feet, and staggers away.

The next morning Scully and Ritter arrive at the crime scene. Crime techs are placing the mugger's knife in an evidence bag.

"The prints are Alfred Fellig's," says Ritter, smugly. "Positive match right off his 1964 background check."

"You're thinking this is Fellig's work?" says Scully.

"It's a lock," says Ritter. "The wound measurements match with the knife. I'd say he's gotten pretty sloppy in his old age."

About eight feet from the victim's body, Scully spots a pool of blood on the sidewalk.

"What's this?" she asks.

"A whole lot of blood," says Ritter, breezily. "It's pretty clear he took a second victim."

"Where's the second body?" says Scully.

Ritter shakes his head. An NYPD detective approaches him. He tells them they've collared their suspect.

"Fellig? Where?"" asks Ritter.

"Home watching TV," says the detective. "They're bringing him in now."

At a precinct house interrogation room Scully watches silently while a pumped-up Ritter double-checks his tape recorder. A virtually expressionless Fellig, walking stiffly and slowly, is led into the room. He sits.

"Hello," he says, into the tape recorder's microphone.

Ritter brandishes a file.

"You're a photographer," he says.

Fellig nods almost imperceptibly.

"I've seen some of your work," says Ritter, tossing several crime scene photos onto the table. "You specialize in some pretty dark subject matter. You're around death a lot. It must fascinate you."

Fellig says nothing.

"Am I boring you, Mr. Fellig?"

"Ask me a question already," replies Fellig, emotionless.

"All right," says Ritter. "I want to know how you always happen to be Johnny-on-the-spot every time somebody dies. You're always there to take the picture. How does that happen?"

"I have a nose for news," says Fellig.

Silence.

Scully steps forward. She asks the photographer why his fingerprints were found on the murder weapon and asks him to account for his movements of the previous night.

"The Bronx," says Fellig. "I was on the job. Saw some jibone stealing a kid's tennis shoes. He chased me. Ran off."

"He ran off?" says Ritter, incredulous. "Some unidentified murderer?"

"I guess I could identify him," says Fellig. "He left the knife behind. I guess I touched it briefly."

"Why would you do that?" asks Scully.

Fellig says nothing.

"Were you injured, Mr. Fellig?" says Scully. Silence.

"You seem to be in pain. Were you attacked? We found a lot of blood at the crime scene, and when we have it tested, I'm wondering whether we're going to find that it's yours."

Fellig looks up at Scully, his expression guarded.

"I got cut some."

"May we see?"

Fellig removes his dress shirt. There are several distinct traces of blood on the back of his undershirt. On his bare skin are several long, partially healed scratches.

Ritter summons an NYPD officer to take Ritter to have his blood drawn and his back photographed. After the photographer is led away, he turns to Scully angrily.

"I'm confused," he says. "I thought we were trying to bust this guy. Not look for reasons to let him go."

Replies Scully, "I thought we were looking for the truth."

Early that evening Mulder sits at his desk placing a phone call. Scully answers. Mulder speaks playfully, in a nasal, semi-goofy voice.

"Hi. My name is Fox Mulder. We used to sit next to each other at the FBI? How's your X-File comin'?"

"Mulder, it's not—"

Scully's voice trails off. She scans the precinct house to make sure that Ritter is out of earshot, then tells her partner that they've made no headway and are releasing Alfred Fellig for lack of evidence.

"You can't hold him? What about the stabbing?" asks Mulder.

"How do you know about that?" says Scully.

"I told you I was nosy," says Mulder.

Scully sighs, then tells Mulder that a second set of prints, belonging to a convicted murderer named Malcolm Wiggins, was found on the knife. This confirms Fellig's alibi.

"But you still think Fellig's a murderer, huh?" says Mulder.

"I don't know what to think," says Scully. "He's, uh, unusual."

> **"I HAVE SPENT TIME WITH THIS MAN, AND HE CAN'T BE MORE THAN SIXTY-FIVE YEARS OLD."** —Scully

"As in he plugs up like a cork when you stab him?" says Mulder.

Annoyed, Scully asks Mulder where he's getting his information.

"Well, young man Ritter's been sending progress reports to Kersh," says Mulder. "My computer may have inadvertently intercepted a few of those. He's got nice things to say about you, though. Mostly."

He adds, "Why don't you let me do a little background check on Fellig for you. C'mon! That's what I do now. I'm getting good at it."

That night Ritter sits in his unmarked sedan, staking out Fellig's apartment at 3650 Dean Street in Brooklyn. Scully arrives to relieve him; the FBI agent tells her that their subject has been asleep for the past four hours, and leaves. Scully stares up at Fellig's darkened window, sighs, and pages through a pile of his crime scene photos. She glances back up at the window and sees the faint glint of a camera lens pointing back at her.

A few moments later she is knocking loudly at Fellig's apartment door. The photographer opens it. Scully holds up the photo of Mrs. Stoller.

"What?" asks Fellig.

"You took that photo an hour before police arrived," says Scully. "You then purposely covered up that fact by photographing that scene again."

"I don't think I remember that one," says Fellig, softly.

"You have, Mr. Fellig, a long and uncanny history of being the first person on the scene of a death. You also have a history of covering up that fact. Why?"

Fellig asks her if he's under arrest again.

Scully asks him if he's a murderer. Fellig shakes his head.

"Well, then, explain yourself, sir," says Scully. "Because I promise you until you do, you will not get a moment's peace."

Fellig thinks for a moment, then picks up his satchel.

"You wanna take a ride with me?" he says. "You come with me. I'll show you."

An hour later Fellig is at the wheel of his large 1970s automobile, Scully in the passenger seat, driving through a dangerous-looking neighborhood.

"This is it," says Fellig. "This is what I do. Looking for the shot."

"What shot?" asks Scully.

"*The* shot," says Fellig.

He pulls over to the curb. Across the street, stamping her feet on the pavement to stay warm, is a solitary streetwalker. She is in black-and-white. Fellig points to her.

"Her," he says, matter-of-factly. "She's about to die. It could happen in the next minute or the next hour, but it'll happen. It's as plain as day."

Scully looks at him, alarmed.

"Fellig, I don't know what you're planning, but no one here's going to die."

"I'm not planning anything. I'm just here to tell you what's going to happen."

"That that woman right there will be murdered?"

"I didn't say 'murdered.' She's a smoker. She might die of lung cancer. The how is always a surprise. I just always know when."

Across the street the prostitute is approached by a

young hood, who begins hassling her. Fellig pulls out his camera and charges up the flash. The streetwalker starts to yell in protest, and the hood gets rougher. Scully leaves the car, gun drawn, and races across the street. She grabs the hood, sticks a gun into his neck, pulls a gun out of his pocket, and cuffs him.

"Are you all right?" she asks the streetwalker.

"I'm outta here," replies the woman.

The prostitute steps off the curb and is run down by a speeding garbage truck, its horn blaring. Scully looks back toward Fellig. He starts his car and drives slowly away.

At dawn Scully is in the precinct house booking the hood she's arrested. Ritter rushes in, furious that she hadn't notified him and had blown off the surveillance of Fellig.

"No offense," replies Scully, impatiently, "but the surveillance was blown before I got there."

"So you blew off the surveillance yourself?" says Ritter, incredulously. "And what? Took a little joy ride with him?"

"I confronted Fellig," replies Scully, angry herself now. "I questioned him further as to his involvement in the deaths he photographed. Is that okay with you?"

"What did he say?"

"He said that he can tell when people are about to die."

Scully adds, "Look, if New York passes a Good Samaritan law, we might be able to nail him on that. But other than that—I doubt we're ever gonna get him for murder."

"Wrong," says Ritter. "Let me show you something."

He takes Scully to the observation window of the interrogation room. Seated inside is Malcolm Wiggins, the man who killed his mugging victim two days earlier.

"They picked up Mr. Wiggins last night," he says. "Now, he says that it was Fellig that killed that kid in the alley, not him. He said he just happened along and had to fight for his life."

Scully looks at the FBI agent suspiciously.

"Tell me, Ritter," she says. "Did he have any help concocting that story?"

Ritter turns to face her, somewhat uneasily.

"Look, Fellig is a murderer. Whether or not he did this specific one, I don't care. Not if it buys me a few days in the box with him."

"No judge is going to issue a warrant based on this," says Scully.

"No, no," says Ritter. "I know the judge. We'll have it by noon."

Scully, disgusted, walks away. Ritter pursues her.

"You know, Kersh warned me about you," he says. "You and your partner—God knows his reputation precedes him. I guess I should have seen this coming.

> "HER. SHE'S ABOUT TO DIE. IT COULD HAPPEN IN THE NEXT MINUTE OR THE NEXT HOUR, BUT IT'LL HAPPEN. IT'S AS PLAIN AS DAY."–Alfred Fellig

You muck up my case—and Kersh'll hear about it. Are we clear, Dana?"

"It's Scully," says the agent, contemptuously. "And we're done with this conversation."

Ritter stalks away. Scully's cell phone rings. It's Mulder, at his desk.

"Hey, Scully," says Mulder. "How's that X-File coming? And before you tell me it's not—"

"It is," says Scully, abruptly. "Alfred Fellig seems to know an awful lot about death."

"Oh, yeah?" says Mulder, "Well, that's not surprising, given that he's reached the ripe old age of one hundred and forty-nine."

He adds that he's done a laborious background check and came up with the interesting fact that a man named Henry Strand—whose fingerprints match Fellig's—applied for a Jersey City press pass in 1939 at

the age of 53. In 1903, a man named L. H. Rice—whose thumbprint matches Fellig's—took a New York State civil service exam. Rice was born in 1849.

Scully is confused.

"I have spent time with this man," she says, "and he can't be more than sixty-five years old."

"I think that's what he wants you to think," says Mulder. "Now, we're talking about a guy for whom the phrase 'life in prison' carries some seriously weighty connotations. I think you should get to him before he vanishes and becomes someone else."

Later that morning the newly released Fellig walks slowly toward his apartment. A grim-faced Scully is waiting for him on the front stoop. Without saying a word Fellig leads her into his apartment.

"You are going to be arrested, Mr. Fellig, in two hours," says Scully. "Charged with murder. And this time you won't be able to change your name."

"I showed you what I do last night," murmurs Fellig. "I just take the pictures."

"What you showed me," says Scully, "was a contemptible lack of compassion for another human being. You showed me that you profit off of people's deaths. Now, why shouldn't you go to prison?"

Fellig eyes Scully with what might even be emotion.

"What do you want? You want me to cry for them? You want me to make like I feel sorry for them? I don't. Lucky bastards, every one of them."

"Lucky?"

"I'm just there to get the shot. I don't take those people. *He* does."

"Who is 'he'?"

Fellig hesitates, then leads Scully through a black velvet curtain and into his darkroom. On the table is an 8x10 print of the elevator crash carnage. Around the head of the dead secretary is a slight white blur. Fellig points to it.

"That's him. He's the one who takes them," he says.

"You're saying that this is a photograph of Death itself?" says Scully.

"It's a glimpse," says Fellig. "Just a glimpse. But it's closer than I've gotten in—I can't even count the years."

"And this is 'the shot' you spoke of?" says Scully. "This is what you try to get?"

Fellig nods. Scully suggests that the blur of light is a lens flare. Fellig barely even reacts to this suggestion.

"Okay," says Scully. "For the sake of argument— why bother? Why take a picture of Death?"

"So I can look into its face," says Fellig. "So I can die."

Scully stares at him, shaken. Fellig shakes his head. "Pills don't work. Razors, gas, bridges—I can't tell

"WHAT YOU SHOWED ME WAS A CONTEMPTIBLE LACK OF COMPASSION FOR ANOTHER HUMAN BEING. YOU SHOWED ME THAT YOU PROFIT OFF OF PEOPLE'S DEATHS. NOW, WHY SHOULDN'T YOU GO TO PRISON?" –Scully

you how many bridges I've jumped off. But all I get is wet. *I got left behind.* I don't want to be here anymore. I can't even remember a time when I did. This is all I know to do."

"You know, I don't believe you," says Scully.

"Sure you do," says Fellig. "It's why you're here."

Considerably unnerved, Scully leafs through a photo album. She comes across a 1920s-era shot of a female murder victim, and is transfixed.

"How is it you know when people are about to die?" she asks.

"Oh," says Fellig, softly. "Chase it long enough, you pick it up."

Scully spots something written in white ink on the lower corner of the photo. The inscription reads: LOUIS BRADY PHOTOG., 1928.

She closes the album, excuses herself, leaves the darkroom, and dials Mulder's number on her cell phone. She asks her partner whether Fellig might have previously gone under the name of Louis Brady. Mulder says he hasn't found any evidence of that, but there's a gap in the records prior to 1939. Scully asks him to check out the name, then hangs up and rejoins Fellig in the darkroom.

The photographer bumps into her in the semidarkness, surreptitiously lifts her cell phone, and places it on a shelf.

In the bowels of the FBI Building, Mulder pages through a leather-bound book filled with ancient crime reports. He finds what he's looking for: a yellowed form stating that a fifty-eight-year-old man named Louis Robert Brady is wanted by the FBI. The charge is double murder; the year is 1929.

Mulder dials his cell phone. Ritter answers; he is in his car somewhere in New York City. Mulder asks him if he knows where Scully is; Ritter replies that he hasn't been able to locate her.

"Me neither," says Mulder. "D.C. Cellular says her phone is turned off."

"What can I do for you, Agent?" says Ritter, impatiently.

"You can find her for me," says Mulder.

"Listen, Agent Mulder," says Ritter, bristling. "I'm on my way to arrest Alfred Fellig."

"Good," says Mulder, quickly gathering up his files and preparing to leave the office. "Because that's where I think she is. And you were right. Fellig is a murderer. Under the name of Louis Brady, he suffocated two patients in a Connecticut hospital. He said he meant to 'catch up with death.' One year into his prison sentence he walked off a work detail. The manhunt never officially ceased."

"When was this?"

"Nineteen twenty-nine. Look, Ritter, don't sweat the math. Just find Agent Scully."

In Fellig's darkroom a deeply pensive Scully watches Fellig work.

"You know," she says, "most people want to live forever."

"Most people are idiots," says Fellig, "which is one of the reasons I don't."

"I think you're wrong," says Scully. "How can you have too much life? There's too much to learn, to experience."

"Seventy-five years is enough," says Fellig. "Take my word for it. You live forever, sooner or later you start to think about the big thing you're missing and that everybody else gets to find out about but you."

"What about love?" asks Scully.

"What? Does that last forever?" asks Fellig. "Forty years ago I drove down to City Hall, down to the hall of records, record archives, whatever they call it. To look up my wife. It bothered me I couldn't remember her name. Love lasts about seventy-five years, if you're lucky. You don't want to be around when it's gone."

Fellig grimaces, looks up, and glances at Scully. She is in black-and-white.

"Count your blessings," he says.

A few minutes later Fellig switches on the red light in his darkroom. Scully watches him methodically load his camera with film.

"Why are you this way?" she asks. "Give me something in the way of proof. Help me find some science that I can hang this on."

"It's got nothing to do with science," says Fellig. "Somebody took my place."

"Took your place?"

"I don't remember her name. I don't think I ever knew it. I had yellow fever, way the hell back when it killed half of New York. Washington Square Park was a common grave, they had so many bodies. They'd bury them shallow. They wrapped them in yellow sheets, the yellow sheets would stick up out of the mud.

"I was in a city-run contagion ward. And I saw him—I saw Death. I wish I'd had a camera then. First I just saw him out of the corner of my eye. But then he got bolder, and he'd start flitting around the room and he'd take this person, and he'd take that person. And I never saw his face. I didn't want to see his face. I figured if I saw it, he'd take me, too."

"But he didn't." says Scully.

"No. There was a nurse. She did the best she could. Back then, medical science—they couldn't find their ass with both hands. They still can't. But she did the best she could. She sat with me, held my hand.

"I was on my deathbed, and he came for me. I didn't look at him. Closed my eyes, turned my head. I didn't tell her not to look at him—I wanted her to look at him. I wanted her to look at him instead of me."

Fellig pauses to lock a lens onto the front of his camera.

"When I came to, the fever broke," he says. "They were carrying her out in a yellow sheet. Since

"I WAS ON MY DEATHBED, AND HE CAME FOR ME. I DIDN'T LOOK AT HIM. CLOSED MY EYES, TURNED MY HEAD. I DIDN'T TELL HER NOT TO LOOK AT HIM—I WANTED HER TO LOOK AT HIM. I WANTED HER TO LOOK AT HIM INSTEAD OF ME."–Alfred Fellig

that time I realized you've got to be careful what you wish for. I missed my chance. You're very lucky, you know that?"

"What do you mean?" asks Scully.

Fellig says nothing. He slips the camera strap around his neck. Beginning to suspect the awful answer, Scully approaches him.

"Wait a minute," she says. "Say what's on your mind. You mean lucky like the others? You want me to believe I'm about to die?"

"I just want to take the picture," says Fellig, softly.

He turns on the camera flash. Scully yells at him to stop. He refuses. She pulls out her handcuffs and chains him to a table. She reaches in her pocket for her cell phone. It's not there. She asks Fellig why he took it.

"Please, just give me a chance," pleads Fellig. "He's coming and you should just make your peace."

"Shut up!" shouts Scully, panicking.

There is a sound of a door being kicked in.

"He's here," says Fellig, his voice trembling.

The velvet curtain parts, and white light pours in. Scully squints into the brilliant glare. Fellig raises his camera with his free hand. A man appears in the doorway, and a shot rings out. It goes through Fellig's camera lens. He falls, revealing that the bullet has gone through Scully, too.

Scully stares, transfixed, at the doorway. Standing there is Agent Ritter, smoking gun in hand.

Blood spreads quickly across Scully's shirt. She slides slowly to the ground. Shocked and panicked, Ritter rushes to her and stanches the blood with his hand. He checks frantically for a pulse, then runs for help.

Slowly, Fellig raises his head, removes the camera from his neck, grabs a tiny Leica from the table, and peers at Scully through the viewfinder. She is still black-and-white.

He doesn't shoot.

"Did you see him?" he whispers. *"Did you see him?"*

Scully shakes her head almost imperceptibly.

"Don't look," says Fellig, gently.

He clasps her hand—and the color drains out of his arm and into hers. He looks up, enraptured, toward something magnificent just above him.

One week later Scully lies in a hospital bed at NYU Medical Center. Mulder stands gazing in at her through a window. A still-frightened Ritter enters the room. Mulder turns to him.

"You're a lucky man," says Mulder.

Ritter leaves, chastened. Mulder takes Scully's hand.

"The coroner's report came back on Fellig," he says quietly. "It says he died of a single gunshot wound. That's all it said."

He adds, "I talked to your doctor. He said you're doing great. You're making the fastest recovery he's ever seen."

Scully closes her eyes wearily, deep in thought.

"You know, Mulder," she says, finally. "I don't even know how I entertained the thought. People don't live forever."

Mulder smiles gently and shakes his head.

"No, I think he would have," he says. "I think Death only looks for you once you seek its opposite."

BACK STORY/6X09

This moody, darkly gripping drama is based on three nuggets of real-life history.

They are:

(1): Arthur Fellig (1899–1968), better known as Weegee, was a Ukrainian immigrant who became one of America's most famous photographers. Prowling the nighttime streets of New York City in a battered Chevy coupe equipped with a police radio, Weegee supplied the tabloid newspapers of the 1930s and 1940s with remorselessly flashlit photographs of the blood-covered victims of gangland rubouts, traffic accidents, and domestic altercations. He also captured thousands of revealing glimpses of the daily lives of New Yorkers rich and poor. Weegee's work—collected avidly by museums and individuals alike—received nationwide exposure via his 1945 book *Naked City.* A contemporary admirer is *X-Files* producer John Shiban, who in 1998 lent his copy of a newer Weegee biography/compilation to his friend and coworker, co-executive producer Vince Gilligan.

(2): The ancient Greek myth of Tithonus, son of the king of Troy. He was a particular favorite of Eos, goddess of the Dawn, who persuaded Zeus to grant her new boyfriend immortality—but somehow forgot to include eternal youth in the package. Eventually Tithonus turned white-haired and feeble, Eos lost all interest in him, and he was doomed to watch the sunrise every morning and pray desperately for death. "Tennyson wrote a poem, 'Tithonus,' that's a favorite of my girlfriend Holly Rice," says Vince Gilligan. "She introduced me to the character."

(3) The New York City yellow fever epidemic of the early nineteenth century. Victims were indeed wrapped in yellow sheets and buried in shallow graves in what is now Washington Square Park in New York's Greenwich Village. The park is just a block or two from New York University, where Vince Gilligan attended film school. "The NYU guy leading me through orientation told me the story," says the writer/producer, "and I never forgot it."

Fueled by these prepackaged elements, recall various members of the *X-Files* brain trust, the basic plotline took shape in a quick jumble of storyboarding and story meetings.

"For years we'd been talking about doing a story about immortality," says executive producer Frank Spotnitz. "But the problem was it's very hard to make immortality scary. After all, most people think that not dying is a good thing. When we figured out that the Weegee-like figure was trying to photograph death so he could die himself, that solved that problem nicely."

Added to the mix were several *X-File*-specific fillips including the Mulder-Scully separation, which exacerbated the tension created by their probationary status established in 6X01 (and gave David Duchovny a relatively "light" week workwise); the customary conflict between Mulder's open-mindedness and intuition and Scully's believe in scientific detection; and references to Scully's own miraculous escape from death—from cancer—during Season Four.

"Also," says Spotnitz, "we came up with the idea of making 'Tithonus' sort of a bookend to 'Clyde Bruckman's Final Repose' (3X04), in which Bruckman had told Scully that she wouldn't die. Here we could kind of answer that, and it was very satisfying."

Quite welcome as well was the fact that 6X09 was primarily a character-driven hour, *sans* elaborate sets and expensive locations, and would be relatively easy on the show's ever-stressed budget. Which didn't, of course, mean any kind of vacation at all for many of the cast and crew members involved.

Casting director Rick Millikan, for one, had some tense moments after asking actor Geoffrey Lewis—best known to the public as the comic sidekick in several Clint Eastwood movies of the late 1970s but to Hollywood insiders as a serious-minded, extremely talented character actor—to audition for the crucial role of Alfred Fellig.

"But he loves the show and loved the part, so he agreed to come in, thank goodness," says Millikan.

"Oh, boy. 'Tithonus!'" recalls property master Tom Day, shaking his head at the memory.

He adds, "This was the only time the entire season where I saw a script in its first rough draft. Somebody in the production office gave me a heads-up call several weeks before I would have normally even begun thinking about that episode. He said, 'Tommy, you gotta see this. You are *huge* in this show.'

"And he was right. And to their credit, the producers realized this, and let me hire the extra people I needed."

Traditionally, a TV series or movie props department is responsible for all the original photographs and documents seen onscreen. In the case of 6X09, that meant all of the pictures taken by and of the immortal photographer Alfred Fellig in his nearly century-long career—as well as all the decades' worth of press passes he'd held and press pass applications he'd filled out.

Says Day, "We had to think about this very carefully, and figure that whatever city commission was involved would for one reason or another come along and reformat the entire document every few years. We had to research the popular government typefaces and printing technologies of the time, make our best estimate as to when Fellig's mug shot would change from black-and-white to color, and properly yellow each document according to its supposed age."

Working closely with the hair and makeup departments, Day and his photographers painstakingly changed actor Geoffrey Lewis's appearance for each era-specific head shot. Fellig's crime scene photographs—each one a freeze-framed movie scene in miniature, utilizing actors, costumes, scenery, lighting, makeup, etc.—was shot using cameras, films, and printing techniques appropriate to the era it was supposedly taken.

"And then," says Day, "we had to come up with all the cameras that Fellig actually used, rig them to flash without making sound during filming, make rubber dummies of them for the stunt scenes, and get extra lenses so the special effects guy could drill them and fill them with blood for the shooting scene. It was a great challenge. But it was a huge, huge mountain of work."

Also deeply involved in what he calls "a killer episode" was set decorator Tim Stepeck, who had the job of filling Alfred Fellig's claustrophobic darkroom with a century's worth of cameras, developers, miscellaneous photographic equipment, and photographs.

"There was just no way we could have gotten that stuff through the normal channels from manufacturers." he says.

Instead, says Stepeck, he had his boss Corey Kaplan—a much-exhibited photographer as well as The X-Files's production designer—call in a favor. Kaplan has taught at the University of California at Riverside's Museum of Photography—possessor of a ten thousand item collection of vintage and antique cameras and photographic equipment. "I think they emptied out that whole museum just for us," marvels Stepeck—who says that inventorying, guarding, and returning all that irreplaceable equipment cost him a few nights of good sleep.

He adds, "The old photographs—boxes and boxes and boxes of them—we got from Corbis [the online photographic agency founded by Bill Gates]. We probably ended up using about 150, hanging them on Fellig's darkroom clothesline and all around his studio. We're still trying to figure out how much money we owe."

Budgeted more carefully, hopefully, were the dozens of stab wounds—constructed in precisely graduated sizes to chronicle the process of Alfred Fellig's miraculous healing—applied to Geoffrey Lewis's body by makeup department head Cheri Montesanto-Medcalf.

Undoubtedly the biggest line item for visual effects producer Bill Millar was the postproduction transformation into black-and-white instead of color of the individuals, including Scully, whom Fellig sees as doomed. "We used a technique very similar to the one used to wreck all those old movies by colorizing them," says Millar. "In fact, it's basically the same, only in reverse,"

Millar explains that the painstaking procedure of decolorization involves outlining the portion of the digitized color image you want to turn into black-and-white; selecting a few key frames to set a "histogram" of the tones and shades desired; then letting loose a complicated computer program to complete the job.

Millar, who first used this method on an episode of the short-lived NBC series *Nightmare Cafe* in 1992,

noted that the hit movie *Pleasantville,* released within a week or two of the night "Tithonus" first aired, was much praised for its innovative use of decolorization, while its employment on 6X09 passed virtually without notice.

"Interesting, don't you think?" he says, smiling wryly.

The name "Alfred Fellig" is a combination of the real last name of Weegee and the first name of another famous photographer whom Vince Gilligan admires: Alfred Stieglitz (1864–1946), an artist, writer, and gallery owner who produced and championed some of the best American photography of the early twentieth century.

The scene in which the streetwalker was run over by a garbage truck was filmed at night directly in front of the executive office building at Twentieth Century Fox Studios.

Set decorator Tim Stepeck has a master's degree in landscape architecture, and considerable experience as a truck driver, which was his entry-level job in the TV-movie business. He has also worked in various capacities as an art director, production designer, and set decorator on various TV movies, feature films—including Stephen King's *Night Flier*—and the TV series *American Gothic* and *Dawson's Creek.*

Some of the other New York scenes were filmed on sets borrowed from *NYPD Blue,* located on the other side of the Fox lot from the *X-Files* sound stages.

Vince Gilligan saluted his girlfriend Holly Rice in "Tithonus" by making one of Fellig's aliases "L.H. Rice"—and on one press pass application giving him the same birthday, April 4, as Holly's.

Gilligan notes that Geoffrey Lewis was one of the rare actors to contact him and discuss the fine points of his character before shooting started. "We even stayed in touch for a while after the episode was finished," says the writer. "He's a very interesting, talented man. And a nice guy, too."

Co-executive producer Michael Watkins, for whom "Tithonus" was the second *X-Files* he directed, also has a few qualms— albeit less specific ones—about how 6X09 turned out. "It's rare when you get a piece of work that's written so perfectly," he says. "I wish I could have done an equally perfect job directing it, that's all."

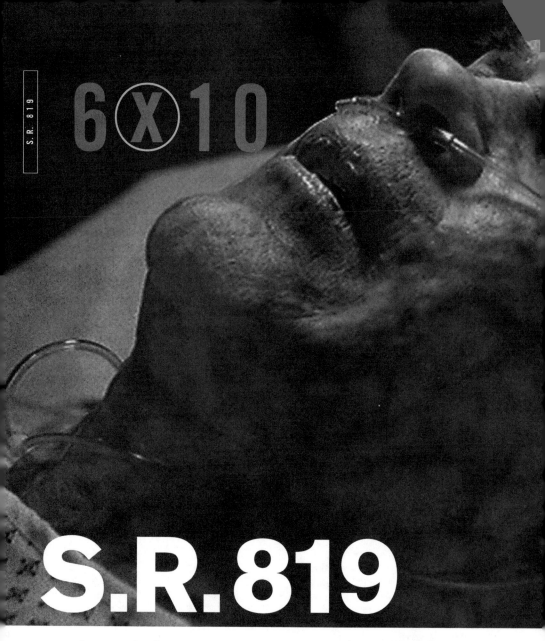

6⊗10

S.R.819

An unknown, deadly microorganism—connected to a shady U.S. government trade deal—is found replicating in Walter Skinner's bloodstream. In just a few precious hours Mulder and Scully must identify the bioagent, discover its human propagators, and save their friend and former supervisor.

EPISODE: 6X10
FIRST AIRED: January 17, 1999
EDITOR: Heather MacDougall
WRITTEN BY: John Shiban
DIRECTED BY: Daniel Sackheim

GUEST STARS:
Mitch Pileggi (AD Skinner)
Nicholas Lea (Alex Krycek)
Kenneth Tigar (Dr. Plant)
Jenny Gago (Dr. Katrina Cabrera)
John Towey (Kenneth Orgel)
Raymond J. Barry (Senator Matheson)
Arlene Pileggi (Skinner's Secretary)

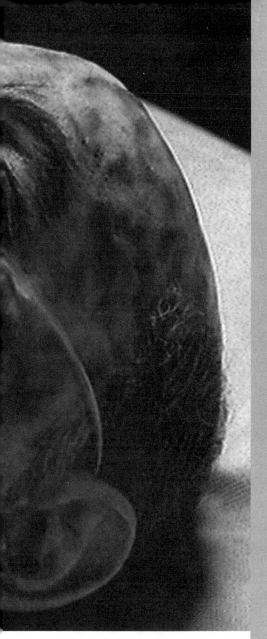

S.R. 819

At St. Katherine's Hospital in Washington, a young male intern confers with an attending physician named Katrina Cabrera. As they stride quickly through the complex, he briefs her on a patient who's waiting for them in the E.R.

"Who transferred him from I.C.U.?" asks Cabrera.

"I did," says the intern. "He was scheduled for therapeutic plasmapheresis. They were prepping him when he went into shock."

"What are his vitals?"

"Not good. His pulse is forty, blood pressure eighty over fifty, GCS is six."

"Okay," says Cabrera. "Get on the phone to the FBI. There's an Agent Scully who needs to be notified. This man is an FBI agent."

"But what's wrong with him?" asks the intern.

"What's wrong with him is he's going to die."

In the trauma room the doomed patient they've been talking about lies on a gurney. His heart monitor beeps erratically. Webs of purple and red distended veins, knotty and thick as pencils, crisscross his arms and face. The man, however, is still recognizable: He is Assistant Director Walter Skinner.

Dr. Cabrera stares at him for a second, then asks him if he can hear her. Skinner's lips mouth something; the doctor bends over to hear.

"What did he say?" asks the intern.

"A name—" says Cabrera.

At that moment a heart monitor alarm sounds— and Skinner's heart rhythms go flat.

"He's coding on us!" yells the intern.

He grabs the crash cart, charges up the defibrillator, picks up the paddles, and tells Cabrera to stand clear. She does not move.

"Dr. Cabrera!" pleads the intern.

"Let him go," says the doctor, solemnly.

Skinner lies motionless, eyes open. As he does so, we hear what may be his last thoughts. They are:

"Every minute of every day we choose: Who we are. Who we forgive. Who we defend and protect. To choose a side, or to walk the line. To play the middle. To straddle the fence between what is and what should be.

"This was the course I chose. Trying to find the delicate balance of interests that can never exist. Choosing by not choosing, defending a center which cannot hold. So death chose me."

A nurse slowly pulls a sheet over Skinner's ravaged face.

Twenty-four hours earlier at the busy South Street Gym, a grizzled old trainer laces up a pair of boxing

Mickey Knox (Trainer)
Donna Marie Moore (ICU Nurse)
Tim Van Pelt (Young Surgeon)
Keith Coulouris (Intern)
Julie Hubert (Exam Room Nurse)
Al Faris (Silk Shirt Man)
Jonathan Fraser (Uniformed Cop)

PRINCIPAL SETTINGS:

Washington, D.C; Chevy Chase, Maryland

"IN THE HALLWAY, THERE WAS A MAN. HE STOPPED ME. HE WANTED TO KNOW THE TIME." —AD Skinner

gloves on Skinner, who's wearing boxing trunks, a T-shirt, and protective headgear. The AD climbs into the ring. Several spectators and kibitzers—including a long-haired, bearded man in a hooded sweatshirt—watch him.

Skinner spars against a younger, well-toned opponent. He gets in a few good shots then, even though he's defending himself well, he begins to feel woozy and disoriented. He backs off, shakes his head clear, resumes boxing, and is nailed with a left to the gut and a right to the head. He gasps, staggers, and is knocked out by a right cross.

He regains consciousness in a hospital examination room. A pretty nurse smiles down at him.

"Mr. Skinner. Hi!" she says, cheerfully. "Are you going to stick with us now? Do you remember what happened?"

"I was boxing. I must have gotten tagged," he says.

"Yes, you did," chirps the nurse. "At least you didn't get your ear bitten off. That's something, right?"

She smiles brightly, tells him that a Dr. Plant will see him soon, and leaves. Skinner struggles to a seated position. He glances at a wall clock, which reads 9:34. His cell phone rings. He reaches into his gym bag and answers it.

"Walter. Skinner," says a staccato computer-generated male voice.

"Who is this?" he replies.

"Have. You. Heard. The. News? It's. In. You."

"What is this?"

"You. Have. Twenty-four. Hours. To. Go. You. Are. Already. Dead."

The connection clicks off. As Skinner is still trying to make sense of this, Dr. Plant enters. He shines a light into Skinner's eyes.

"Well, the good news," says the doctor, "is your dilation's back to normal, plus you still have both your ears."

Skinner smiles gamely.

"I heard that one," he says.

"I'm going to release you," says Plant. "But I suggest you rethink the boxing. You're not twenty anymore."

"There's nothing wrong with me?" says Skinner.

"You got your bell rung," says the doctor. "Otherwise you're fine. You might want to ice that bruise."

Plant lifts the front of Skinner's T-shirt. There is a fist-sized contusion on the right side of his torso.

At 10:21 that evening Skinner walks slowly and painfully toward his office at FBI headquarters. He passes the darkened bullpen in which Mulder is seated, idly tossing pencils at the ceiling. Mulder spots the assistant director and goes to his office.

Looking ill, Skinner sprawls on his couch.

"I just thought I'd poke my head in and say, 'Hey,'" says Mulder.

"Hey," says Skinner, listlessly.

He tries to stand, then slumps back on the couch.

"Are you sleeping one off?" asks Mulder, smiling.

"No," says Skinner. "I'm just having trouble seeing. I didn't think I should drive."

"Are you going to be all right, sir?" says Mulder.

Skinner does not reply.

Shortly afterward Scully arrives at the FBI Building and walks quickly to Skinner's office. Skinner's condition has not improved. Scully asks why all the lights have been turned out.

"He's having trouble with his eyes," says Mulder. "He's also got a nasty bruise on his rib cage."

"What'd you do?" asks Scully.

"It's nothing," says Skinner

Scully lifts up his shirt. The bruise is twice as large, and twice as ugly, as before. Skinner protests that the doctor who discharged him said he was all right.

"That was the second opinion," says Mulder. "The first was unsolicited—a phone call to the hospital. A scrambled voice telling him he had twenty-four hours to live."

Again Skinner struggles to reach a sitting position, but Scully places her hand on his shoulder and pushes him back easily. She checks his pupils and asks if he'd eaten anything strange-tasting or out of the ordinary in the past forty-eight hours. He says he hadn't. Scully asks him if his blood had been tested at the hospital. He replies that it was and that it had checked out fine.

"Well, if you were poisoned," says Scully, "it could have been overlooked."

"If they did," says Skinner, "why call and tell me at the hospital?"

"To scare you," says Mulder. "To see what you'd do. Who you'd turn to."

Skinner frowns.

"Oh," he says to Mulder. "This is about you."

"Or the X-Files," says Mulder.

Skinner struggles to sit up, shaking his head.

"You are so paranoid, Mulder," he says. "You're not even on the X-Files anymore," he says.

"But you are," says Scully. "You still supervise them."

Arms folded, Mulder looms over Skinner and asks him to carefully recount all of the day's events. After more resistance—and more stern urging from Mulder and Scully—he starts to chronicle his activities. Skinner tells them he woke up, drove to the office, had a few meetings, went to the gym, was knocked out, landed in the hospital, and then walked back to his office.

"Just slow down," says Mulder. "One step at a time. How'd you get from the parking garage to your office?"

"I took the elevator," says Skinner.

"And then what?" says Mulder.

Skinner sighs. "I walked up the hallway," he says. "I passed the same dozen people I pass every morning."

"I said hello to my secretary. She said hello to me. I returned some calls, I did some paperwork, and I was there for the rest of the day."

Skinner thinks harder.

"In the hallway, there was a man," he says. "He stopped me. He wanted to know the time."

"Did he touch you?" asks Mulder.

"He grabbed me," says Skinner. "By my right wrist."

He turns his wrist over and looks at it. Scully tells him that an intentional poisoning wouldn't necessarily leave a mark—some poison substances are absorbed through the skin.

Mulder looks at Skinner.

"What time was it?" he asks.

Shortly afterward they watch a surveillance tape of the FBI lobby. The tape shows Skinner passing through a metal detector. The running time code at the bottom reads 09:06.

The tape runs on. Peering into the monitor, Skinner spots the man who grabbed his arm: a gray-bearded middle-aged man in a business suit. The time code reads 09:07:30. Startled, Scully asks for the tape to be rewound. She watches the bearded man enter one more time.

"It can't be," she says. "That's Kenneth Orgel. Advisor to a Senate subcommittee on ethics and new technology. A physicist, very well known as far as physicists go."

Mulder grabs the sign-in sheet, reads it, and tells the other two agents that Orgel was signed in as a visitor to Skinner's office.

"Why was he coming to see you?" asks Scully.

"I'd like to ask him that myself," says Skinner, grimly.

Later that night Skinner and Mulder stand on the front porch of a house in Chevy Chase. Skinner pounds on the door. A man—Dr. Orgel—opens it.

"Do you know who I am?" asks Skinner.

Orgel appears fearful at the sight of the assistant director.

"No," he says.

"My name is Walter Skinner. I'm an assistant director of the FBI."

Orgel does not respond.

Says Mulder, "Dr. Orgel, you visited the FBI this morning. You came to see Mr. Skinner."

"No, you must be mistaken," Orgel replies nervously. "I'm sorry. You'll have to come back another time."

Orgel closes the door. Mulder draws his gun and

> **"IT'S CARBON. PURE CARBON! HOW IN THE WORLD WOULD THAT GET INTO HIS BLOODSTREAM?"**–Dr. Plant

> **"HOW IS IT WORKING AS A POISON?"**–Scully

tells Skinner to go around to the back. He knocks loudly. When an annoyed Orgel opens up, Mulder puts a shoulder to the door and pushes—only to be brought up short by a bullet passing through the wood above his head.

On the back porch Skinner reacts to the gunshot by kicking in the kitchen door. He shouts that he's a federal agent, then trains his gun on Orgel, who's being dragged away by a man in a black silk shirt and black jacket. At that moment someone pistol-whips Skinner on the back of the head, sending him crashing to the floor. The assailants drag Orgel out the back door as Mulder rushes in through the front.

"Go!" groans Skinner as Mulder rushes past him.

Mulder races out the back and catches the silk-shirted man just as Orgel is hustled into a waiting car and driven quickly away.

Back in the house, Skinner grimaces with pain. The veins on his neck are dark and distended. He can make out Mulder dragging his prisoner back into the house, but his vision is badly blurred.

A few minutes later Mulder hustles the silk-shirted man onto the front porch. The man spouts off defiantly in Arabic; Skinner searches his pockets and finds a passport.

"Let him go, Agent Mulder," he says. "He's got diplomatic papers. It's our mistake. You can go. Just let him go."

The man quickly departs. Skinner turns to the astonished Mulder.

"Get in the house," he says. "The police are going to be here any moment and I don't have time to stick around and answer any questions."

Skinner adds, "His name is Alexander Lazreg. L-A-Z-R-E-G. He's a cultural attaché with the Tunisian Mission here in D.C. See what else you can find out about him."

Mulder takes a long look at Skinner's neck bruise.

"You need to get to a hospital," he says.

"No," replies Skinner, leaving. "I'm trying to stay out of one."

At 1:06 A.M. Scully confers with Dr. Plant at St. Katherine's. She tells him she suspects Skinner's been poisoned. He reveals that—because Skinner belongs to a government HMO—no one's bothered to test his blood sample. Over Plant's objections, Scully retrieves the vial of blood from a lab refrigerator. She holds it up to the light. The bottom of the vial contains a dark layer of what looks like sludge.

At 2:33 A.M. Mulder sits in Dr. Orgel's home office and—over a uniformed cop's objections—goes through the files in the scientist's desk. He stops, intrigued, when he finds a photograph of Dr. Orgel. The physicist is posing with a jut-jawed, distinguished-looking gray-haired man. They are holding some kind of award or certificate.

"A FRIEND OF MINE IS GOING TO DIE BECAUSE OF S.R. 819.
I DON'T KNOW HOW, I DON'T EVEN KNOW WHY. BUT I'M BETTING
YOU DO."–Mulder

"Hello, Senator," says the agent, quietly.

At St. Katherine's, Scully injects a sample of Skinner's blood into a liquid chromatograph. After a few seconds the machine produces a spiky, oscilloscope-like line. Plant looks at the readout with puzzlement and dismay.

"It's carbon," he says. "Pure carbon! How in the world would that get into his bloodstream?"

Asks Scully, "How is it working as a poison?"

Plant shrugs. He places a petri dish into a computerized imaging system, types some commands on a keyboard, and produces a highly magnified picture of Skinner's blood. In addition to platelets, white blood cells, and red blood cells, there are tiny specks of carbon, like grains of black sand.

"Look at them," says Scully. "They're just rattling around in solution."

At that moment the number of black specks doubles, startling the two doctors. As they watch, the specks double again. Plant types in more commands, increasing the magnification. The shape of each grain can now be seen: they are rounded, symmetrical, vaguely gearlike objects. They vibrate, then double again.

"What the hell are they?" whispers Plant, astonished.

At 4:01 A.M. Mulder is let into an upscale house by a servant. Down a grand staircase walks a gray-haired man—the same man as in Orgel's photograph. He is U.S. Senator Matheson, last seen in "Nisei"(3X09).

"I don't have to tell you how late it is, do I, Agent Mulder?" says Matheson, acidly. "But I suspect that wasn't even a consideration of yours."

"Actually, time is my only consideration," says Mulder, handing him the photograph.

Mulder adds, "This was taken only three days ago. It's of you and Dr. Kenneth Orgel holding a Senate resolution—S.R. 819, I think it's called. What is it?"

"A funding bill," says Matheson. "What is this all about?"

"A friend of mine is going to die because of S.R. 819," says Mulder, forcefully. "I don't know how. I don't even know why. But I'm betting you do."

"What are you talking about?"

"I don't even really know yet," says Mulder. "I've only got a few pieces—all leading up to a plot to kill an assistant director of the FBI. Does that make sense?"

Matheson shakes his head dismissively.

"The bill you refer to will provide money and supplies to the World Health Organization. Medical technology to third world countries."

Mulder has no reaction.

Adds Matheson, "I have aided you in the past with

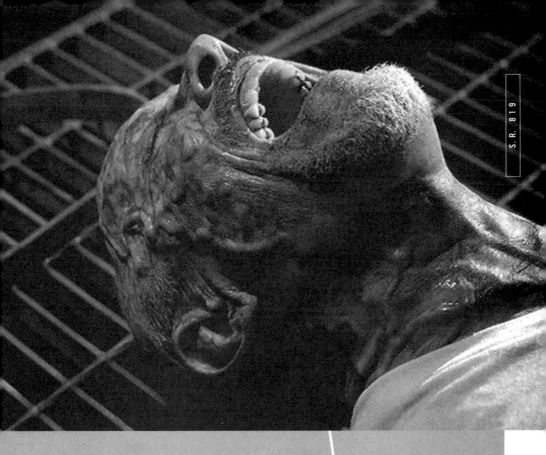

information, Fox. And advice, which is right now to leave here at once, and never again suggest to anyone my involvement in any such dark intrigue. Am I understood?"

"This man may die," says Mulder. "He may only have a few hours to live."

Matheson is unmoved.

"My intention is to save lives, Fox," he says. "But I can't save his. Good night, Fox. Drive safely."

At 5:10 A.M. a Lincoln Town Car enters the Embassy Row parking garage. Inside is the silk-shirted man. A few seconds later Skinner, at the wheel of his car, follows. He scans the diplomatic plates of the parked cars, then looks at himself in the rearview mirror and grimaces at the spreading bruise on his neck.

A bullet whizzes past him and exits through his windshield. The Tunisian stands behind his car, gun in hand.

Skinner sinks to the floor of his car. His assailant approaches the driver's window cautiously—and is greeted by two shots from Skinner. They miss. The Tunisian disappears.

Skinner—shaky and with blurry vision—exits his car and scans the garage for the gunman. The silk-shirted man is behind him, preparing to fire. At that moment a car races through the garage and directly into the Tunisian, knocking him up and over its wind-

shield. The car speeds off, and the gunman lies motionless on the floor. Skinner gets a blurry glimpse of the departing driver: a bearded man with very long dark hair. Gun in hand, the AD staggers against a parked car and slumps to the ground, helpless.

At 6:10 A.M. Scully is still at St. Katherine's, examining a sample of Skinner's blood under a stereoscopic microscope. The gearlike carbon constructs are still multiplying wildly. She calls Dr. Plant to her side.

"I think I found it," she says. "I think I found what the carbon is doing. It's not just reproducing itself. It has behavior. It's creating something—a matrix, stimulated by blood flow in response to movement. It's multiplying, then solidifying in an orderly fashion. It's building valves, or dams, in the vascular system."

"It's building a heart attack," says Plant.

A nurse enters the lab. She tells them that Skinner has been picked up at the parking garage by paramedics, and is headed for D.C. General Hospital. Scully rushes away.

At D.C. General shortly afterward, an unconscious Skinner—his arms crisscrossed by black distended veins—is prepped for surgery by Dr. Cabrera and her colleagues. Scully and Plant rush into the operating room and tell the doctors to stop. The surgeons protest vehemently.

"If he's going to live," says Cabrera, "he's going to have to lose his arms."

"No! That's not going to save him," says Scully. "It's his blood. You're not going to solve anything unless you get a scope into him. Nothing else is going to work. Look, if you want to save this man, listen to what I'm saying."

A few minutes later a barely conscious Skinner is being rolled on a gurney, back to another room. Scully walks alongside him. Using much of his remaining strength, Skinner raises his head from his pillow.

"Who did this to me?" he says.

"That's what Mulder's trying to figure out right now," says Scully. "We're going to take good care of you—I promise. We're going to do everything we can."

At 8:58 A.M. Skinner's secretary enters her office to find Mulder rifling Skinner's desk drawers.

"Agent Mulder? What are you doing?" she asks, alarmed.

"AD Skinner's in the hospital. Somebody poisoned him," says Mulder.

"Poisoned him? Why?"

"For doing his job. I'm looking for anything that relates to a Senate resolution—S.R. 819. If you want to save his life, you'll help me open this drawer."

"I don't have the key," replies the secretary.

Mulder strides into the outer office.

"Is he going to be all right?" asks the secretary, fearfully.

Mulder doesn't answer. On the secretary's desk is a letter opener—perfect for forcing a lock—and a large envelope from the U.S. Senate. He rips it open, pulls out a letter, and reads it.

Later that morning Mulder joins Scully in the D.C. General I.C.U. He asks her about Skinner's present condition.

"It's stable, but it's not good, Mulder," she says. "He's got extreme vascular trauma and distention. His blood has become a weapon against his body."

"Well, can you fight it?" asks Mulder.

"We don't know what it is. The best that we can do is keep lasering his arteries open. But it's only a matter of time before we lose. It's building walls in his vessels faster than we can tear them down and we just don't have the technology to combat it."

"Maybe we do," says Mulder.

He shows Scully the letter to Skinner from the Senate.

"He was doing a security check on the Senate bill for violations of trade laws involving sensitive technology," says Mulder. "This bill was going to a vote in the Senate and all it was waiting on was Skinner's review and an analysis by Dr. Kenneth Orgel."

"You're saying that Dr. Orgel poisoned Skinner in order to cover up his analysis?"

"No," says Mulder. "Orgel didn't poison anybody. Orgel came to the FBI to tell Skinner what he knew— that there was a gross violation of export laws involving new technology. You know what that means?"

"I think I might," says Scully.

A nurse interrupts the agents. She hands Skinner's cell phone, which is ringing, to Mulder. He clicks it on and places it to his ear.

"Might. As. Well. Give. Up," says the computer-synthesized voice. "You. Can't. Stop. It."

"Who is it?" asks Scully.

"Somebody who must know he's here," says Mulder.

"Your. Time. Is—" says the voice.

As Mulder hears this, the same words appear on the glowing screen of a Palm PC. Somebody is writing them on the handheld device with a metal stylus. Mulder walks out of Skinner's room, peers down the hospital corridor, and spots him. It is the bearded long-haired man.

The man spots Mulder, and begins to walk away.

"Federal agent! Stop right there!" shouts Mulder.

The man flees. Mulder pursues into a stairwell, up the stairs, and into a parking garage. Gun drawn, Mulder scans the garage, with no luck. There is a sound behind him. He whirls and aims his gun—at a nurse leaving her car. He lowers his weapon, silently reassures her, and resumes his search.

A car starts up behind him. Driven by the bearded man, it pulls out of its slot and hurtles past Mulder toward the exit. Mulder runs to the stairwell and sprints upward toward the exit level. At a card-key exit the bearded man's car sits idling, its passenger door opened, while a female driver, complaining to the parking lot attendant, screams loudly in Spanish. Mulder peers cautiously into the empty getaway vehicle.

On a suburban Maryland road, Senator Matheson, at the wheel of his car, picks up his ringing cell phone.

"The bill is in danger, Senator," says a filtered male voice. "A new threat has emerged. Blood will be on your hands."

"I don't buy your hollow threats," replies Matheson, angrily.

"Dr. Orgel does," says the caller—the long-haired man—at a phone booth. "You can ask him."

"What have you done with him?" demands Matheson.

"I can tell you where to find him," replies the man.

At 12:11 P.M. a forensic technician at the FBI Impound Garage tells Mulder that the long-haired man's car is leased to a fleet service that serves the diplomatic counsel corps. The only forensic evidence: several loose hairs from an expensive wig in the interior, and, caught in the tire treads, traces of PCBs,

"FEDERAL AGENT! STOP RIGHT THERE!"–Mulder

"THEN TELL ME WHAT YOU KNOW, SENATOR! THIS IS ABOUT S.R. 819, ISN'T IT? WHAT THE HELL DID THEY PUT IN SKINNER?"–Mulder

banned in the 1970s by the EPA—most probably from a demolition site or an old power plant.

At 2:04 P.M. a Mercedes pulls to a stop at a power plant. Senator Matheson gets out, looks around to see if he's being followed, and walks inside. In the deserted facility, strapped face up to a small table, is a man.

"Who's there?" he moans. "Is someone there?"

Matheson approaches the table. The captive is Kenneth Orgel. His face is bruised and his veins distended, like Skinner's. He begs to be released, and for water.

Matheson loosens the straps holding Orgel to the table.

"Who did this to you?" he asks.

"Hurry. Please!" says Orgel. "It's killing me."

"They believe you've exposed them to the FBI. To Walter Skinner," says Matheson.

"I told the FBI nothing!" says Orgel. "I told them nothing! Please, I promise not to expose anyone!"

On a balcony high above them someone is watching everything. It is the long-haired man, holding the Palm PC. He touches the stylus to the screen. A jolting spasm grips Orgel. He screams in agony. On the Palm PC's screen a trapezoidal bar graph rises, thermometer-like. Matheson backs away in horror.

At 5:32 P.M. Skinner lies in his bed in the I.C.U at D.C. General. His condition has clearly deteriorated. Scully enters, crosses to his bedside, and proposes a radical treatment: therapeutic plasmapharesis, which involves filtering all the blood in his body. She tells him that there is a strong danger of him going into shock during the procedure. Skinner smiles faintly.

"I'm in your hands," he whispers.

Scully blinks back some tears and prepares to leave. Skinner stops her.

"I think I owe you an apology, Scully," he says. "You and Mulder."

"Sir—?"

"I've been lying here thinking," says the AD. "Your quest—it should have been mine. If I die now, I die in vain. I have nothing to show for myself. For my life."

"Sir, you know that's not true."

"It is. I can see now that I always played it safe. I wouldn't take sides, wouldn't let you and Mulder pull me in."

Scully gazes down at him sadly.

"You've been our ally more times than I can say."

"Not the kind of ally that I could have been," whispers Skinner.

Scully reaches down and squeezes his hand. At

that moment Skinner flashes back to his original encounter with Orgel and then to his collapse in the boxing ring.

"I remember now," says Skinner, urgently. "I can't see his face. He has a beard. He was at the gym. At the hospital. He killed that man. He was at the FBI when Orgel approached me."

"He was following you?" asks Scully.

"The tape," says Skinner. "He's on the surveillance tape."

Scully pulls away and exits the room immediately.

At 5:56 P.M. Mulder pulls into the power plant parking lot and, spotting its federal license plates, identifies the Mercedes as Matheson's. He enters, draws his gun, and cautiously walks into the room containing the torture table. It is empty. A man stands next to it.

"You must be surprised to see me here," says Matheson. "I'm not the man you're looking for."

Mulder holsters his gun and strides toward the senator.

"Where is he? Where's Orgel?" he demands.

"Orgel is dead," says Matheson.

"I don't believe you," says Mulder. "You lied to me this morning; you're lying to me now."

"Drop this, Fox—"

"Where is Orgel? I need to know what he knows. A friend of mine is dying!"

"I tell you they killed him," says Matheson, evenly. "What Orgel knows died with him."

Mulder grabs Matheson by the collar and lifts him off his feet.

"Then tell me what you know, Senator! This is about S.R. 819, isn't it? What the hell did they put in Skinner?"

Matheson sneers, and pushes Mulder off him.

"I'm sure you already have some idea, Fox," he snarls.

Says Mulder, "It's the same technology S.R. 819 will export."

Says Matheson, "Technology the world believes is purely theoretical."

Mulder pauses, stunned.

"Nanotechnology!" he says. "Microscopic, atom-sized machines. Machines can be stopped."

Matheson stares at him.

"Your friend is already dead," he says.

"I don't believe that."

"If you pursue this, Fox, they will kill you."

"Not before I expose you and your role in this."

Mulder turns to leave.

"My role?" shouts Matheson, after him. "I am a victim here. Don't you understand that? I'm fighting for my life!"

"I *will* stop this!" shouts Mulder.

"It's too late, Fox. It's too late!"

At 9:33 P.M. at D.C. General a heart monitor alarm

sounds and Skinner's heart rhythms go flat.

"He's coding on us!" yells the intern, grabbing for the crash cart. He charges up the defibrillator, picks up the paddles, and tells Cabrera to stand clear. She does not move.

"Dr. Cabrera!" says the intern.

"Let him go," she says, solemnly.

The intern pronounces the time of death. A nurse slowly pulls a sheet over Skinner's ravaged face.

Somewhere nearby someone is holding the Palm PC. He moves his stylus over the screen. This time the trapezoidal bar graph descends toward the bottom.

At that moment Skinner's heart rhythms begin again. The AD gasps and coughs. Cabrera pulls the blanket down, and the astonished medical team races into action. Skinner opens his eyes and spots the long-haired, bearded man. A second later, the man is gone.

Three weeks later Skinner sits at his desk in FBI headquarters. Mulder and Scully sit across from him.

"Sir, I've spoken with your doctors, and their prognosis is excellent," says Scully. "Whatever you were infected with appears to be dormant and your recovery is being hailed as a miracle."

"The man who poisoned you was at the FBI that day," says Mulder. "Scully was able to pull these off the security videotapes. We hoped that these might jog your memory and help us identify this man."

Skinner looks at the video grabs showing the long-haired man. He says, flatly, that he doesn't recognize him. Mulder shakes his head. He tells Skinner that S.R. 819 was withdrawn by committee earlier that evening without explanation.

"Good," says Skinner, "So this man failed then."

"If that was his true purpose," says Mulder.

He adds, "But if he wanted to poison you to prevent you from investigating S.R. 819, why call you to tell you that? This man worked for the government that was to receive this technology—he drove one of their cars—and he killed one of his own to save you."

Skinner frowns.

"So you still think this was about you. About the X-Files."

"Yes!" says Mulder. "And I have an idea who may be behind all this. But I need your authority to continue the investigation."

Skinner pauses, then looks down at his desk.

"I have neither the authority nor the will to allow your continued inquiry into this matter. You will perform your duties as directed by AD Kersh—and only AD Kersh. This matter is closed, Agents. Am I clear?"

That night Skinner walks to his car in the FBI parking garage, unlocks it, and slips behind the steering wheel. He senses someone behind him.

"I've been expecting you to show up," he says, grimly.

In the back seat a short-haired man, his clean-shaven face in shadow, clicks open a Palm PC with one gloved hand.

"You know I can push the button at any time," says the man, chillingly.

Skinner turns to face him, bitterly angry.

"What do you want from me?" he says. "What's this about, Krycek?"

Alex Krycek leans forward and levels Skinner with his gaze.

"All in good time," he says.

He pushes open the rear door and exits, leaving Skinner alone. The AD starts the engine and drives away.

BACK STORY/6X10

Walter Skinner lives!

Interestingly, the exclamation above does an equally good job of summarizing (1) the conclusion of "S.R. 819;" (2) the episode's pivotal long-range impact on the rest of The X-Files's season and series; and (3) the joyously relieved reaction of several million of the uptight bureaucrat's fervent admirers.

In a slightly bigger nutshell: the outcome of 6X10 meant, despite previous indications to the contrary, that the tall, bald assistant director would make it to Season Seven, and perhaps beyond.

Ever since "Tooms" (1X20), the first-year episode that introduced the character—and accomplished actor Mitch Pileggi—as Mulder and Scully's FBI supervisor, Skinner has served the show's writers well. His skeptical, by-the-book attitude—punctuated by revealing bursts of self-examination and heroism—has been a useful counterweight to the two agents' passionately contentious relationship. The question of Skinner's ultimate loyalty—to Mulder's crusade, to the organization he works for, or to the nefarious conspirators working behind the scenes—has been a constant topic of discussion among viewers.

But by the beginning of the X-Files's sixth season AD Skinner was in trouble. Over the years, the show's core group of senior writer/producers had begun to believe Walter Skinner had come through in the pinch for Mulder and Scully so many times that the original reason for his existence was disappearing.

"The trouble was," says producer John Shiban, "that by now Skinner meant so much to Mulder and Scully that he wasn't that much of a mysterious figure. He was family, which changed a lot of things."

Changing also, of course, was Skinner's professional connection to the two agents. Mulder and Scully's disciplinary transfer from the X-Files, and their punitive assignment to menial duties under AD Kersh, made the character look increasingly expendable.

"Obviously, I realized that Skinner was going to be out of the picture for a while," recalls Mitch Pileggi. "Earlier Frank Spotnitz had told me they were going to do this. He and Chris had always made it a given that the character wasn't going anyplace. But then again, in this business, who knows?"

Certainly "S.R. 819" author John Shiban didn't—at least until the exciting last scene of this real-life cliffhanger. By the fall of 1998, while Pileggi was enjoying some time off with his wife Arlene and new daughter Sawyer, the writer was wrestling with a plotline borrowed from D.O.A., a 1950 film noir potboiler starring Edmond O'Brien and a cast of dozens. A remake, starring Dennis Quaid, surfaced briefly in 1988.

"To be honest, neither of them are good movies," says Shiban. "They're both pretty bad. But the central idea is interesting: a guy who's been poisoned has only a short time to live and has to use that time to find out why and by whom he's being murdered."

Shiban first pitched the story with Mulder as the poison victim. "But then Frank said to me: 'We can't do that. The audience will never think we're gonna kill Mulder. They'll know he's going to be all right.'

"Then he suggested we do it with Skinner, which solved that problem perfectly. Because there's always a possibility that we'll kill a secondary character. We've done it before, haven't we?"

With Skinner's fate now definitely in question, Shiban reconfigured D.O.A.'s plot to X-Files specs by incorporating Mulder's and Scully's different approaches to Skinner's crisis; folding in the nanotechnology plot device, which had been kicking around various writers' offices for a season or two; and—most importantly—making Alex Krycek the man behind the conspiracy and giving the one-armed assassin continuing control of the microscopic killing machines in Skinner's bloodstream.

This was, in fact, the masterstroke that rescued Walter Skinner.

Says Shiban: "We realized that now Skinner has this very dangerous relationship with Krycek, who has the power to bring him under his heel and use him as a pawn. It gives Skinner an agenda that Mulder doesn't know about, which gives back some mystery to his character and some conflict to their relationship. Which was something we ultimately used again in the seasonender, and will carry us into next year."

Their most immediate task, however, was to carry off a typically demanding mid-season episode. Shiban recalls a particularly difficult time getting all the parts of the complicated plot to fit together properly. Along the way, a potentially time-consuming and expensive fight scene between Skinner and Krycek was cut for budgetary reasons.

However, another fight—the one between Skinner and his opponent in the boxing ring—proved surprisingly easy to stage. Mitch Pileggi's father fought professionally when he was a young man; the actor himself boxed competitively in college. Before filming for the episode began, Pileggi (already a certified fitness fanatic) went for a refresher course to the famous Goosen Gym in Los Angeles.

"It makes me happy that some people will assume there was a stunt double in the ring," he says. "There wasn't! As a matter of fact, before I took my little dive, I hit that guy I was boxing with a couple of good ones. We both had a great time."

Pileggi has an altogether different set of recollections about waking up in the middle of the night, driving into the studio, and sitting motionless long past sunrise while wide-awake *X-Files* makeup artists glued monstrous black veins onto his face, arms, and torso.

"They did a beautiful job and it looked awesome, but man, I hated it! I really don't know how those guys on *Star Trek* or *Babylon 5* can stand having that done to them every day. I just wouldn't work if that's what it took.

"There was one positive aspect, though. I was so wiped out by the process that it really helped me play dead and dying. Remember that shot where the camera pulls back from my open eye? The truth is, I was having a hard time keeping even one eye open."

For the record, Pileggi's chief tormentor on "S.R. 819" was special effects makeup supervisor John Vulich, who constructed Skinner's ravaged features from a latex mask of the actor's face shot through with hollow rubber veins—many of them hooked up to hand-operated air bulbs to make them pulse and quiver on command. "He was covered with a lot more rubber than you would probably think," says Vulich, proudly. "The only part of his actual face that you really see are his nose and upper lip."

To show Skinner (and the unfortunate scientist Kenneth Orgel) progressing from extreme illness to near death, Vulich constructed two entirely different sets of makeup. For the scene in which Krycek tortures and kills Orgel by remote control, visual effects producer Bill Millar morphed the two levels of makeup together electronically in postproduction. Millar also designed the bloodstream-borne nanobots ("It took a few tries. One of our attempts looked too much like the CBS eye," he says); inserted them in actual through-the-microscope footage of blood and plasma; and "cloned" them with a handy computer animation program.

Krycek's lethal palm computer was actually a small working television set, modified and embellished by prop master Tom Day's minions. Its screen displayed graphic images broadcast from a computer—programmed and operated by consultant John Markham, who was located just out of camera range. "It was amazing," recalls Day, with relish. "John could enter his commands, change the display on the little TV, and get instant feedback by watching what the TV camera attached to our film camera was showing."

Location manager Ilt Jones, in contrast, remembers 6X10 as "the damn parking lot episode." He says

grumpily, "There were three or four of the damn things in the script. Above ground. Below ground. Big. Small.

"You wouldn't believe how many we scouted for each one we finally chose! I'm now the world's greatest expert on the parking lots of Los Angeles. I started to wake up screaming about barriers and parking tickets and entrances and exit ramps."

As for set decorator Tim Stepeck, the teeth-gritting tension of "S.R. 819" centered around the real-life electronic blood analyzer, borrowed from a friendly medical device manufacturer, used in the scene with Scully and Dr. Plant. The $12,000 device worked perfectly during filming, then vanished into thin air.

"We looked frantically for it everywhere, for weeks," says Stepeck. "All around our office. All our storage facilities. We even went over to *Chicago Hope*, which shoots on the Fox lot also, to see if somebody had taken it by mistake.

"We didn't find it until we were wrapping the whole season. By mistake, somebody had taken it away and dressed it into the Lone Gunman set. I guess they felt it fit just right with all that junk and weird equipment on their shelves."

Special makeup effects supervisor John Vulich is the founder and owner of Optic Nerve Studios, a Sun Valley, California–based firm that provides makeup, prosthetics, and other related nondigital special effects for movies and TV series. He and his company have won Emmys for their work on *Buffy the Vampire Slayer* and *Babylon 5*.

"S.R. 819" is the third "Skinner episode" in *X-Files* history. The first two were "Avatar" (3X21) and "Zero Sum" (4X21).

Composer Mark Snow says that his complex score for "S.R. 819," filled with tension and foreboding, was inspired by Daniel Sackheim's subtle direction and "a lot of big-time feature-like action." It was nominated for an Emmy for Outstanding Music Composition for a Series (Dramatic Underscore).

Dr. Katrina Cabrera, one of the physicians who treats Skinner, was named after a current researcher on *The X-Files* staff.

TWO FATHERS

As a prelude to the colonization of Earth, Syndicate scientists successfully create a human-alien hybrid. The slave-race prototype is abductee Cassandra Spender, who returns, reveals many secret conspiracies and connections—and plunges Mulder and Scully into a climactic battle for

global domination.

EPISODE: 6X11
FIRST AIRED: February 7, 1999
EDITOR: Lynne Willingham
WRITTEN BY: Chris Carter & Frank Spotnitz
DIRECTED BY: Kim Manners

GUEST STARS:
Mitch Pileggi (AD Skinner)
William B. Davis (The Cigarette-Smoking Man)
Chris Owens (Agent Jeffrey Spender)
Nicholas Lea (Alex Krycek)
Veronica Cartright (Cassandra Spender)
Mimi Rogers (Agent Diana Fowley)
George Murdoch (The Elder)
Don S. Williams (Second Elder)
Nick Tate (Dr. Openshaw)
Al Ruscio (Third Elder)
Frank Ertl (Fourth Elder)
James Newman (Lead Surgeon)
Damon P. Saleem (Pick-Up Player)

PRINCIPAL SETTINGS:
Arlington, Virginia; Washington, D.C.;
Silver Springs, Maryland

6⊗11

In a brilliantly lit operating room, a team of protectively garbed surgeons focus intently on their task. The lead surgeon, wielding a handheld laser, makes a long, straight incision on his patient's abdomen. The severed flesh emits a sizzling green fluid. The surgeon pauses. As he watches, the razor-sharp cut heals spontaneously, leaving only a faint scar.

At the Potomac Yards in Arlington, Virginia, dozens of rail cars wait out the night on parallel sidings. A gray van bearing the markings of Roush Biolabs, a Syndicate front, is parked nearby. A sedan pulls up; its lone occupant, a middle-aged man, gets out. A still-gowned surgeon steps down from one of the silver-sided cars—the mobile surgical unit last seen in "Nisei" (3X09)—and extends his hand.

"Dr. Openshaw, congratulations," says the surgeon. "Your work—it's completed. You should see her."

Dr. Openshaw climbs into the car, which holds the operating room seen previously. The patient, still unconscious, lies faceup on the operating table.

"Twenty-five years," says the lead surgeon, marveling. "She must seem like an old friend."

"Yes," says Openshaw, nearly overcome with emotion.

The surgeon tells Openshaw that they're going out to celebrate, and invites him to join them. Openshaw declines.

The lead surgeon exits the rail car, and is met by a faceless alien—last seen in 5X13, "Patient X"—holding a small cylindrical weapon. He holds it out toward the surgeon, who bursts into flames, screaming.

The rest of the surgical team is waiting in the gray van. Horrified, they watch the surgeon in his death throes, and are set afire by another faceless alien.

The first alien enters the operating room and sees Openshaw, who is preparing to inject a drug-filled syringe into the patient. The alien slams him to the floor with a vicious backhand blow, looms over him, sets him ablaze, and peers down at the patient. It is Cassandra Spender—last seen being lifted into a hovering spacecraft in "The Red and the Black" (5X14).

At an undisclosed location the Cigarette-Smoking Man leans back, lights a Morley, and exhales. He is addressing an unseen visitor.

"This is the end," he says. "I never thought I'd hear myself say those words after all those years."

He adds, "You put your life into something, build it, protect it—the end is as unimaginable as your own death. Or the death of your children. They could never have scripted the events that led us to this. None of us could—all the brilliant men, the secret that we kept so well.

"It happened simply, like this: We had a perfect conspiracy with an alien race. Aliens who were coming to reclaim this planet and to destroy all human life. Our job was to secretly prepare the way for their invasion. To create for them a slave race of human-alien hybrids.

"They were good plans. Right plans. Kept secret for over fifty years, ever since the crash at Roswell. Kept secret from men like Fox Mulder. Plans that would have worked had not a rebel alien race come to destroy them. Had not my own son chosen betrayal—or chosen to betray more wisely."

In the basement of FBI headquarters Jeffrey Spender sits at Fox Mulder's old desk, writing. He looks up. Walter Skinner is standing in the doorway.

"I didn't hear the elevator," he says, somewhat flustered. "I was working here."

"Working on what, Agent Spender?" says Skinner.

"A progress report on the X-Files. Just for the file."

Skinner is expressionless.

"Well, I wasn't aware that you'd made any progress," he says. "In the months since your assignment I've received but one memorandum. Were you planning to hit me all at once?"

"Ah, it's been slow going," says Spender.

"Truth is," says Skinner, disgusted, "your purpose here is not any progress, isn't it? Truth is, you have no interest in the X-Files—beyond a certain personal case. Your mother's abduction."

"Alleged abduction," replies Spender.

"That's what I'm here about," says Skinner.

Later that morning Skinner and Spender arrive at the Potomac Yard, where firemen are still hosing down the smoldering Roush van. Spender explores the fire-damaged operating room with Skinner close behind him. The AD explains that the entire medical team—save Openshaw, who is on life support—is now dead. The only sure survivor is Cassandra Spender.

On hearing this, Spender rushes outside. His mother, still somewhat dazed, is seated at the rear entrance of an ambulance, being given oxygen by a paramedic.

"Mom, it's me, Jeffrey," he says, near tears. "Mom, what happened to you? You've been gone so long I thought I'd never see you again."

Cassandra smiles.

"Ah, don't cry, honey," she says.

"Where have you been? What did they do to you?" asks her son.

135

"MOM, IT'S ME, JEFFREY.
MOM, WHAT HAPPENED TO
YOU? YOU'VE BEEN GONE
SO LONG I THOUGHT I'D
NEVER SEE YOU AGAIN."
—Jeffrey Spender